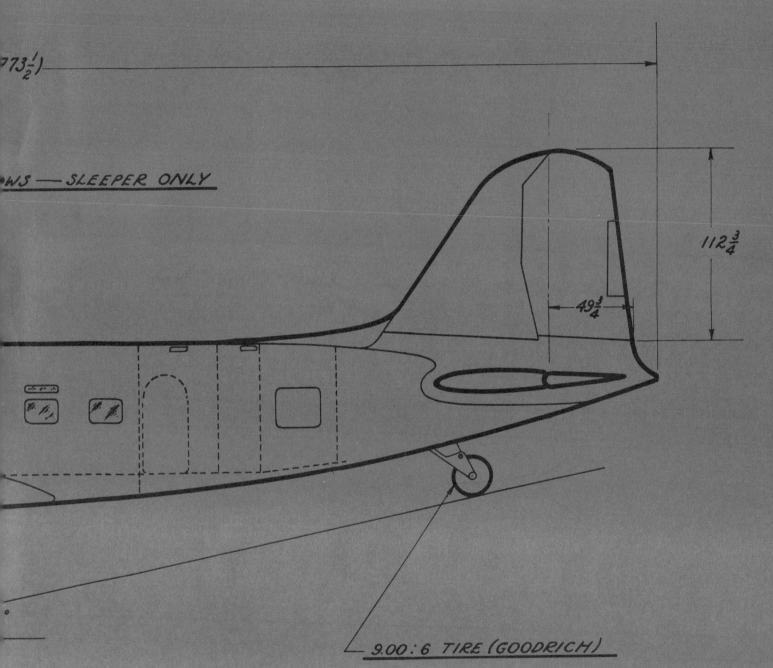

$773\tfrac{1}{2}$)

WS — SLEEPER ONLY

$112\tfrac{3}{4}$

$49\tfrac{3}{4}$

$773\tfrac{1}{2}$

9.00 : 6 TIRE (GOODRICH)

# CALIFORNIA WINGS

*"As the wing flew over the flat land like a great bird, it seemed to me that I was participating in the birth of aviation all over again."*
Theodore Von Kármán

# CALIFORNIA WINGS

## A HISTORY OF AVIATION IN THE GOLDEN STATE

BY WILLIAM A. SCHONEBERGER

WITH PAUL SONNENBURG

"PARTNERS IN INDUSTRY" BY CARTER BARBER

FOREWORD BY ROBERT J. SERLING

PRODUCED IN COOPERATION WITH THE
CALIFORNIA STATE CHAMBER OF COMMERCE

WINDSOR PUBLICATIONS, INCORPORATED
WOODLAND HILLS, CALIFORNIA

*To the host of aviation compatriots with whom I have had a rewarding association for nearly 30 years; to Paul Sonnenburg, Windsor Publications, whose aviation mania is almost as intense as my own; and to Bill, Marion, and Andrew, who I hope will treasure this tome in the years ahead.*

Windsor Publications, Inc.
History Books Division
Publisher: John M. Phillips
Editorial Director: Lissa Sanders
Senior Picture Editor: Teri Davis Greenberg
Editorial Director, Corporate Biographies: Karen Story
Assistant Director, Corporate Biographies: Phyllis Gray
Marketing Director: Ellen Kettenbeil
Design Director: Alexander D'Anca
Production Manager: Dee Cooper
Typesetting Manager: E. Beryl Myers
Proofreading Manager: Doris R. Malkin

Staff for *California Wings*
Editor: Paul Sonnenburg
Production Editor: Annette Igra
Picture Editor: Teri Davis Greenberg
Corporate Biographies Editor: Judith Hunter
Editorial Assistants: Kathy Brown, Patricia Buzard, Lonnie Pham, Pat Pittman
Assistant Art Director: Chris McKibbin
Production Artist: Beth Bowman
Proofreaders: Henriette Henderson, Jeff Leckrone
Typographer: Barbara Neiman

**Library of Congress Cataloging in Publication Data**

Schoneberger, William A., 1926-
   California wings.

   "Produced in cooperation with the California State
Chamber of Commerce."
   Bibliography: p. 182
   Includes index.
   1. Aeronautics—California—History.  I. Sonnenburg,
Paul.  II. Title.
TL522.C2S36  1984    387.7'09794    84-15166
ISBN 0-89781-078-3

*Frontispiece: The Northrop YB-49 Flying Wing is shown during a 1948 flight over Muroc Dry Lake. The 172-foot-span airplane had a takeoff weight close to 200,000 lbs, a maximum speed of 493 mph, and a range of 3,155 miles. Two of these eight-jet variants were flown, conversions from propeller-driven YB-35s. Courtesy, Edwards Air Force Base History Office (EAFBHO). Endsheets reproduced from 1936 service blueprints for Douglas DC-3/ DST. Courtesy, McDonnell Douglas Corporation*

# CONTENTS

Douglas Ettridge's 1983 painting captures a day at the Dominguez Hills Air Meet of January 1910. In the foreground Glenn Curtiss checks the flight of Louis Paulhan's Farman just off his right wing. Below rest a few of the aeroplanes and lighter-than-air craft that delighted hundreds of thousands of Angelenos and visitors from around the world. Courtesy of the artist and the Collection of Si Robin and Betty Bazar

Douglas Ettridge 1983 ©

IN THE EXAMINER IT

# ACKNOWLEDGMENTS

For much of its history the territory now constituted as the State of California has welcomed wayfarers from other places. Paraphrasing an old comment that originally implied religious beliefs, Golden State residents frequently proffer the sharp remark, "I'm a California convert . . . and we're the worst kind!" For all of the same reasons that cause California's continued population growth—temperate weather, the sea, the mountains, and a relaxed life-style—aviation's earliest pioneers were attracted to the state. As a result, more aviation history and accomplishments emanated from the Golden State than perhaps from any other area of the world.

Despite the state's aviation preeminence and the countless books, articles, essays, and features about individuals, companies, and feats, to the best of our knowledge no one has attempted to summarize in one volume California's venerable aviation heritage; for this reason alone *California Wings* should prove useful. We hope so.

. With the advent of *Sputnik, Vanguard,* and *Mercury,* what is now broadly called "aerospace" encompassed the all-inclusive effort of America's scholars, scientists, engineers, technicians, and, of course, the derring-do spirit of its pilots. Our book treats only that segment of aerospace known as *aviation*—man's achievements in gliders, lighter-than-air craft, and aeroplanes, although some segments do touch upon the transition from aviation into space flight.

Readers will quickly recognize that space limitations precluded in-depth analysis or inclusion of much material that many believe should have been included. We agree. But a comprehensive collection of California aviation memorabilia might have yielded a set of volumes weightier than Winston Churchill's chronicling of the Second World War.

*California Wings* has been compiled by two "converted Californians" devoted not only to aviation's colorful, exciting heritage but to its future as well, and the sharing common to both scholarship and aviation combined to make the research (for both text and illustrations), writing, and editing of *California Wings* a great

pleasure for both of us. As it happened, author and editor mined complementary groups of the aviation and academic communities, sometimes overlapping. To both groups, our gratitude is deep for the unfailing generosity and enthusiasm consistently extended to us.

The editor's debt is especially large to: Jean Anderson, Carol Bugé, and Dennis Meredith at Caltech; Rita Mae Gurnee and Wayne Lutz at Mt. San Antonio College: Terry Helwick at USC; Chere Negaard at Northrop University; Clifton Moore, Eddie Holohan, and Ethel Pattison at LAX; R.E.G. Davies at the Smithsonian (his books are the starting place for airline history and his generosity gratifying); Dick Hallion at Edwards (another generous scholar with infectious love for his discipline); Bob Ferguson at Lockheed (two days with this skilled and caring veteran in Lockheed's grand archives were a joy); Harry Gann (who one day soon will surely get his *own* book through the press—his colleagues are waiting eagerly); "Bruce" Reynolds at San Diego's Aero-Space Museum (whose kindness and wisdom delight the aero-bibliophile); Ted Poyser and Marge MacKay of Voi-Shan (two erudite and witty colleagues with sound advice); Fran Fox (that great rarity, a truly good man); Nick Galloway; Eleanor "Fergie" Glithrow and Margie Craig at PSA; Linda Dozier at Western Airlines (an elegant lady whose immense knowledge makes a day in Western's exhaustive files a researcher's delight) and Tom Dozier of GE; Joy Barrett Sabol at the Tigers; Walter Hellman at Republic; Gene Kropf (for whom aviation education has been a lifetime of sharing what he loves with people he cares about); David Kuhner (the paradigm of a gentle bookman whose concern for excellence is contagious), John B. Rae and Iris Critchell (she radiates her faith in students and aviation's ability to make them better people) at Claremont; Col. John Lowman, USMC (Ret.) (the "Ret." is coterie humor); Col. Robert P. Muhlbach, USAF (Ret.); Capt. Jeanne Hoeck, USNR (Ret.); Carolyn Kozo, Gloria Barajas, and Bettye Ellison at the Los Angeles Public Library; Theron Rinehart at Fairchild; Marsha Toy (nurse, air hostess, teacher, educator, tireless aviation booster, people person, and grand lady); William Wagner; Gordon Williams (if you're serious about aero research, you eventually find Gordon and wish you'd located his encyclopaedic mind and ebullient interest earlier); Clarence Belinn; Douglas Ettridge (the discovery of whose painting for our dust jacket gave us all fresh determination); Si Robin and Betty Bazar at Sensor Systems; Bob Conrich; Kevin Cavanaugh of the Windsor staff; Bob Moffatt (whose indefatigability helped to make the book a reality); Carter Barber (veteran journalist and diligent researcher); and Lissa Sanders.

The author's work was inspired by a host of pioneers and other enthusiasts who have been instrumental in keeping California in the vanguard of aviation progress. My personal motivation reached a zenith during the hours I spent interviewing and just talking with John K. Northrop, the design genius whose career touched those of most of his fellow aviation pioneers. Jack Northrop was associated with the Lockheeds, Don Douglas, Jerry Vultee, Claude Ryan, Bill Boeing, Ed Heinemann, Amelia Earhart, Howard Hawks, Wiley Post, Bernt Balchen, Roscoe Turner, and hundreds of others still active in the industry.

I've had the opportunity to probe, always on an informal and relaxed basis, the unparalleled experiences of Richard W. Millar, an aviation pioneer who was present at Dominguez Hills, witnessed Cal Rodgers' last flight, was a Don Douglas confidant and board member during the formative "DC" years, was president of Vultee, an associate of Howard Hughes, and a member of Maddux Air Lines board and later chairman of the Northrop Corporation board.

Jack Northrop's and Dick Millar's personal recollections were invaluable in this work. Most important, they triggered the realization of the intertwining relationships that characterized California's pioneering aviation "fraternity."

My first aviation inspirations came from GE's jet-engine genius, Gerhard Neumann, largely responsible for the company's preeminence in the worldwide jet-engine business. I had the opportunity of talking at length with Sir Frank Whittle, British inventor of the turbojet and acknowledged "father," with Germany's Hans Von Ohain, of the jet age. Valuable insight came from talks with Ed Heinemann, Max Stanley, Clete Roberts, Tony LeVier, Ted Coleman, Jim Greenwood, Peggy Hereford, Marvin Miles, Al Cline, Vern Haugland, and one of my favorite aviation buffs, Charley Barr.

Much credit for initial inspiration, and particularly attention to detail, is due my longtime friend and professional associate, Eric Falk, who is the most fastidious, precise, and often-harsh critic of aviation history that I know. Eric provided basic photo and document research as well as critical analysis of the book's approach, continuity, and accuracy.

Those dedicated journalists who cover aviation and aerospace as a profession are fonts of information and personal inspiration. I'm particularly indebted to Bob Ropelewski, Phil Geddes, Paul Turk, Norm Lynn, Bob Hotz, Bill Gregory, Don Fink, Lou Davis, Bob Stanley, Jim Woolsey, Ed Tripp, Bill Hall, Rich Tuttle, Jim Skinner, Jeff Lenorovitz, Bill Scott, Bob Parrish, Sam Jones, Warren Goodman, Larry Levy, Lew Townsend, and dozens of other intrepid newspersons who have contributed to my sum of aviation knowledge.

Having spent most of my career on what is oft-characterized as "the other side of the desk," I am particularly sensitive to the "over and above" efforts of the corporate, association, and government communications, or public relations, professionals whose responsibility it is to assure a truthful and positive projection of their product or service. In *California Wings* we are particularly indebted to Ginny Black, Lee Pitt, Earl Blount, Grover Nobles, Jim Ragsdale, Roy Blay, Don Hanson, Jim Corfield, Larry Peeples, Bob Scholl, Ben Scarpero, Dave Wright, Don Arney, Paul Weeks, Joe Lipper, Tom Sprague, Herb Rosen, Rob Mack, Jack Hefley, Matt Portz, Nissen Davis, Bruce Plowman, Alan Wayne, Julian Levine, Jerry Ringer, Ben Cook, Dick Larrick, George Mulhern, Don Page, Ira Chart, Tony Cantifio, Bill Hastings, Bill Dick, Warren Hanson, and, most particularly, the Public Affairs officers at California's

widespread, diversified U.S. Air Force, Navy, Marine Corps, and Army facilities.

In addition to the Windsor staff, the initial research, original drafts, re-drafts, editing, rework, and extensive writing involved in a compilation of this magnitude would never have been possible without the loyal services of my own staff—Judy Miller, Sally Berns, Suzanne Fickinger, and Leanne Silver.

The most rewarding facet of my nearly 30 years of association with world aviation has been the opportunity to meet and talk with giants whom I hold in awe, people who literally made history. I have had the good fortune to be exposed to these giants at Paris, Farnborough, and Hanover air shows, at Edwards AFB, at the National Air and Space Museum, at dozens of civil and military airfields in the U.S. and overseas. However, I knew that my roots had been firmly planted in California aviation when my son, daughter-in-law, and I had the privilege one golden spring afternoon of viewing from the air in the Goodyear blimp the panorama of the

*From period photographs Douglas Ettridge captured the excitement of Transcontinental Air Transport's coast-to-coast, air-rail inaugural flight from Glendale's Grand Central Terminal on July 8, 1929. At the center is TAT's Ford Tri-motor with pilot Lindbergh; at the left is a trim Lockheed Vega. The Jenny overhead, Ettridge confesses, is pure artist's nostalgia. Courtesy of the artist and the Collection of Si Robin and Betty Bazar*

Los Angeles basin and, in particular, the site of the 1910 Dominguez Hills Air Meet. My son photographed Dominguez Hills and the Spruce Goose display site, while I had the opportunity to "pilot" this behemoth of the air. It was one of my most memorable aviation moments.

It was fun. But then, aviation is fun.

William A. Schoneberger
Malibu, California

# FOREWORD

You are about to read a unique book, one that could not have been written about any other state in the union.

This is not to say that California has a monopoly on aviation tradition, history, and contributions to aeronautical science. Yet in most states, aviation lore has been confined to one particular city or area. Kansas, for example, where Wichita is a kind of general aviation capital. Washington State, whose largest city—Seattle—is almost synonymous with mighty Boeing; the late Senator Henry "Scoop" Jackson for years was known as "the senator from Boeing."

Try Pennsylvania. One thinks of tiny Lock Haven where Mr. Piper and his ubiquitous Cubs flew their way into fame. Illinois? Well, Chicago is United's home base and O'Hare is the nation's busiest airport. Period.

You might make a case for Florida. It's aviation-oriented and aviation-minded, and the U.S. scheduled airline industry got its start there in 1914 when a pilot named Tony Jannus and a lone passenger made the world's first scheduled airline flight, over an 18-mile route from St. Petersburg to Tampa across Tampa Bay. The inaugural ticket cost $400, which added up to a price tag of $22.00 a mile.

How about New York? True, Long Island is home plate for Grumman, whose Navy fighters and torpedo bombers helped defeat Japan. And there's New York City itself with its myriad corporate headquarters—except that TWA and Pan Am are the only major airlines with corporate command posts still situated in the Big Apple; Eastern moved to Miami years ago, and American is happily residing in Dallas/Fort Worth.

Alaska must be mentioned with its rich bush pilot background—this was a state literally built by the airplane. And we must not forget North Carolina's claim to aeronautical fame, for Kitty Hawk was the birthplace of powered flight.

The point is, however, that California's love affair with flight encompasses *every* phase of aviation—airlines, manufacturing, sports flying, lighter-than-air, aerobatics, stunting, airports, military, experimental, and space exploration.

Add the inevitable wedding of the motion picture to the airplane—the overwhelming majority of classic (and also some abysmal) aviation films were made in California, the outstanding exception being *Wings*, which was filmed largely near San Antonio.

More than any other single state, California epitomized Franklin Roosevelt's bell-ringing "Arsenal of Democracy" phrase (which, incidentally, wasn't FDR's creation but that of a French diplomat named Jean Monnet). When Herman Goering told Hitler that Roosevelt's promise of 50,000 planes a year was so much propaganda, he hadn't reckoned with the productivity of U.S. airframe manufacturers—the bulk of them located in the Golden State.

Florida may have been the cradle of the airline industry, but the baby never really got out of the crib; the St. Petersburg-Tampa Airboat Line didn't last very long, and we could make a strong case for establishing California as the launch pad for *modern* commercial aviation. In 1928, a time when most air travelers were parked on top of mail sacks and passengers were strictly an afterthought, Western Air Express established the "Model Airway"—an experimental, all-passenger service between Los Angeles and San Francisco—including comfortable seats, in-flight meals, and cabin attendants.

This book tells the Model Airway story, along with fascinating accounts of all the other carriers whose roots in California aviation are deep and so often dramatic, including some almost forgotten airlines with names kept alive solely by the sentiments of those who served them. Transocean comes to mind—pilot/author Ernest Gann flew the Pacific for this line, and an experience on one flight furnished the plot basis for his superb novel (and later film) *The High and the Mighty*.

As you progress through these well-written, scrupulously researched pages, history will come alive through California's army of magnificent aviation characters. You'll meet the legendary Howard Hughes, for example, but don't expect a sleazy, gossip-saturated hatchet job—Bill Schoneberger is a *professional* aviation writer of integrity who paints an objective portrait of the real Hughes: an eccentric, yes, but a vastly underrated contributor to aeronautical science.

The cast also includes Continental's Bob Six, who once told reporters that Pan Am's 747 interior must have been designed by a mail-order house. Colorful, beloved Francis Fox, onetime head honcho at Los Angeles International Airport who was the prototype for the hero of Arthur Hailey's *Airport.* Cecil B. De Mille, who once owned the biggest airfield in Southern California and was a true aviation pioneer in the state, yet ironically never made an aviation spectacle for the films. Claude Ryan, who built the most famous single aircraft in history—Lindbergh's *The Spirit of St. Louis,* which justifiably could have been named for the city in which it was made: San Diego. Manufacturing giants like Donald Douglas and Allan and Malcolm Loughead, who changed their names into a symbol of aerial progress: Lockheed.

Travel via Schoneberger's facile pen to the vast desert dry lakes now known as Edwards Air Force Base, where in 1942 America's first jet—disguised during preparation with a dummy propeller—made its initial flight. Visit the wartime aircraft assembly plants where thousands of Rosie the Riveters first began the eventual demolishing of male chauvinism. Ride with the pioneering airmen whose willingness to face death paid off in the supersonic warplanes and magnificent airliners of today—the barn-stormers, the early Pacific fliers, the test pilots who knew each flight could be their last.

Stand alongside those early designers who used to test structural integrity by kicking at an airframe. Relive the exciting dawn of naval aviation, born in California with the world's first landing of an airplane on the deck of a crudely modified warship. Witness firsthand the incredible development of great airports like Los Angeles and San Francisco International. Be present at the creation of America's oldest airline—Los Angeles-based Western Air Express; still in existence as Western Airlines, it owes its start to pure civic jealousy: it was founded because some Los Angeles citizens were incurably envious of San Francisco's status as the West Coast terminus of the transcontinental airmail route.

Go behind the scenes at the filming of Hollywood's great aviation movies like *Hell's Angels,* although remember that the motion picture industry—even though it is part of California's aviation history—has too often distorted that history. Technical inaccuracies plague virtually every aviation film (*Airport* and *The High and the Mighty* were welcome exceptions) and cause airplane buffs to wince.

*California Wings* is the perfect example of bringing history to life via the printed word—factual yet exciting, a story whose drama and romance lie in the power of untinted nostalgia and unvarnished objectivity.

Every state can produce its own archives of aerial lore, each fact, figure, and anecdote fitting into the mosaic that forms the image of America's role in the conquest of the skies. This writer's own Tucson, for example, boasts the modest accomplishment of operating the country's first municipally owned airport.

But until *California Wings,* no one could have grasped the enormity of what the Golden State has contributed to that mosaic. California has always been known as a place of paradoxes, anomalies, and inconsistencies. Not, however, when it comes to its part in aviation progress. The dauntless spirit of its first settlers was to be reflected in the equally undaunted resolve of its aviation pioneers. They trod no less a precarious path than those who arrived in the golden land via covered wagons taking months to cover the mileage a jet travels in a few hours.

In that juxtaposition of time lies the real story not merely of Califoria's wings but of all aviation. Yet reading Bill Schoneberger's brilliant account may generate a perhaps sacrilegious "what if" thought . . .

. . . what if Orville and Wilbur had first dreamed their dream in California?

Robert J. Serling
Tucson, Arizona

12

# INTRODUCTION

From the dawn of recorded history man dreamed of flying, challenged at each skyward glance by birds' aerial mastery and the freedom implicit in flight itself.

Wings became synonymous with the dream. Mythology tells of Daedalus and Icarus, who created bird-like wings of feathers and wax. Mercury traveled the world wearing winged cap and sandals and bore a winged caduceus. Pegasus soared about the heavens on widespread wings. This predilection with bird wings occupied more practical thinkers too, including Leonardo da Vinci, who said: "There is in man the ability to sustain himself in the air by the flapping of wings."

In 1783 the Montgolfier brothers finally achieved man's first real-life ascension. Their manned balloon flight from a clearing near the Seine River in Paris was witnessed by America's famed scientist, philosopher, and statesman, Benjamin Franklin. Legend holds that, after descent of the gas-filled balloon, a spectator turned to Franklin and asked, "What good is it?" Franklin replied, "What good is a newborn baby?"

On the sand dunes of Kill Devil Hill, on a December Thursday in 1903, Orville and Wilbur Wright fulfilled the cherished dream of powered flight in a winged vehicle. Orville wrote: " . . . it was nevertheless the first in the history of the world in which a machine carrying a man had raised itself by its own power into the air in full flight, had sailed forward without reduction of speed, and had finally landed at a point as high as that from where it started." A local fellow, with more exuberance if less precision, rushed to the Kitty Hawk post office with the news: "Damn if they ain't flew!"

Today, in the United States alone, nearly 300 million passengers travel more than 250 billion miles by air each year. Military and commercial airplanes traverse the skies at supersonic speeds. Men and women routinely orbit the globe. Humans have walked upon the moon, and earthborn spacecraft probe the galaxy.

## CALIFORNIA AERONAUTICS

Three industries have focused world attention on California: agriculture, motion pictures, and aviation. Like the gulls gliding above its 1,200 miles of seacoast, air-minded men and women were attracted to California's near-perfect climate and topography—ideal for building, promoting, and testing the aircraft that have been the most visible evidence of leadership in aeronautic endeavors.

Led by the growth of aviation-related enterprise since 1910, California has become a high-technology center of the world. In 1980 nearly a quarter of all United States aircraft and parts manufacturing employment and almost half of all the nation's missile, space vehicle, and parts manufacturing employment was concentrated in the state, along with 22 percent of the electronic components and accessories manufacturing employment. In 1982 twenty-three percent of all Department of Defense contracts were awarded to California-based firms as were 44 percent of all National Aeronautics and Space Administration (NASA) contracts.

California's aviation industry grew explosively from 1920 through the '40s, a powerful magnet for the westward migration of the engineers, entrepreneurs, technicians, and scientists who built the sophisticated companies linked together today in "the aerospace industry," encompassing all facets of airframe and component manufacturing.

The work of Martin, Curtiss, Douglas, the Lougheads, Northrop, Ryan, Vultee, Fleet, Hughes—men whose names are synonymous with aviation progress—remains the touchstone of California aviation history. Their genius and energy, added to the legacy of their predecessors, generated scientific, technological, and managerial creativity and productivity that remain unparalleled in our time. Their accomplishment, and what they began, is the foundation upon which uncounted collaborators in related aeronautical disciplines have continued to build, assuring California's central place in aeronautical history.

# PART ONE: BEGINNINGS

*Dirigible pilots needed fine coordination, judgment, and agility as Lincoln Beachey demonstrated at Dominguez Hills in January 1910. The engine turned a propeller (hidden at right by the sun's glare); directional control came from the rear rudder assembly (left); altitude and climb angle were changed by dropping sand ballast (in bags at the rear), releasing hydrogen from the vents just above the pilot, and shifting the center of gravity by clambering back and forth along the trestle. Courtesy, Security Pacific National Bank Photograph Collection, Los Angeles Public Library (SPNBPC/LAPL)*

# CHAPTER ONE

# DIRIGIBLES AND GLIDERS

## JOHN MONTGOMERY

Octave Chanute, the French-born bridge builder who pioneered theoretical and practical flight efforts in the United States, noted in an 1896 essay that his studies were based on observing sea gulls at San Diego. One of Chanute's correspondents was young John J. Montgomery, who moved with his family to San Diego in the early 1880s while he was an undergraduate at St. Ignatius College in San Francisco. Montgomery was enthralled by the uncannily proficient soaring of the southern coast's abundant sea gulls and vultures. Chanute and Montgomery, the two foremost American proponents of glider flight in the 19th century, by studying the flight of California gulls helped pave the way for Orville and Wilbur Wright.

Many historians, including Victor Lougheed (brother of Allan and Malcolm Loughead), author of the authoritative 1909 *Vehicles of the Air*, credit Montgomery with the first successful U.S. glider flight in 1883 near San Diego, in a craft he named *Gull Glider*. By the early 1890s Montgomery was teaching at Santa Clara College and testing glider models. In 1905 he had great success with a 22-foot-span biplane incorporating such sophisticated elements as a rear rudder and elevator, suspension of the operator below the wings for a low center of gravity, and controls to warp the wings in coordination with the rudder movement for lateral stability.

Montgomery had flown his own gliders, but he considered himself essentially a designer and scientist. So when circus performer J. Daniel Maloney, who specialized in parachuting from free balloons, showed up between engagements,

Montgomery promptly hired him—almost certainly California's first "test pilot." On April 29, 1905, Maloney ascended in his employer's balloon-suspended glider to about 4,000 feet before cutting loose. Diving and leveling out, he worked the controls to glide silently to earth in a flight of some 19 minutes over a distance of 7-1/2 miles.

Despite this success, disbelievers persisted, and on July 18, 1905, another flight was attempted with release at about 1,800 feet. Apparently problems with the controls induced a dive too steep for recovery, and Maloney plunged to his death. Although deeply disturbed by the tragedy, by 1909 Montgomery conceived with Lougheed a machine intended for powered flight. After 51 successful unpowered flights, Montgomery—now 53, and warned by his physician not to pilot further flights—insisted on a farewell appearance. As his glider sped down the inclined track and rose into the air, he slumped over the controls and the craft faltered and crashed. On October 31, 1911, John Montgomery died in the Santa Clara Valley he loved so well. Columbia Pictures' 1946 film, *Gallant Journey*, is based on his life story.

## FREDERICK MARRIOTT

To California in the mid-1800s came Frederick Marriott, who had worked in England with early aero experimenters John Stringfellow and William Henson. A journalist—he founded *The Illustrated London News*—Marriott settled in San Francisco where he edited the San Francisco *News Letter* and formed a stock company to finance a dirigible that he planned to design and build. His *Avitor Hermes, Jr.* (intended as a model for a larger airship) was completed in June 1869.

The craft, a cigar-shaped, gas-filled bag 37 feet long, was fitted with wings for stability and lift, and a rear-mounted elevator and rudder. Below hung a carriage housing a miniature steam engine designed and built by G.K. Gluyas, president of the California Steam Navigation Company. On July 2, 1869, the *Avitor* flew at Shellmound Park across the bay from San Francisco. *Scientific American* in its issue dated July 31, 1869, gives this account of the first flight of a lighter-than-air vehicle in the western hemisphere:

*The morning was beautiful and still—scarcely a breath of air stirring. The conditions were favorable to success. The gasometer was fully inflated and the model was floated out of the building. In six minutes steam was got up—the rudder set to give a slight curve to the course of the vessel—and the valves opened. With the first turn of the propellers she rose slowly into the air, gradually increasing her speed until the rate of five miles per hour was attained. The position of the rudder caused her to describe a great circle, around which she passed twice.*

Buoyed by success, Marriott and his backers pressed forward and by 1875 had raised money enough for a new vehicle that Marriott called an "aeroplane," in some historians' view the first use of the term. In 1881 Marriott formed a company to finance and build a triplane, to be named the *Leland Stanford,* but in 1883 the Patent Office denied the application on grounds of "impossibility." Discouraged and depressed, Marriott died in San Francisco in December 1884.

## THOMAS SCOTT BALDWIN

For most early practitioners flying was serious business, but a link between daredevils and ballooning, with its obvious drama, under-standably persisted. Thomas Baldwin combined the gifts of a center-ring showman with those of an imaginative and determined inventor to earn lasting distinction as a builder of dirigibles.

In January 1887 Baldwin made his first parachute jump from a balloon, leaping over the gondola's side from 3,000 feet to dazzle a San Francisco audience. But public enchantment with free balloons deflated, and in 1903 Captain (a rank freely accorded to balloon pilots of the era) Baldwin visited Europe to study the dirigibles (steerable lighter-than-air craft) of Count von Zeppelin and Alberto Santos-Dumont. When he came home to California to implement his own ideas with two young helpers—earnest Roy Knabenshue and feisty, redheaded Link Beachey—he soon met a frustration well-known to his aeroplane-building counterparts: the absence of light, powerful, reliable engines.

Glenn Curtiss biographer Alden Hatch engagingly sketched the 48-year-old Baldwin trying to launch an early dirigible one spring day in 1903. The crowd of disappointed Oakland ticket-holders was growing surly when the balky engine repeatedly refused to start. The timely arrival of a motorcyclist whose engine ran sweetly compelled Baldwin to ask the name of its maker. "Glenn Curtiss of Hammondsport, New York," came the reply.

Soon after, Baldwin visited the Curtiss home in New York. Uncle Tom (as he was called by his friends) spent the rest of the summer working with Curtiss to adapt a motorcycle engine for aero installation. A few months later Knabenshue and Beachey welcomed their mentor at the Oakland station, the precious engine crated in the baggage car, and history waiting.

On July 29, 1904, the *California Arrow* was ready. Below its 54-foot-long gas envelope of yellow Japanese silk hung a framework containing space for the operator and the 10-horsepower, 60-pound engine geared to a reversible propeller mounted at the front. With the Curtiss motor's steady beat generating power and confidence on that sunny afternoon in Idora Park, Captain Tom Baldwin happily piloted *California Arrow* on its initial course out over San Francisco Bay and back—the first successful controlled rigid dirigible flight in America. The *Arrow* was demonstrated at the 1904 St. Louis World's Fair with Knabenshue at the controls; and Baldwin and Beachey subsequently toured the Orient with the durable little ship.

In February 1905 Knabenshue raced the *Arrow* against one of the era's fastest automobiles, a Pope-Toledo, from Chutes Park in Los Angeles to the Raymond Hotel in Pasadena. Bucking a threatening side wind, he landed the *Arrow* on the hotel grounds a full two minutes ahead of the car. Arthur Raymond, whose father ran the hotel and who would become chief designer of the immortal DC-3 and other Douglas airplanes, dates his devotion to aviation from his watching Knabenshue's exploits.

Baldwin joined with Curtiss to build and sell the first dirigible to the U.S. Army and went on to design an airplane, the *Red Devil*, which he flew in exhibitions around the world. He was a consultant to the Japanese government in the construction of that nation's first dirigible and served in World War I as the U.S. Army's Chief of Balloon Inspection and Production, retiring with the rank of major. Unlike so many of his fellow early aviators, Baldwin died of natural causes in May 1923.

Glenn Curtiss was significantly influenced by his encounter with the irrepressible Baldwin, who became his lifetime friend. And from 1903 Curtiss' commitment to aviation never swerved, carrying him in 1910 to San Diego for a portentous rendezvous with the United States Navy.

By 1909 the devoted competence and imagination of Montgomery, Marriott, Baldwin, Curtiss, and others had materially advanced a fledgling art and craft from a primitive struggle with the unknown to a practicable, even respectable, science and technology. Other Californians began to appreciate the potential of powered flight not for mere entertainment but as practical transportation.

The initial spark that ignited international interest in aviation was struck in 1909 at the world's first air meet in Rheims, France. But on a windy mesa near Los Angeles, an American match was truly about to set off an aviation explosion.

*Frederick Marriott's dirigible,* Avitor Hermes, Jr., *flew near San Francisco on July 2, 1869, the first flight of a lighter-than-air vehicle in the western hemisphere. Courtesy, Smithsonian Institution*

*Piloted by Roy Knabenshue on February 5, 1905, Thomas Baldwin's 54-foot* California Arrow *raced an auto from Chutes Park to Pasadena. Arriving a full two minutes before the car, the dirigible drew throngs of admirers. Courtesy, SPNBPC/LAPL*

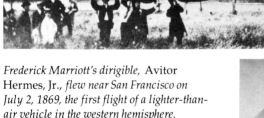

*Captain Thomas Scott Baldwin is pictured here in Manila, Philippine Islands, on tour with the* Red Devil *biplane of his own design. He became the U.S. Army's Chief of Balloon Inspection and Production in WWI and retired with the rank of major. Courtesy, SPNBPC/LAPL*

J. Daniel Maloney was hired to pilot John Montgomery's gliders and did so with great success in April 1905 with a 19-minute flight. Here, on July 18 at the San Jose Fairgrounds, Maloney begins an ascent to some 1,800 feet. Upon release, apparent problems with the controls induced a dive too steep for recovery, and Maloney plunged to his death. Courtesy, SPNBPC/LAPL

Montgomery's 1911 glider, Evergreen, made 51 successful flights in the Santa Clara area. In what he ironically planned to be his farewell appearance, the professor died in a lift-off crash of Evergreen on October 31, 1911. Courtesy, Northrop Corporation (NC); Jim Spurgeon Collection

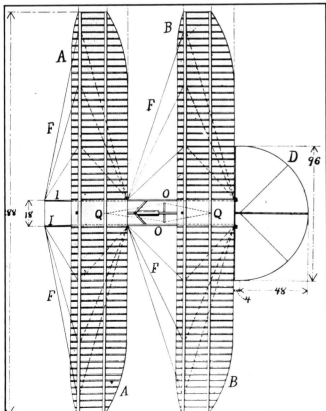

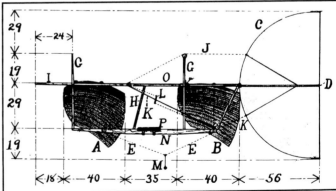

*Top: John J. Montgomery (far left) studied soaring birds so abundant near San Diego. He incorporated what he saw into his successful glider designs, such as in this model photographed in San Jose in 1905. Courtesy, James R. Greenwood*

*Left and above: Victor Lougheed's 1910* Vehicles of the Air *shows the layout of John Montgomery's* Gull Glider. *Many authorities believe that the* Gull Glider *made the first successful man-carrying glider flight in America when it flew in 1883 near San Diego. Courtesy, CALAC*

# CHAPTER TWO

# EARLY PIONEERS

After the Wrights' success at Kitty Hawk, America's epidemic flying fever was nowhere more virulent than in California. A frequent symptom was the outbreak of groups devoted to aviation. The Aero Club of California was established in Los Angeles on March 26, 1908, among the first in the United States. An organizer of the Junior Aero Club at Los Angeles Polytechnic High School, Harry La Verne Twining, a physics instructor and California correspondent for *Aeronautics* magazine, encouraged his students in the new science of aeronautics. An ornithopter designed by Twining, despite its inability to fly (Twining wrote, "I could beat the wings some 52 half beats per minute, and . . . take the wind out of me in about 10 seconds"), was depicted in the second volume of *Jane's All the World's Airships.*

The Aero Club sponsored the first aviation show in California when its members exhibited their work on May 1-2, 1909, including gliders of Edgar S. Smith and W.J. Cochrane, a full-scale model of a J.H. Klassen helicopter called the "Gyroplane," and a gasless airship designed by A.L. Smith.

In May 1910 the Club obtained acreage for a flying field called the Los Angeles Aerodrome, California's first airport worthy of the name. Club members began in earnest to build flying machines, Twining joining forces with Warren F. Eaton to construct a conventional monoplane powered by a Model T Ford motor.

Spurred by the formation of Los Angeles' organization, Cleve T. Shaffer of San Francisco founded the Pacific Aero Club in March 1909. William Crocker of the Crocker Bank made rooms available in his bank building, and the new group held displays of its members' work in August 1909 and again in May 1910.

AMERICA'S FIRST AVIATION MEET
World interest in aviation received tremendous impetus with the first aviation meet at Rheims, France, August 22-28, 1909. The Wrights at the time ran a flying school near Rheims, an operation characterized by Charles Gibbs-Smith as seminal in the development of European aero technology. But Wilbur and Orville, in keeping with their generally secretive ways and lack of exhibitionism, had elected not to participate. The lone U.S. representative was Glenn H. Curtiss of Hammondsport, New York. With his "Golden Flyer," he won the newly created Gordon Bennett trophy for aeroplane speed with a record 46.5 miles per hour. He returned to the United States in September, and the news of his great success in Europe was enthusiastically reported across the nation.

The idea for an American aviation competition arose during shop talk between two pilots "on the circuit" at a 1909 Kentucky air display. Roy Knabenshue, by now one of America's premier exhibition fliers, and Charles Willard, a Curtiss associate who would soon join Glenn Martin's fledgling aircraft company, found themselves with no worthy prospects for the coming winter season. Roy's Los Angeles background may have colored their discussions, but somehow the talk led to an appealing idea: how about some sort of show in sunny Southern California? Everyone was talking about Rheims, of course, and the next step was a phone call to Hammondsport. Curtiss delightedly agreed to meet his friends in Los Angeles, and the airmen promptly turned to the vital matter of financial backing.

Knabenshue's first contact was Dick Ferris, a Los Angeles businessman and aviation devotee with a reputation for civic promotion. Sold on the idea straightaway, Ferris took charge to plan a far grander event than Knabenshue and Willard had envisioned, and he vowed to give Los Angeles an extravaganza to surpass the Rheims show. Ferris approached the young and energetic Los Angeles Merchants and Manufacturers Association (LAMMA), which agreed to raise the needed money. Curtiss and Willard soon arrived, and the aviators and sponsors selected an ideal site owned by Joseph and Edward Carson, a mesa on the Dominguez Ranch between Compton and Long Beach.

A part of the Rancho San Pedro, with a railroad siding nearby, the bluff was high enough so that the public could not see the flying without paying admission to the site. Money was initially raised by public subscription, and an engineer was contracted to lay out the site, construct the grandstand, and build pylons to mark the course. Dates were set for January 10-20, 1910.

LAMMA formed an aviation committee including Courtland F. Bishop, Edwin Cleary, and Jerome S. Fancuilli (who would later become a publicity man for Curtiss), with Dick Ferris as its chairman, to develop the program and rules and to organize the distribution of prizes. The committee invited the celebrated French aviator Louis Paulhan, offering him a $50,000 guarantee if he would compete, and so assure the international flavor of the meet. Paulhan, greatly admired on the Continent and fondly called "Le Petit Meccano" because he had been a dirigible mechanic, shipped two Farman biplanes and two Bleriot monoplanes to Los Angeles, then departed with Madame Paulhan for the United States in December 1909. Among the entourage were two mechanics and student pilots, the Baron and Madame de Pennendreff, and the Paulhan's poodle.

On his arrival in New York, the great airman was met by a court injunction obtained by the Wright brothers, who sought to prevent Paulhan from flying his aeroplanes, claiming patent infringement. The restraining order, part of the Wrights' continuing legal efforts to protect their patents, did not extend to California and so did not prevent Paulhan from flying at Dominguez Hills. Curtiss, whose career was long complicated by charges from the Wright Company that his hinged ailerons impinged upon their lateral control patent (which depended upon the interaction of wing warping and simultaneous rudder movement), learned at this meet of a judge's decision upholding the Wrights' claim. Before one Dominguez flight, Curtiss immobilized his rudder with tape to effectively demonstrate that his opposite-acting ailerons functioned independently of the rudder, thus hoping (futilely, it turned out) to settle the dispute.

With careful preplanning by the Dominguez Hills Executive Committee under D.A. Hamburger's chairmanship, the site was ready for opening-day ceremonies on the 10th of January. Eleven aeroplanes were to be flown by 10 pilots (Paulhan had one entry each for the Farman and Bleriot aircraft); lighter-than-air entries included three dirigibles and seven balloons. One balloon was named the *City of Los Angeles,* another the *City of Oakland,* and a third the *Dick Ferris.*

Special Pacific Electric Railway cars carried a steady stream of spectators to Dominguez Hills. By noon the crowd was estimated at 20,000, probably not one person among them who had ever before witnessed an airplane in flight. Promptly at one o'clock a yellow-winged Curtiss biplane was rolled before the grandstand. With Glenn Curtiss at the controls, a mechanic swung the propeller, and the engine coughed to life. Curtiss taxied away, took off, and gracefully rounded the course in shallow banks over a distance of about 5/8ths of a mile at a height of 50 feet or so, landed, and rolled to a gentle stop within 300 feet of his starting point.

The crowd roared its approval and amazement. Here was exhilarating proof that man could be propelled into the air in controlled flight, maneuver his craft, and return near where he started. America's first air meet was under way.

But Paulhan was the star that day. Unobtrusively leaving his tent on the field, he had his mechanics tow his aeroplane to a gully hidden from the grandstand. While the spectators had their eyes glued on dirigibles piloted by Knabenshue and Beachey, Paulhan started his engine, took off in the backstretch, made a far turn, and roared by directly in front of the astonished crowd. Quickly circling out over the countryside, he passed again in front of the grandstand and landed in the center of the field. He had succeeded in completely upstaging Curtiss, Willard, Knabenshue, and Beachey. Later that day Paulhan made three more flights, while Curtiss, with considerably more caution, made but one more.

By the second day crowds had swelled as word spread through Los Angeles of excitement not to be missed at Dominguez Hills. By one o'clock the grandstand was completely filled despite gusty winds that buffeted spectators as they disembarked from the big red Pacific Electric cars.

Such elevating goings-on were not neglected by Los Angeles' social set, for whom the grand events of the day compelled suitable evening celebration. And so was convened at the Hotel Maryland in Pasadena what may have been America's first aviation ball, a charity event for the Children's Training Society of Pasadena. The grand march was led by the French aerial knight and Madame Paulhan, new idols of Pasadena and Los Angeles society.

To promote the theme of progress in transportation, the aviation committee arranged for an Oregon Trail ox cart (with oxen, of course) to be brought to the mesa, and photographers had a heyday shooting pictures of the cart and the newfangled aeroplanes. Paulhan refused to pose with the animal and venerable cart despite an explanation of the pioneering role played by such transport. Said he, "What is an Oregon?"

Gallic hauteur, however, did not deter a more durable contribution to the advancement of aviation—the conversion to aviation enthusiast of one of America's most influential men. William Randolph Hearst was among the passengers Louis Paulhan carried during demonstrations at Dominguez Hills. Naturally,

the newspaper tycoon's venture aloft was attended by a host of writers, photographers, and editors. As the machine was about to take off, one of Hearst's minions dashed from the sidelines, shouting over the clatter of the engine, "W.R.!" "What is it?" the great man called. "Mrs. Hearst says for you to tuck in your coat tails!" W.R. complied, exchanged his black sombrero for Paulhan's little felt cap, and the Farman taxied away, the press lord's progress to be duly reported throughout the Hearst empire. Later that year Hearst established a $50,000 prize for the first coast-to-coast flight to be completed within a 30-day period by October 10, 1911.

By any measure, the 11 days of flying at Dominguez Hills were a resounding success. Paulhan won $14,000 in prize money; Curtiss, $6,000; Hamilton, $3,500; and Willard, $250. Aggregate attendance was 176,466; receipts totaled $137,520, against expenses of approximately $115,000.

In his address at the closing ceremonies, chairman D.A. Hamburger waxed prophetic:

*There has just passed in review before you the evolution of time, from the slow moving oxen to the speedy aircraft, the future possibilities of which are beyond even the fertile imagination of man. Time is too short to dwell upon the immensity and the possibility of what the future may bring forth in the utilization of the air as a popular highway of navigation. Certain it is that we have seen demonstrated before our very eyes that machines can fly. It only awaits the ingenuity and fertility of man's inventative and practical genius to make this mode of transportation a mercantile fact. The people of Los Angeles should feel proud that it was, and is, the only place in this broad land of ours where in the month of January the atmosphere is balmy, light and warm enough to permit of such a successful meet.*

Even in 1910 Californians recognized the potential of the site and the future of aviation.

## AN INDUSTRY IS BORN

From among the entrepreneurs, designers, and aviators in California who were accomplishing much, the man who must be credited with establishing the state's aviation industry is Glenn Luther Martin.

Born in Macksburg, Iowa, on January 17, 1886, Martin grew up in Kansas, spending his earliest days in Liberal, attending high school in Salina. He studied business at Kansas Wesleyan University for a time, before his mother Minta's health motivated the family's move in 1905 to Santa Ana, California.

Closely following the work of Chanute and Lilienthal, Glenn had built box kites (and sold quite a few to classmates as well) and recognized that the Wright Flyer closely resembled some of his own designs. When only 19, Glenn joined his father Clarence (known as C.Y.) in opening a garage and securing a dealership for Ford and Maxwell autos and invested some of his money in his secret love, aviation. With the help of his mother (Minta, later to be called "The First Lady of Aviation," was unfailingly supportive of her son's aeronautical ambitions from the beginning until her death in 1953 at the age of 89) and his friend and mechanic at the garage, Roy Beall, Martin spent a year working in his spare time on a monoplane design to be powered by a Ford engine. An instructor in mechanics at the local YMCA, Charles Day, carved the laminated wood propeller as the airframe neared completion. In July 1908 the aeroplane was ready for tests and was towed behind Glenn's Ford roadster to a local pasture. But during a ground taxi run, the engine stalled at the pasture's far edge. Glenn, not waiting for Roy to reach him, got off his seat and swung the prop, which instantly spun. Before the startled pilot-to-be could remount, the machine lunged out of control and crashed without lifting off the ground. Angry but determined, Martin vowed he'd try again, despite the fact that his glasses were lost, his clothing ripped, his hands cut, and nearly $2,000 and months of hard work gone in a sad little heap of broken pieces.

Glenn sought approval from the Wright brothers before proceeding with his next design, a pusher-type biplane. Orville wrote back, saying: "I and my brother have no objections to your building a plane according to the design you have outlined to us."

Martin rented (for $12 a month) an abandoned Methodist church at Second and Main streets near his Santa Ana garage in which to work secretly on his new airplane. When it was complete, Martin and his crew (Minta, Day, and Beall) performed what has since become a virtually compulsory ritual for airframe builders, "the rollout," one summer midnight in 1909. Pushing the plane along, in Orange County aviation historian Vi Smith's words, "like a mother pushing a baby carriage," they set out on the four-mile trip to a 160-acre lima bean field belonging to James Irvine, Jr., the largest landowner around Santa Ana. Irvine had understandably declined 23-year-old Glenn's invitation to be his first passenger.

Checking the plane carefully as a few well-wishers watched, Martin's group awaited first light. At dawn Beall swung the prop. Although he had never actually piloted an aircraft into flight, Martin decided this time not to risk taxi tests. Instead, he touched the throttle and the plane lurched across the field. Advancing the throttle further and adjusting his controls for the wind, he whispered to himself, "Now!" Abruptly the violent bumping stopped. He was airborne. With characteristic cautiousness, he quickly cut the throttle and let the plane settle back to earth. On August 1, 1909, Martin had flown 100 feet, about eight feet high, for some 12 seconds—the first powered flight of a heavier-than-air machine in California and the third in the United States, after the Wrights and Curtiss.

Martin sailed exuberantly ahead, and by late 1910 he had built an entirely new plane with a 60-horsepower motor manufactured by the Hall-Scott Motorcar Company of San Francisco, the first production engine specifically designed to power aircraft. Until then, aero engines were principally of French origin, but in 1909 E.J. Hall developed a four-cylinder aircraft engine that was extraordinarily light, powerful, and reliable.

From December 24, 1910, to January 2, 1911, Los Angeles' second air meet hosted more than twice as many aviators as the first Dominguez Hills gathering, and Glenn Martin's 12-minute flight in the novice category earned him $450 in prize money. By this time Martin had gained enough experience to travel east to compete in exhibition meetings on a level with Curtiss and the Wrights, and in August 1911 he received Expert Pilot's License No. 2 from the Aero Club of California. He was granted U.S. Pilot License No. 56.

Resourceful, energetic, and imaginative, Glenn Martin in the next few years was practically an industry of his own. In 1910 he and his mechanics, Roy Beall and Charlie Day, moved the airplane operation from the church to an abandoned cannery and incorporated the Glenn L. Martin Company. By early 1912, with a growing roster of employees, still larger facilities were needed, and Martin moved his operation to an industrial warehouse in nearby Los Angeles.

While aircraft construction continued in the factory at 943 South Los Angeles Street, Martin was in the field with seemingly endless exhibition flying. He completed a record-setting, 37-minute over-water flight from Newport Beach to Catalina Island with his new Martin Hydro-Aeroplane on May 10, 1912. He opened his own flying school, advertising his company's flying fields as "Griffith Park and Los Angeles Harbor."

At the factory Martin and his engineers developed the Martin "Model T," a tractor biplane with a Curtiss engine and four-wheel landing gear, with which in 1913 he set a new American altitude record with passengers aboard, flying to 9,800 feet. Martin eventually delivered dual-control Model Ts, the first Army Signal Corps training aircraft, to North Island, San Diego, and the Army bought 17 Model T and improved Model TTs in one of the first quantity military aircraft orders.

Recognizing the value of the parachute, Martin demonstrated its capabilities with an eye to publicity. On June 21, 1913, eighteen-year-old Georgia "Tiny" Broadwick floated into the record books as the first woman to parachute from an airplane (Tiny had performed the feat before from balloons) when she jumped from an airplane piloted by Glenn Martin over Griffith Field, Los Angeles.

On April 4, 1914, together with his colleagues, including Charlie Willard and Floyd Smith, Martin provided headline-making evidence of the military capabilities of aircraft with his cleverly staged "Battle of the Clouds." As part of opening ceremonies sponsored by the local chamber of commerce at "The World's Greatest Speedway" at Pomona, Martin and his ground crew built an imposing fort of plywood, chickenwire, and pâpier-maché on the fairgrounds. With much brouhaha, Martin and Smith circled the structure in their Martin-built Army Scouts and unleashed a cascade of bombs made of sacks filled with oranges and flour, all accompanied by spectacular explosions, which he later revealed were detonated by remote control. The "fort" was flattened, and the "battle" made fine press and good conversation long afterward.

Martin provided training ground for several men who would themselves earn great distinction. His first shop foreman in Los Angeles was Lawrence Bell, whose Bell Aircraft Company would later build America's first jet, the XP-59A Airacomet of 1942, and the X-1, the first aircraft to fly faster than the speed of sound, on October 14, 1947, at Muroc Army Air Field. Donald Douglas did his first aircraft engineering for Martin in 1915, and William E. Boeing, founder of the Boeing Company, was an early student at Griffith Park.

In August 1916, persuaded by an Eastern syndicate, Martin merged his company with that of the Wrights, and the Glenn L. Martin Company became a subsidiary of the Wright-Martin Company of New York. The merger was never a happy one: Douglas soon left to serve with the Army Signal Corps' Aviation Section, and Martin chafed at his subordinate role. When his old friend Frank Garbutt arranged financial backing through a group of Ohio industrialists, Martin left Los Angeles to form a new Glenn L. Martin Company in Cleveland. The company moved to Baltimore, Maryland, on October 27, 1929, to enjoy years of success, particularly with the famed Clipper flying boats for Pan American Airways in the 1930s and such honored World War II designs as the B-26 Marauder and the

Mars flying boats. Although it defied the more usual pattern by its eastward move, Glenn Martin's company holds honored pride of place as California's pioneer airframe manufacturer.

## CURTISS' SECOND BASE
Glenn Curtiss in the winter of 1910 began developing an airplane to operate from the water, a project little aided by the local Hammondsport, New York, weather. Happily, Curtiss and his group were invited back to California to the January 1911 San Francisco air meet, and California's climate proved ideal for his aviation plans. And so, after a survey of potential sites for his hydroplane project, Curtiss opted for San Diego. There the Spreckrels family (noted for their sugar company) provided an area near Spanish Bight on North Island at Coronado, and a field was cleared on which the Aero Club of San Diego constructed hangars and sheds. During his San Diego affiliation Curtiss would earn the title, "Father of American Naval Aviation."

## AVIATION AND THE NORTH
In February 1912 an Oakland meet was the first major competition dominated by airplanes powered by engines especially designed for aviation, some 70 percent of the aircraft being equipped with the Hall-Scott engine. And California's first female aviator, Blanche Scott of Los Angeles, was the star of the show, making several flights in a Glenn Martin machine and significantly spurring the interest of women in the new sport of flying.

San Francisco's first major meet was held at Selfridge Field, between Tanforan and South San Francisco, January 7-25, 1911. (The new field had been named to honor Lt. Thomas E. Selfridge, military aviation's first fatality. The Army's devoted young aero advocate and colleague of Alexander Graham Bell and Glenn Curtiss was killed at Fort Meyer on September 17, 1908, while observing aboard the first Wright plane delivered to the Army. The crash, which severely injured pilot Orville Wright, was caused by a collapsing wing support.) Among the world-renowned aviators

present was Hubert Latham of France with his Antoinette monoplane. The Wrights entered an aircraft flown by Walter Brookins and Philip O. Parmalee; and the Curtiss operation was represented by Lincoln Beachey, Hugh Robinson, and Eugene Ely.

## FRED WISEMAN, ICONOCLAST
At Santa Rosa one of the state's best-known aviation pioneers developed his skills. Fred J. Wiseman, originally an auto-racing driver, heard about the flying achievements of the Wright brothers while racing at Dayton, Ohio, and returned to Santa Rosa determined to build his own aircraft. Wiseman assembled photos of existing aircraft, finally deciding to build one similar to a modified French Farman, using a Hall-Scott engine. Wiseman first flew his airplane on May 30, 1910.

Describing his embryonic efforts, Wiseman was candid: "We didn't have any blueprints. We stuck an elevator out in front because everyone else did. All it was was a kite with a motor in it." In February 1911 Wiseman flew some 12 miles from Petaluma to Santa Rosa, showing his hometown folks the capabilities of his aircraft. As a stunt, Wiseman carried groceries, newspapers, and mail for delivery in Santa Rosa: the flight is now recognized by the National Air and Space Museum as the first airmail flight in the world.

## $50,000 CROSS-COUNTRY INCENTIVE
Although Hearst's $50,000 prize for the first coast-to-coast crossing of the United States within a 30-day period was to expire October 10, 1911, it was not until a month before the deadline that three aviators, two starting from the East and one from the West, took off in an effort to win the prize.

From San Francisco on September 11, 1911, Robert Fowler, a student of the Wrights, took off, circled the Golden Gate, and ultimately reached Sacramento that same day. Although making it up to 8,000 feet in the Sierra's Donner Pass, Fowler was forced back and out of the contest. On September 13 ex-jockey James J. Ward headed west in a Curtiss aeroplane out of New

York, lost his way in the fog over New Jersey, and landed only 20 miles away, then cracked up in New York State and abandoned the quest. Neither man completed even one-tenth of the route.

But these ill-fated efforts dimmed not one bit the gritty determination of a gentle, jovial giant whose success transcends mere contests. Calbraith Perry Rodgers, a former Columbia University football player and yacht and car racer, was one of the Wrights' prize pilots. He soloed in 1911 at the Wrights' school after but 90 minutes of instruction. At 32 Rodgers was a happy-go-lucky, cigar-smoking aviator who stood six foot four and whose hearing was nearly gone from a childhood bout with scarlet fever.

For their star pupil, the Wrights built a Model EX Flyer, a single-seat version of their Model B with a top speed of 60 miles per hour. Rodgers made a deal with the Armour Company of Chicago to promote their soft drink called "Vin Fiz" by naming his aeroplane the *Vin Fiz Flyer*. Accompanied by a special train with Pullman car and day coach for his wife, mother, and crew, and with plenty of spare parts, Rodgers set out from a racetrack near Sheepshead Bay, New York, on Sunday, September 17, 1911. The first leg of the flight was smooth and uneventful, hardly a portent of things to come, and his landing 84 miles later at Middletown, New York, was perhaps his last calm moment of the trip.

Rodgers had his first two incidents while still in New York State, was storm damaged in Indiana, and finally landed in Chicago on October 8 with only two days remaining till the Hearst deadline. Said Rodgers: "Prize or no prize, I mean to get there!"

On across Missouri, Kansas, Oklahoma, Texas, into Southern California via the Salton Sea, and through the San Gorgonio Pass near Palm Springs, Rodgers pressed on to land on November 5, 1911, at Pasadena's Tournament Park, the original site of the Tournament of Roses, having covered 4,231 miles—just 20 miles short of the Pacific. He'd missed the Hearst prize, but most newspapers and the public considered that he had completed the first coast-to-coast aircraft flight. Rodgers, however, didn't agree. A week later he took off from Pasadena to fly to the water's edge at Long Beach. At Compton, 12 miles short of his destination, his reconditioned engine failed and Rodgers crashed into a plowed field. Recovering consciousness in the hospital, with internal injuries and a broken ankle, he announced his determination to complete the flight.

On December 10, crutches strapped to the wings, Rodgers flew to Long Beach, landed on the sand, and touched *Vin Fiz's* wheels in the surf of the Pacific. The trip had taken 84 days, but the gallant airman had averaged a mile a minute while in the air, had overcome five major crashes, a host of lesser accidents, in-flight engine failures, and hospital time.

One youngster who almost every day poked around the old factory where Cal Rodgers kept and repaired his airplanes was Richard Millar. Later a member of the Douglas Aircraft and Northrop Corporation boards of directors and president of Vultee Aircraft, Millar vividly recalls Rodgers' ruddy face lined from racing and flying, and the inevitable cigar and checkered cap with the peak turned round.

Sadly, Millar was also witness to Cal Rodgers' last flight. Sitting on the beach in front of the big bathhouse on the Long Beach Pike, Millar watched on April 3, 1912, as Rodgers flew an exhibition to celebrate his successful transcontinental flight the previous year. Rodgers buzzed the crowd at the amusement park, then flew seaward at about 50 or 75 feet. Then, according to the *New York Herald*, "Seeing a flock of gulls disporting themselves among the great shoal of sardines just over the breakers, Rodgers again turned and dived down into them, scattering the seafowl in all directions." Rodgers' body and the wreckage of the plane were later recovered from the water.

APPROACHING TAKEOFF
Still a long way from maturity, California aviation had outgrown its infancy. Major strides had been made at Dominguez Hills, at San Diego, at San Francisco, at Oakland, at Santa Rosa, at Long Beach.

By the end of 1912, two thousand four hundred eighty-two aviator certificates had been awarded in the world, principally in France, Great Britain, and Germany, but only 193 in the entire United States. Even in the absence of records to indicate geographic distribution of these licensed fliers, reasonable speculation suggests that because of Curtiss, Martin, and others who had begun to teach flying in California, in the early days of this century most of America's aviators were California's aviators.

California wings were stretching in the skies over the United States and would soon spread worldwide.

*Top left: Mrs. Dick Ferris, wife of the January 1910 Dominguez Hills Air Meet's principal organizer, cheerily converses with Louis Paulhan before her flight in Paulhan's Farman in which she became the first American woman to fly in an airplane. Courtesy, SPNBPC/LAPL*

*Top right: As pilot Louis Paulhan and the ground crew ready the Farman for flight at Dominguez Hills in January 1910, W.R. Hearst settles in for his first trip aloft. Clearly seen are the aircraft's large ailerons, the first efficient ones fitted to any airplane. Courtesy, SPNBPC/LAPL*

*Above: An Oregon Trail ox cart, featured in the Dominguez Hills Air Meet parades, provided a vivid contrast to the swift aeroplanes that so delighted spectators. French aviator Louis Paulhan, declining to pose for photographs, asked "What is an Oregon?" Courtesy, SPNBPC/LAPL*

Piloting a plane of his own design on March 14, 1915, Lincoln Beachey took off before a crowd of 50,000 at San Francisco's Panama-Pacific Exposition. From 6,000 feet he began a dive over the bay during which the plane's wings collapsed and Beachey was killed. Courtesy, Smithsonian Institution

Soon after arriving in San Diego from New York early in 1911, Glenn Curtiss began the historic sea and land plane flights that persuaded the U.S. Navy of the practicability of the aeroplane for Naval service. Here a crew eases a Curtiss pusher hydroaeroplane into the water for a test flight at North Island. Courtesy, SPNBPC/LAPL

Cal Rodgers, star pupil of the Wrights, soloed after 90 minutes and later won the nation's heart for his courageous trip in the Vin Fiz Flyer in 1911, the first coast-to-coast flight. One accident broke his ankle, but on December 10, 1911, with crutches strapped to the wings, Rodgers flew the last 12 miles to touch his plane's wheels in the Pacific. Courtesy, CALAC

Glenn Martin flew at the second
Dominguez Hills meet in December 1910
(when this photo may have been taken). As
able a publicist as he was a builder and
flyer, Martin did much to achieve public
acceptance of flying. He was known as ''The
Flying Dude'' because of his stylish flying
attire. Courtesy, SPNBPC/LAPL

In the summer of 1909 Glenn Martin
rented an abandoned Methodist church at
Second and Main streets in Santa Ana to
work on his second plane with his friend
and assistant, Roy Beall. The biplane,
shown under construction here, was
Martin's first successful design. Courtesy,
SPNBPC/LAPL

CHAPTER THREE

# GIANTS OF AVIATION'S GOLDEN AGE

The years from 1927 through the 1930s are sometimes characterized as America's Golden Age of Aviation. For California, however, that Golden Age glimmered first with the work of Glenn Martin and Glenn Curtiss in the years just before World War I. The glow began to radiate in earnest during the the 1920s.

With the end of the "War to End All Wars," hundreds of young men who had tasted the romance of flight in the skies over France or at hastily built training fields in the United States returned to civilian life. And an uncounted horde of war surplus airplanes sold for as little as $300 apiece.

Airplanes, aviators, and grass or dirt strips were very much a novelty to most Americans, and airplanes and the men who flew them became the "stars" of county fairs and local carnivals while airports blossomed in open fields all over California.

In the broader national context, a necessary framework was being assembled to support both potential suppliers and users of aeronautical goods and services. The Air Commerce Act of 1926 became effective January 1, 1927, providing for federal regulation of interstate air commerce, for the examination and licensing of all airmen and aircraft engaged in interstate activities, and for the implementation of vital navigation and terminal services. The nation's growing prosperity combined with aviation's increasingly evident potential in the 1920s to make capital available from previously indifferent financial institutions for many aviation projects, particularly development of aircraft for the transport of mail and passengers on newly established air routes. And the military

complex was fast forging powerful links to aviation which would do more than any single factor to irrevocably establish aircraft manufacturers as legitimate participants in the nation's economic establishment.

## CALIFORNIA INDUSTRY EMERGES

The interrelationships among America's aviation pioneers from the early 1900s on are striking, particularly in California. Direct associations link almost every major figure— Douglas, the Lockheeds, Northrop, Vultee, Ryan, Hughes, and Kindelberger—and Glenn Martin's Los Angeles factory was an early hub of the network, having provided both base and training ground for several "giants" of aviation.

## DONALD WILLS DOUGLAS: THE ARCHETYPE

One of the most imposing figures at Martin's company was Donald Wills Douglas, who had attended the U.S. Naval Academy but resigned to enter the Massachusetts Institute of Technology where he received MIT's first BS in Aeronautical Engineering in 1914. Teaching at MIT for a year, Douglas was also a consultant to Connecticut Aircraft Company. In August 1915 Martin hired Douglas as his chief engineer for the new Los Angeles plant, marking Douglas' debut in California.

Douglas journeyed to Washington in November 1916 to become chief civilian aeronautical engineer for the Aviation Section of the Army's Signal Corps. In 1917 he rejoined Martin, who by then had relocated in Cleveland. Douglas remained with Martin until 1920 when, well aware of the climatic advantage for aircraft manufacturing, he established his own company in Southern California. Setting up headquarters in the back room of a downtown Los Angeles barbershop, Don Douglas set out to acquire financial backing for his newly formed company. Introduced to Southern California aviation circles by Bill Henry (later a nationally recognized journalist and political commentator) of the *Los Angeles Times*, Douglas met David R. Davis.

Davis received *his* aviation orientation in 1909-1910 doing odd jobs around Martin's Orange County shop. In 1915 Davis bought a half interest, with Lawrence Bell, in a Curtiss pusher aircraft. By 1920 Davis was able to put up $40,000 to form the Davis-Douglas Aircraft Company with the intent of building a biplane to be called the Cloudster and designed for transcontinental nonstop flight. The airplane was built on the second floor of the Koll Lumber Company in Los Angeles and lowered piecemeal down the freight elevator.

The Cloudster, unique at the time for its ability to lift its own weight in payload, flew in February 1921, the first product of Davis-Douglas. A nonstop transcontinental flight attempt in June by Davis and chief test pilot Eric Springer ended after 8-1/2 hours at El Paso, Texas, with a stripped timing gear. Meanwhile, in May 1923, Army lieutenants Oakley Kelley and John Macready achieved Davis' dream in a Fokker T-2, flying from New York to San Diego on their third try. The Douglas airplane was eventually rebuilt and used for sightseeing trips around Santa Monica and Venice and bought in 1924 by Claude Ryan who converted it to an 11-passenger layout for his Los Angeles-San Diego airline.

Davis, keenly disappointed by the Cloudster failure, sold his interest in the company to the Douglas family, and in 1922 the business was moved to an abandoned motion picture studio at Wilshire and 26th Street in Santa Monica. Douglas already had a contract to build a new torpedo plane, the DT-1, for the Navy. Follow-on contracts funded 44 DT-1 and -2 aircraft.

Donald Douglas' familiarity with the Eastern establishment and Washington, D.C., acquired at Annapolis, MIT, and the Signal Corps, served his company well throughout a career in which he personally participated in his company's civil and military marketing efforts.

In 1924 four modified Douglas DT aircraft, named Douglas World Cruisers, undertook the first around-the-world flight. To honor the country's four principal regions, the ships were christened (with water from the closest river, ocean, or lake) *Boston, Chicago, New Orleans,* and *Seattle.* Departing from Santa Monica's Clover Field on March 17, 1924, Army pilots flew to Seattle to officially begin the circumnavigation attempt on April 6. Five months (actual flying time was 15 days, 11 hours, and seven minutes) and 27,553 miles later, *Chicago* and *New Orleans* (*Seattle* was lost early in the trip, *Boston* in the Atlantic, their crews unhurt) returned to Seattle on September 28, 1924. The airplanes were flown to Clover Field to salute the men who had built them, and were greeted by a crowd estimated at 200,000, described by the *Chicago's* commander, Lieutenant Lowell Smith:

*All around was a heavy line of guards. As we crawled out of our cockpits, the crowd went wild. With a roar they knocked down the fence. They knocked down the police. They knocked down the soldiers. They knocked us down. They tried to pull our ships apart for souvenirs, but somehow we fought them off.*

With the success of the World Cruisers, Douglas entered the international market when Norway ordered modified versions of the DT. In 1924 the U.S. Army awarded Douglas a contract for the 0-2 advanced observation aircraft. In early 1925 Douglas won its largest single production contract yet, and entered commercial aviation with its first mail plane, the M-1. In November 1925 Western Air Express (today's Western Airlines) became Douglas' first commercial customer when it ordered six M-2s (an M-1 derivative with larger wing and more powerful Liberty engine), one of which made the first Douglas aircraft civil flight from Salt Lake City to Los Angeles in April 1926.

From the Wilshire Boulevard plant all the

Douglas airplanes were towed to Clover Field for assembly and flight, the short grass landing strip adjacent to the Wilshire facility having been deactivated and aviators warned against using it. Nonetheless, one day early in 1927 a young pilot erroneously landed at Wilshire Boulevard. The pilot introduced his passenger, former Douglas engineer Donald Hall, now working for Ryan Airlines in San Diego, who had business with Mr. Douglas. When asked if he himself worked for Ryan, the pilot said no, that he actually had been flying the mail for Robertson Aircraft Corporation in the Midwest. "My name is Charles Lindbergh," he told the Douglas people, and so among the hero's many honors are listed the final landing and takeoff from the old plant. In 1929 Douglas moved his entire company to the Clover Field site, which it occupied until the 1970s.

In his book, *Climb to Greatness, The American Aircraft Industry, 1920-1960,* John B. Rae notes the significance of the Douglas selection of Southern California as an aircraft manufacturing site:

*The successful establishment of Douglas Aircraft in Southern California was an event of historic importance in the history of the American aircraft industry, far out of proportion to the size of the company at the time. It was the first effective step in the process of geographical concentration that by 1940 would give Southern California 45 per cent of the nation's airframe manufacturing facilities. California has a long history of aeronautical development, including such famous names as John J. Montgomery, Glenn L. Martin, and the Loughead (subsequently Lockheed) brothers, Allan and Malcolm. But Montgomery's gliding experiments were largely forgotten, Martin moved east (or was moved), and the original Lougheed firm in Santa Barbara folded in 1921. Douglas was the first to get into business in Southern California and stay. Donald Douglas also appears to have been the first airframe manufacturer to make a deliberate choice of location. Earlier companies were established where their founders happened to live, financial support was offered, or manufacturing facilities were readily available. Douglas chose the Los Angeles area and*

*then sought his backing and his factory space. In the aircraft industry, accessibility to materials and markets is a negligible factor in determining location, and capital is usually procurable from local sources in a company's early days. A climate that permits year-round flying has been mentioned as one desideratum; the other major one is an adequate supply of skilled and semiskilled labor. Los Angeles had both, and a substantial part of Douglas' success must be credited to his appreciation of these factors as well as to his own talents as an aeronautical designer.*

## THE LOUGHEADS BEGIN IN SAN FRANCISCO

In 1912 the Alco Hydro-Aeroplane Company was founded in San Francisco by Allan and Malcolm Loughead. On June 15, 1913, the two brothers—Allan, a self-taught barnstorming pilot, and Malcolm, a mechanical wizard who subsequently moved to Detroit to perfect the hydraulic automobile brake he invented—launched their Model G Hydro-aeroplane. (The "G" was intended to suggest to prospective buyers a lineage of six worthy predecessor designs.) The wood and fabric seaplane they had designed and built in a garage first flew over San Francisco Bay, and transported more than 600 paying passengers, at $10 for a 10-minute ride, during the 50 days of the 1915 Panama-Pacific International Exposition in San Francisco, and provided the capital for a second business venture.

In 1916 the Lougheads moved to Santa Barbara and established the Loughead Aircraft Manufacturing Company and began work (again in a garage) on the F-1, a twin-engine, 10-passenger flying boat, which first flew in March 1918. The Lougheads continued to carry passengers on sightseeing trips of the Santa Barbara area.

In addition to being astute designers, manufacturers, and pilots, the Lougheads recognized talent. When the company was first established, they hired Anthony Stadlman, who had known Allan in Chicago, had first soloed in 1912, and was already an accomplished mechanic and craftsman. Stadlman, in charge of production at

Santa Barbara, became factory superintendent at the Hollywood Lockheed plant in the 1920s and stayed in the aviation industry through his entire career, working with North American Aviation during World War II.

Another Loughead hiree was a young Santa Barbaran named John K. "Jack" Northrop. In Jack's words, "I was hired to do mechanical drawings of various parts of the F-1, particularly the wing fairings." But he was soon to contribute far more to precedent-setting Lockheed designs.

During World War I the Lougheads built two Curtiss HS-2L flying boats for the Navy, performing their first military "rollout" in 1918. Even with the industry's bleak plight after the war, the Lougheads saw a market, and soon Jack Northrop designed the first of the uncluttered, stylish aircraft that would mark the Lockheed/ Northrop association. But with its $2,000 price tag, the resulting S-1 couldn't compete with the glut of bargain war surplus aircraft, and Loughead Aircraft closed its Santa Barbara doors in 1921.

Malcolm went to Detroit with his automobile brakes, Allan left for Hollywood and the real-estate business, and Jack went to work for his father in Santa Barbara. (The Loughead name is pronounced, and the spelling was changed to, Lockheed, first by Malcolm in Detroit, then by Allan in Hollywood in December 1926. The elder Victor used the variant "Lougheed" in his published works.)

Combining Northrop's design concepts and Stadlman's production techniques, the Lougheads had experimented in Santa Barbara with the monocoque fuselage, which employs its external covering as a load-bearing structural component. The concept, although assayed by German and French designers, had not yet been utilized for production civil aircraft. Believing that together they could produce a successful monocoque fuselage airplane from designs he'd been working out on his kitchen table, in 1926 Jack Northrop (who since 1921 had worked first for his father's construction outfit, then for Donald Douglas in Santa Monica) sought out Allan. The pair enlisted Kenneth Jay as financial organizer, the three formed Lockheed Aircraft

Company, and construction of the first Lockheed Vega began in Hollywood, the building . . . a garage.

In addition to its sleek monocoque fuselage, formed by molding laminated wood veneer in massive presses, the Vega featured cantilevered wings with no supporting struts. Allan worried that the airplane would never sell without wing struts, even if only for the appearance of safety. Jack steadfastly maintained that struts were unnecessary, and his view prevailed to result in an enormously successful design called by the National Air and Space Museum (NASM), "that beautiful Lockheed Vega."

The airplane was not merely radical in concept and attractive to the eye, but a stellar record and headline maker for nearly two decades. The first Vega was sold to George Hearst, son of William Randolph, for $12,500—something less than its cost of manufacture, but a shrewd trade-off for the saleable glamour of the Hearst name. Vegas were flown by Frank Hawks, Wiley Post, Charles Lindbergh, Amelia Earhart, Sir George Hubert Wilkins, and Roscoe Turner. The airplane set so many records, including Wiley Post's round-the-world flights, that one ad boasted: "It takes a Lockheed to beat a Lockheed."

In 1927 the Hearst-owned Vega flown by Jack Frost, with Gordon Scott as navigator, vanished over the Pacific during the ill-fated California-to-Honolulu Dole Race in which several other crews were lost. Despite that setback, in 1928 Captain George Hubert Wilkins and Ben Eielson flew a Vega across the Arctic. Later that year they took two Vegas to the Antarctic, making the airplane the first to fly over both polar regions.

Wiley Post, who had been a Lockheed test pilot in 1929, set an around-the-world record in the Vega *Winnie Mae* in 1931, then broke his own record in 1933. In 1932 Amelia Earhart made two historic flights, the first solo flight by a woman across the Atlantic and the first solo flight by a woman across the United States, both in the Vega now in the NASM. In 1935 she flew alone from Hawaii to the United States, the first person to do so.

From the Vega, most examples of which were built after the Lockheed factory was moved to

Burbank in 1928, came a number of derivatives, including the Sirius used by Charles Lindbergh and his wife, Anne Morrow Lindbergh, in 1931 and 1933 to survey overseas airline routes. In 1931 the Lindberghs made their famous "North to the Orient" flight, the first east-to-west by the northern route from Maine, across Canada to Alaska and Siberia, then to Tokyo and Nanking, to demonstrate the feasibility of using the "Great Circle" route to reach the Far East. In 1933 the Lindberghs (Charles was then technical advisor for Pan American Airways) flew from New York, up the eastern coast of Canada to Labrador, across the northern route, and into the major cities of Europe as far as Moscow. From there they flew down the west coast of Africa, across the South Atlantic, down the Amazon River, and then north through the Caribbean to return to the United States, having covered 30,000 miles and touched four continents.

In 1929 the flourishing Lockheed operation caught the eye of Detroit Aircraft Corporation, a holding company with dreams of becoming the General Motors of the air, which bought control of Lockheed and 11 other companies. The stock market collapse scuttled Detroit Aircraft's dreams of empire, and the overextended company went into receivership, much to the disgust of the Lockheed people whose operation was healthy enough. Lockheed's general manager, Carl Squier, struggled to keep the plant operating and even sold some additional aircraft to airlines, the military, and private buyers.

Nonetheless, in the heart of the Depression a federal receiver offered the assets of Lockheed for sale. A group headed by Robert E. Gross assembled a consortium and $40,000 to buy Lockheed's assets. The present company dates from this 1932 reorganization.

## AT THE INDUSTRY'S CENTER: JACK NORTHROP'S CAREER

Fascinated with the exhibition flying of a touring aviator in 1911, eleven-year-old John Knudsen Northrop vowed that he'd somehow get into aviation. That vow was fulfilled indeed by a prodigious array of aircraft design achievements during a singularly productive career.

Northrop's first job was as mechanical draftsman-engineer with the Lougheads. To augment his high school education, Jack had experience with his father in architectural design and construction, and mechanical skills honed while he worked as a garage mechanic during high school.

For the Lougheads, Northrop designed the wings of the F-1 flying boat, but his real breakthrough as a designer was the revolutionary S-1 sport biplane, which first revealed the uncluttered look characteristic of his subsequent work. When Loughead folded, Jack stayed briefly in Santa Barbara to work with his father, but in 1923 ventured down the coast to Santa Monica where the young Donald Douglas had his plant. Jack was hired personally by Douglas, and a friendship began that would last their lifetimes.

Assigned to design fuel tanks for the Douglas World Cruisers, Northrop later said: "I'd had experience designing things such as wings and even entire airplanes with the S-1. But I had never designed a fuel tank. The thought of it made me physically ill and I left work early to go home and be sick."

Northrop stayed with Douglas through 1926, but the designs then prevalent at Douglas did not accord with his "clean" airplane concept, and at his famous kitchen table he continued to commit his ideas to paper. With Don Douglas' reluctant blessing, Northrop sought out Allan Loughead to bring those ideas to fruition in the illustrious Lockheed Vega.

In addition to the monocoque fuselage, Northrop had been developing multicellular construction for load-bearing wings and tails, a technique employing a series of thin, nested U-shaped metal forms, which produced airfoils at once both light and strong. Although Lockheed was doing well with the Vega, Jack wanted to develop his advanced notions. And now another dream was taking shape, an airplane reduced to its essence—a pure and elegant single wing. So, in 1928 Jack Northrop left Lockheed to form, with Ken Jay, the Avion Corporation in Burbank.

Northrop's achievements at Avion were

commercial as well as artistic successes. He designed, built, and tested his first flying wing. Although it was not a "pure" wing because it had two booms to hold a tail assembly, the Avion flying wing that took to the air in 1929 demonstrated several aerodynamic concepts, particularly Northrop's conviction that "the cleaner the airplane, the better it will fly."

The Avion craft had multicellular construction in wing and tail assembly, and its first flight was made by Eddie Bellande, a major participant in Vega flight testing who would later test many Northrop designs. In addition, Bellande was a Transcontinental Air Transport pilot who flew in the right-hand seat next to Charles Lindbergh when TAT (later Transcontinental and Western Airlines) inaugurated its west-to-east transcontinental service in 1929.

Avion's commercial success was the Northrop Alpha, which represented a complete transition in air transport manufacture, including all-metal design, the Northrop multicellular cantilever wing, a semi-monocoque fuselage, and streamlined NACA cowling. Its landing gear fairings reduced drag without the weight and complexity of a retractable undercarriage.

In Avion's Burbank factory the Alpha was produced for TWA, the Department of Commerce, and the Army Air Corps. Because it could carry only four passengers, it was eventually transferred to freight service, flying regularly coast-to-coast in 23 hours to bring perishable commodities from California to New York, and was used on TWA's mail routes as well.

So successful was the Alpha, called "one of the most beautiful airplanes in the museum's collection" by the National Air and Space Museum staff, that William Boeing, then president of Boeing Aircraft and Transport Corporation (a division of the giant United Aircraft and Transport Corporation), recommended to his Eastern management that Avion be made a part of United Aircraft. Northrop saw a chance for the infusion of fresh capital and the opportunity to expand his horizons. He accepted, and Avion became the Northrop Aircraft Corporation, a division of United Aircraft. However, in 1932 United consolidated Northrop with its Stearman Aircraft division in Wichita. Having no desire to move to Kansas, Northrop sold his interest in the company.

Banker Richard Millar, then on the board of Douglas Aircraft, heard about Northrop's availability. Would Douglas be interested in again establishing a relationship with Jack? "Would I?" replied Douglas with great enthusiasm. Millar arranged for the two to get together, and in 1932 a new Northrop Corporation was established in partnership with Douglas Aircraft as a division located in El Segundo, with Douglas owning 51 percent, Northrop 49 percent.

From this partnership emerged a new all-metal aircraft, the Gamma, derived from the Alpha. The Gamma was best known for its pioneering TWA flights as the "Experimental Overweather Laboratory" directed by D.W. "Tommy" Tomlinson. Equipped with GE turbo-superchargers, the plane demonstrated high-altitude flight possibilities.

The restored association with Douglas produced important new applications of Northrop's clean design concept, particularly to the famed Douglas series of DC (Douglas Commercial) aircraft that revolutionized world-wide civil air transport. Douglas said of his friend in the 1940s, "Every airplane flying today has some Jack Northrop in it."

By 1938 the Northrop division of Douglas was doing more production than development work and again Northrop wanted to move on to more creative matters, particularly his flying wing. Millar, who had officiated in 1932 at the "marriage," was called in to engineer the "divorce." When Millar talked to Douglas about handling the arrangements for the sale, it had all the prospects of a tough negotiation. As Millar was about to leave Douglas' office to go negotiate, Douglas called him back and said quietly, "Lean Jack's way."

In 1939 Northrop formed the third company to bear his name (the fourth in which he had participated in creating), the Northrop Aircraft Corporation in Hawthorne, California. This would be the start of the present Northrop Corporation and the platform from which Jack could launch his Flying Wing and the P-61 Black Widow night fighter/interceptor.

## A FLIGHT THAT CHANGED HISTORY

Charles A. Lindbergh's nonstop solo flight across the Atlantic from New York to Paris in May 1927 at a stroke captured the world's imagination and powerfully accelerated popular acceptance of air transport. Whatever else the achievement may represent, it was a triumph of aviation's most enduring values—sound technical conception and execution, meticulous attention to detail, methodical planning, skilled airmanship, resolute determination, and great courage. Lindbergh's gifts were many, but his contribution to aviation derived substantially from his remarkable capacity to generate cooperation among his colleagues and trust from the general public through his unfailing insistence upon thoroughgoing excellence. The name Lindbergh became synonymous with aviation progress. And with it went the name Ryan.

## "RYAN, THE AVIATOR"

T. Claude Ryan was yet another transplanted Midwesterner, whose family had moved from Kansas by way of Vancouver, Washington. Influenced early by the work of Glenn Martin in Santa Ana, young Claude Ryan dedicated his energies to an aviation career, even applying for work with the fledgling Martin Company in Los Angeles where he was turned down as too inexperienced.

After several attempts to sign up for military pilot training at San Diego's Rockwell Field during World War I, Ryan was finally accepted three days before the Armistice was signed. His orders were promptly cancelled, but he persevered and began Army Air Service flight training in 1920 at March Field.

In 1922 Ryan ventured once again to Rockwell Field where he met the commanding officer, Major Henry H. "Hap" Arnold. Buying a surplus Jenny for $400, he opened Ryan Flying Company in September 1922 to launch his

"empire" with barnstorming and demonstration passenger flights. A leaflet dropped over towns announced his arrival in bold circus lettering: "FLY WITH ME. TAKE A Real Trip Thru The Clouds. RYAN, The Aviator is in Your City." He eventually acquired several Standard J-1 biplanes that he converted for passenger service and began his Los Angeles-San Diego Air Line with headquarters in both cities.

One mechanic in the Los Angeles shop was Douglas Corrigan, who would gain fame in the late 1930s as "Wrong Way" Corrigan. Refitting an old plane at Ryan's San Diego shop, but warned against making a transatlantic flight, he flew from New York to Ireland, contending upon touchdown in the land of the Blarney Stone that he thought he'd been headed for California.

By now Ryan had been joined by a fellow pilot and playboy, B. Franklin Mahoney, who provided financing for the company. In 1925 Ryan designed an airplane called the M-1. After some discussion the partners decided to go ahead and produce the aircraft; in 1926 the first M-1 was rolled out. It flew, but needed engineering refinements beyond the knowledge of Ryan and his colleagues. Ryan called his friend Jack Northrop, then working for Douglas, for help. "If it's OK with Doug, I can sure use the money," said Jack. Douglas admonished Ryan, "Remember now, Claude, just weekends." And so Northrop and his friend Art Mankey began working Saturdays and Sundays in San Diego. They redesigned the wing, reducing overall weight by 200 pounds, and other refinements contributed substantially to the outstanding performance of the M-1, its successor M-2, and its most prestigious variant, Lindbergh's *Spirit of St. Louis*. The Ryan M-1/M-2 became the first production monoplane in the U.S. and was used to open the Los Angeles-Seattle airmail service operated by Pacific Air Transport.

Having found little interest among the major aircraft manufacturers to build a machine to his demanding specifications, Lindbergh ventured to San Diego to talk with the management of relatively unknown Ryan Airlines. On February 24, 1927, he wired his backers in St.

Louis: "BELIEVE RYAN CAPABLE OF BUILDING PLANE WITH SUFFICIENT PERFORMANCE. STOP. COST COMPLETE WITH WHIRLWIND ENGINE AND STANDARD INSTRUMENTS IS TEN THOUSAND FIVE HUNDRED EIGHTY DOLLARS. STOP. DELIVERY WITHIN SIXTY DAYS. STOP. RECOMMEND CLOSING DEAL. LINDBERGH." The 60-day race was on.

Lindbergh, with the support of his St. Louis backers, while in San Diego "really wrung out" the M-1. He was happy with the results, and work quickly began on the N-X-211 Ryan NYP (New York to Paris) with Lindbergh working constantly with Donald Hall, engineer in charge of the design modifications, and the factory staff. The aircraft was constructed at the Ryan plant and then towed to Dutch Flats Airport for its maiden flight on April 28, 1927, exactly 60 days after the awarding of the contract. Following several days of flight tests, Lindbergh flew to St. Louis and on to New York, establishing records as he went. At 7:52 in the morning on May 20 he took off from Long Island's Roosevelt Field for his rendezvous with history.

Just before the contract to build the "Spirit," Ryan had sold his interest in the company he had founded to Mahoney for $25,000 and an M-2 plane, but remained as general manager for some time. Twenty-six years after the event, Ryan wrote to Lindbergh, "Although I no longer owned a financial interest in the company during the period your plane was being built, I had the satisfaction of knowing that I had developed a team which had the ability, confidence, enthusiasm, and energy to do the job."

In a presentation copy for Ryan of his book, *The Spirit of St. Louis*, Lindbergh inscribed these words: "To Claude Ryan, who built the company that built the 'Spirit of St. Louis.' With best wishes, Charles A. Lindbergh 1953."

Ryan continued to make important contributions to California aviation through his various enterprises in San Diego. The company derived from the original Ryan venture is now known as Teledyne Ryan Aeronautical.

## THE STEEL WORKER'S SON

Among California's eclectic aviation pioneers, national origins were diverse—Scotch, Scandinavian, Irish, English—and one with a legacy of strict German work discipline. James Howard ("Dutch") Kindelberger, born in Wheeling, West Virginia, the son of a German immigrant steel molder and his wife, quit school at 16 to work as a foundry apprentice. Young Kindelberger took correspondence courses, became a civilian draftsman/inspector with the Army Engineering Corps, continued working nights until he completed high school, then passed the entrance examination for Pittsburgh's Carnegie Institute of Technology. Kindelberger stayed for his freshman year at Carnegie Tech, leaving to join the Army in 1917.

Like so many others, Kindelberger found his call to aviation in the military. Enlisting in the Engineers, he soon transferred to the Aviation Section of the Signal Corps. Sure, he had seen Lincoln Beachey flying at the Wheeling Fair Grounds, but it was the Army that gave him his chance to fly. Learning on the ubiquitous Jenny, Kindelberger received ground training at Ohio State University, preliminary flight familiarization at Dallas, and early flying practice at Park Field, Memphis, Tennessee. He didn't make it to France.

With the romance of flight still coursing through his veins, the returning veteran said, "I decided to try my luck with the very young, and very small aircraft industry. . . ." That industry was so small that Kindelberger was immediately initiated into an elite fraternity in Cleveland, Ohio. The fraternity, of course, was the Glenn L. Martin Company, and its cadre was Martin, Donald Douglas, and Larry Bell.

When Douglas returned to California, he asked Kindelberger to come along. Kindelberger told Douglas he would prefer getting more experience with Martin but might come later. At Martin in 1920 he became chief draftsman and assistant chief engineer. His years there saw the advent of the all-metal seaplane, heavy bombardment aircraft, and the MB-2 bomber General Billy Mitchell would use in 1922 to demonstrate the capabilities of air power.

Kindelberger's experiences at Martin served him well. In the 1920s there were some 300 aircraft factories in America, including, as Kindelberger put it, "those where you had to shove the cow aside to see the airplane." Fortunately, Kindelberger was able to move from one major airplane manufacturer to another. Although he'd never been to California, he picked up his option in 1925 when he joined Douglas as chief engineer, and in 1928 was named vice-president of engineering. The Douglas staff then included not only Kindelberger, but Jack Northrop, Ed Heinemann, and John Leland (Lee) Atwood, a quiet Texas mathematician who had joined from Moreland Aircraft. Responding to the incentive of management advancement, but particularly to the challenge of running his own company, Kindelberger reluctantly resigned from Douglas to move east as president of newly restructured North American Aviation (NAA). Lee Atwood and Douglas engineer J.S. "Stan" Smithson went with him, and within the year they would return to California, bringing North American Aviation with them.

During his NAA years Dutch Kindelberger made a telling contribution to American preparedness for World War II. In June 1938 Dutch was in England discussing trainer aircraft sales, and as he toured he noted the handcrafting techniques used in British aircraft factories. Then, trading on aviation's camaraderie, and doubtless his German heritage, Kindelberger fulfilled a secret Army Air Corps request to visit Germany. He received a cordial invitation from Ernst Udet, World War I German ace and an air show acquaintance. Under Udet's aegis (he was high in the Nazi war machine) he was the first outsider to see what was happening at Messerschmitt; at Heinkel he compared production techniques with his Inglewood factory and was told Germany had copied American production methods. Udet showed him production lines able to turn out 1,000 aircraft per month. Reporting his observations and astute conclusions about German and British aviation preparations for a war sure to come, Kindelberger in 1938 provided the U.S. Army Air Corps with intelligence it could not otherwise

have uncovered.

At Douglas and at North American, Kindelberger was a motivator, a driver. During World War II, as first president of California's Aircraft War Production Control Council (representing all the state's aircraft manufacturers), Kindelberger personally badgered the nation's War Production Board for materials, machinery, and priorities. He nagged, chided, stormed, and slashed at red tape, the automotive industry's "blacksmith" techniques, and draft boards for taking engineers he considered indispensible to the war effort. At Kindelberger's insistence, his company astounded industry and government alike when it returned to the U.S. government $14 million saved by increased efficiency in trainer aircraft manufacturing.

Ingenious, bold, and persevering, these men established an industry and shaped an era.

*Introduced in 1919, the innovative Loughead S-1 Sport Biplane with a $2,000 price tag could not compete with bargain war surplus aircraft, even when promoted by publicity photographs such as this one with a movie actress in front of San Francisco City Hall. Courtesy, CALAC*

*Top: Allan (left) and Malcolm Loughead's second successful aircraft project was the 1918 F-1, a 10-passenger flying boat with a 74-foot wingspan. The big boat attracted the Navy's interest and was put through lengthy acceptance trials at North Island. When the Navy chose Curtiss' H2-SL instead, the Lougheads converted their airframe to the F-1A, a landplane. Courtesy, CALAC*

*Above: The Loughead brothers' initial aircraft, the Model G Hydroaeroplane, powered by an 80-hp water-cooled Curtiss V-8 engine, first flew on June 15, 1913, from San Francisco Bay. Its second flight, with Allan piloting and Malcolm as passenger, lasted an impressive 20 minutes. Courtesy, CALAC*

39

*Above: Claude Ryan bought the Davis-Douglas* Cloudster *for his Los Angeles-San Diego Airline and converted the mammoth biplane into a luxurious, 10-passenger airliner—the first of the Douglas line of big passenger planes. Courtesy, Gordon Williams*

*Opposite, top: In 1924 four Douglas World Cruisers undertook the first around-the-world flight, departing from Santa Monica's Clover Field on March 17 in U.S. Army Air Force colors.* Chicago, *shown here, was one of the pair which completed the flight five months (flying time 363 hours) and 27,553 miles later. Courtesy, McDonnell Douglas (MD)*

*Jack Northrop poses with the first incarnation of his dream—the flying wing—at the Avion Corporation plant in 1929. Although not a pure wing (it had a boom-supported tail), the ship allowed Northrop to test his ideas, which would find ultimate expression in the massive YB-49 almost two decades later. Courtesy, NC*

*In 1920 David Davis invested with Donald Douglas to form the Davis-Douglas Aircraft Company, intending to build a biplane for a coast-to-coast nonstop flight. The resulting* Cloudster *flew in February 1921 but was beaten across the continent by an Army Fokker T-2 in May 1923. Disappointed, Davis sold his interest in the company to Douglas. Courtesy, MD*

*Before beginning Pacific Air Transport's Los Angeles-San Francisco-Seattle route in September 1926 with Ryan M-1 monoplanes, Vern Gorst (left) engaged Claude Ryan himself (right) to conduct meticulous survey and proving flights. Here the pair arrive in Seattle. Courtesy, Teledyne Ryan*

# PART TWO: BUILDERS

GALCIT Director Theodore Von Kármán (1881-1963), acknowledged by peers as the preeminent aeronautical scientist of his time, was a tireless innovator and leader whose profound contribution to worldwide aviation progress included the grounding of aero education on a firm base of theoretical science. Courtesy, Caltech Archives

# CHAPTER FOUR

# AIRCRAFT MANUFACTURERS

Spurred by venturesome men who imagined great opportunity following World War I, aircraft manufacturing sprang up in garages, hangars, barns, and abandoned buildings around the state, centering in Southern California. Time would glean from these many acorns only a few oaks. But the contribution of these small enterprises was by no means negligible in the grander scheme. Often the tiny springs of imaginative design, manufacture, and operation made possible the rivers upon which the dominant builders launched their technological triumphs.

## NAMES LONG FORGOTTEN

Those who took up aviation's challenge in 1919 hoped to succeed in a marketplace just discovering aeronautics as it emerged from the realm of theory into practical technology. There were abundant aviators who had tasted the romance of flight either in the skies over France or at stateside training fields. Added to California's appeal as a place to begin were glowing reports of men who had trained at San Diego and Los Angeles. And there was plenty of challenge for all.

In 1919 Waldo Waterman established W.D. Waterman Aircraft Manufacturing Company in Venice, California, to design and build the sleek Mercury Gosling for Cecil B. De Mille's Mercury Aviation Company. Later an engineer and test pilot for Bach Aircraft Company, in 1928 Waterman helped establish Metropolitan Airport at Van Nuys, where he later became general manager.

Kinner Airplane and Motor Corporation produced "business, pleasure and sport" aircraft, including engines, first in a downtown Los Angeles factory, with flying operations at the Kinner Air Drome in Long Beach; later the factory was moved to Glendale Airport. Their best-known model was the Airster, advertised in 1925 as "America's foremost sport plane, a lady's plane as well as a man's," one example becoming Amelia Earhart's first personal airplane. By 1933 Kinner had formed Security National Aircraft Company in Downey, offering a low-wing, single-place monoplane, the Security Airster.

Otto Timm was known for his unique aircraft, among them the Argonaut, built for Dr. T.C. Young, chairman of the Aviation Council of the California Development Association, and later acquired by famed racer Roscoe Turner. His Pacific Hawk, a twin-engine, six-place biplane, was built by Pacific Airplane and Supply Company in Venice.

In 1921 the Catron & Fisk Airplane and Engine Company was founded in Ocean Park and began producing the CF11, a small sport biplane resembling combat aircraft of the war. Catron & Fisk for its next design added a third wing (not unlike German Fokker triplanes), the aircraft first being powered by three Ford Model T engines, later by two Curtiss OX-5s.

Once established, a production facility often housed successive operations. When Catron & Fisk moved to Long Beach to make the International, then moved to Cincinnati, the plant was taken over by Courier Monoplane Company. Kinner's Downey location became the site for Vultee Aircraft, then for a North American Aviation facility, and today is part of Rockwell.

The post-World War I era produced a mixed bag of airplane designs. Some worked, others didn't. The Belcher California was a boxy monoplane whose distinction was a woven wood veneer fuselage, much like a basket, that proved light and strong. Unfortunately the prototype aircraft crashed, killing the designer, his wife, and son. The largest Southern California monoplane was the Zenith Albatross, built at Midway City in Orange County. With a span of 90 feet and a 47-foot fuselage, the Zenith attempted flight endurance records during 1928, one flight above Imperial Valley lasting 47 hours.

In 1927 Larry Brown built the Brown Mercury *City of Angeles*, an open cockpit, high-wing monoplane that formed the basis in 1929 for the Kreutzer Air Coach, which was first built on the second floor of the Kreutzer Building on South Hope Street in Los Angeles and test flown at Mines Field. The company lasted little more than a year, although there was an unsuccessful effort in the mid-1930s to revive the Air Coach.

California designers created some distinctive airplanes, among them the Maximum Safety Airplane Company's M-3, a four-passenger cabin plane marked by wings angled up steeply from fuselage to tips in 14 degrees dihedral. In Glendale in 1928 William Waterhouse and Lloyd Royer built the Waterhouse Romair two-place, fabric-covered, open-cockpit biplane. In 1926 the W-F-W Aircraft Company of Los Angeles built the racy "Thunderbird, wings of the wind" three-place open biplane. General Western Aero Corporation in 1930 began in Burbank, later in Santa Barbara, to produce the Meteor monoplane, which sold for $3,280.

In San Francisco, Noran Aircraft announced in 1929 its speedy Bat, with a small wing and welded steel fuselage, for only $1,095. In San Bernardino, Federal Aircraft Corporation offered the CM-3, "constructed entirely of chrome molybdenum seamless steel tubing." In 1929 Moreland Aircraft of El Segundo offered a high-wing monoplane to franchise distributors nationwide. Southern California industrialist E.M. Smith in 1928 formed Emsco Aero Engine Company to build a 1,000-horsepower diesel airplane engine and in 1929 purchased Zenith Aircraft to become a pacesetting producer of record-breaking aircraft and introduced the trimotor Challenger, the two-passenger, open-cockpit Cirrus, and the B-3 monoplane.

One company created in California whose name remained in the forefront of light airplane manufacturers was Stearman Aircraft Company. In 1926 Lloyd Stearman joined Fred Hoyt to form a company in Venice. Stearman's C-1, -2, and -3 were each designed, produced, and eventually test flown at Clover Field, Santa Monica. Stearman had migrated to California from Wichita, Kansas, where he worked for Swallow Airplane Company and later for Walter Beech in design and production of the first Beech Travel Air. Hoyt learned to fly in the Army at Rockwell and March Airport, and formed Lyle-Hoyt Aircraft Company to sell Travel Airs. In 1927 Stearman and Hoyt decided to return to Wichita, which had become America's general aviation aircraft center. Stearman designed many best-selling light airplanes, and his company later became a part of United Aircraft and Transport, along with Boeing, United Airlines, and the rest. Stearman in 1932 temporarily interrupted his Wichita general aviation career to return to California as president of newly refinanced Lockheed Aircraft Corporation.

One of the last pre-World War II designs created by a small independent California aircraft company was the Harlow PJC-2, designed under the direction of Max Harlow and his students at Pasadena Junior College and built in 1939 by Harlow Aircraft Company in Alhambra. The PJC-2 was a streamlined, low-wing, two-to-four-place plane, one of the sportiest designs of its day.

In 1939 a map highlighting Southern California aviation noted that 55 percent of the nation's planes were engineered, designed, and built "in the center of America's greatest flying activity." The map was also graphic evidence that small aircraft businesses had given way to the giants: it showed only Douglas, Lockheed, Vultee, Northrop, North American, Menasco, Consolidated Aircraft, and Security Aircraft as airframe manufacturers. As a second world war loomed, the little fellows were few indeed. Aircraft manufacturing in California had become big business.

## A THIRD LOCKHEED AIRCRAFT EMERGES

Like a phoenix, in July 1932 Lockheed Aircraft Corporation was reborn. As a result of the failure of Detroit Aircraft (of which Lockheed had become a part in 1929), the company was in receivership with total assets valued at $129,961. Although some groups had shown interest in the company (one, led by Richard Millar, on the advice of Donald Douglas and Harry Wetzel of Douglas elected not to bid), by June only one offer to buy was forthcoming, from a group headed by Robert E. Gross, a 35-year-old Boston-born, Harvard-educated, San Francisco investment broker. He and his younger brother, Courtlandt, had established the Viking Flying Boat Company in New Haven, Connecticut, to manufacture a small, French-designed flying boat.

Gross' fellow investors included Walter T. Varney, owner of Varney Speed Lines (a Lockheed airline customer), Mr. and Mrs. Cyril Chappellet, R.C. Walker, and Thomas F. Ryan III: their successful bid, $40,000. The investors elected Lloyd Stearman as president and general manager. Carl Squier was named vice-president and sales manager; Robert Gross, treasurer; Cyril Chappellet, secretary; Richard Von Hake, chief engineer; and Hall L. Hibbard, assistant chief engineer.

Their task was formidable. Although the previous Lockheed company had sold more than 150 airplanes, the group's immediate challenge was to complete the limited backlog on order and develop a new product line. The Stearman-Von Hake-Hibbard team at Gross' recommendation developed a twin-engine transport aircraft. The prototype was taken to the University of Michigan's wind tunnel for tests, principally conducted by a talented young engineering student, Clarence L. "Kelly" Johnson, who soon joined the company.

Despite precarious finances and the need to restructure capital investments, the group proceeded with the new aircraft—the Model 10 Electra twin-engine transport, which first flew in February 1934—for which orders had already been received from Northwest Airways. With the company off to a sound new start, Varney left to concentrate on his airline operation, Stearman returned to Wichita, Bob Gross succeeded Stearman as president, and Hibbard became chief engineer. The Model 12 Electra Junior, a scaled-down version of the Model 10, was introduced and 130 units were delivered to civil and military customers between 1936 and 1942.

By 1936 Lockheed had in hand substantial military aircraft orders: Navy XR20-1 and Coast Guard XR30-1 versions of the Electra, Air Corps contracts for high-altitude research aircraft, and three Y1C-36 staff transports; and in 1936 it began design of the Super Electra. Although Lockheed's focus was transport aircraft, in 1937 the War Department awarded the company a contract for a prototype of the Model 22 twin-engine interceptor, first in the famed Lightning series. It was designated XP-38 and truly brought Lockheed into aircraft manufacture's major leagues.

For Lockheed these were exciting times as the company prospered in commercial and military markets alike. In 1982 Cyril Chappellet recalled:

*My happiest times were the very early days when we didn't know from day to day whether the sheriff would take over or we could keep going. We were never more lighthearted. We had a lot of personal enjoyment out of each other's company. We worked long, hard hours. We had a great deal of fun along the way . . . We concocted many plans, some of which came to fruition and some of which didn't.*

Lockheed soon felt the competition from Douglas DC-2s and DC-3s, but the company's fortunes turned sharply upward in 1938 when it received an order from the British Air Ministry for 200-250 B-14s configured as the Hudson general reconnaissance aircraft, which put Lockheed in the international military market at the threshold of World War II.

In 1937 Lockheed formed a subsidiary,

AiRover Company, to study light commercial aircraft. In 1938 AiRover was renamed Vega Airplane Company, and it was as president of Vega that Courtlandt Gross began to serve Lockheed in the home office. Early in the war, Vega Aircraft handled some Lockheed production; in 1943 it was absorbed by the parent company.

Along with military development and production, Lockheed proceeded with commercial aircraft: the Model 18 and the 049 Constellation, first of the prodigiously successful "Connies," which entered production in 1940 when TWA ordered nine aircraft. Immediately before the war Lockheed diversified, purchasing Union Air Terminal in Burbank from United Air Lines and operating it as Lockheed Air Terminal from 1940 until it was sold in 1978 to the Department of Transportation of the cities of Burbank, Glendale, and Pasadena.

Because of sales of Hudsons and Lodestars to Allied nations, assembly plants were established in England, Scotland, and Ireland, the beginnings of what is now Lockheed Aircraft Service Company, to handle international assembly and service of U.S.-built military aircraft. Between July 1940 and September 1945, Lockheed produced some 19,000 airplanes, including 5,600 patrol bombers, 2,750 B-17s, and 10,000 P-38 Lightning fighters, with employment reaching a peak of 93,000.

Production was concentrated at the carefully camouflaged Burbank facilities, but feeder plants included two each in Bakersfield, Fresno, East Los Angeles, and Santa Barbara, and one each in Taft and Pomona, and a service depot at Van Nuys Airport.

In addition to the Constellation, which debuted as the C-69 military transport, two other significant airplanes were conceived during the immediate prewar period: the piston-powered Neptune, which began Lockheed's dominance in naval antisubmarine warfare, and the P-80, the first U.S. operational jet fighter. Lockheed's Hibbard-Johnson team had begun studying jet aircraft in 1939-1940; engineers at the company designed the L-1000 turbojet engine, but because Lockheed's primary concern

was airframes, the engine patents were sold to Curtiss-Wright.

The Army Air Force in 1943 contracted with Lockheed for development of the XP-80, which first flew in January 1944; and more than 8,500 of the P-80 family (including the T-33) had been produced by 1958.

Even in the midst of the inevitable wholesale work-force reduction entailed by cessation of military production, only a few days after V-J Day Bob Gross announced orders from eight major airlines for 103 of Lockheed's triple-tailed Constellations, the largest commercial order up to that time. During 16 years 856 Connies were built for 32 airlines in 21 countries.

The F-80 Shooting Star established the company as America's preeminent jet aircraft manufacturer. An F-80 triumphed in the world's first all-jet air battle, downing a Russian-built MiG-15 early in the Korean War. Through the early 1950s, the Shooting Star was the USAF's first-line jet fighter, and more than 1,700 were built during 16 years.

The F-80 gave birth to the famed T-33 jet trainer, affectionately named the "T-Bird," which provided advanced jet training for 9 out of 10 U.S. jet pilots in the 1950s and '60s. Nearly 6,000 of the T-33 family were produced in Burbank, an additional 866 under license in Canada and Japan.

Under development at Burbank during this period were the XF-90 penetration fighter, the YF-94 interceptor, and the Super Constellations. During the Korean War Lockheed expanded outside California when the Air Force asked the company to reopen a government plant at Marietta, Georgia (now Lockheed-Georgia Company), and an entirely new facility at Palmdale Airport, California, to which T-33 production was transferred in 1953. In 1952 Lockheed Aircraft Service relocated its main base to nearby Ontario.

When the Advanced Development Projects section headed by Kelly Johnson began its super-secret development of the XP-80, facilities at Burbank were crowded. Looking for a place to do his cloak-and-dagger work, Johnson created a space next to a wind tunnel, using Wright engine packing-boxes for walls and a rented circus tent for a roof. As the project took shape, curiosity mounted. Someone wondered aloud what Johnson was "brewing up" in there, and soon some wit compared Johnson's operation with the foul-smelling location in Al Capp's "Li'l Abner" comic strip where Kick-A-Poo Joy Juice was brewed, the Dog Patch Skunk Works. Although Johnson at first bridled at the nickname, it stuck, and "Skunk Works" became synonymous with secret aviation development at Lockheed.

From the Skunk Works came remarkable airplanes. Following the P-80, in 1954 came the world's first Mach 2 (twice the speed of sound) fighter, the F-104 Starfighter. The stubby-winged creation, dubbed "the missile with a man in it," swiftly captured world speed, time-to-climb, and altitude records. The Starfighter became practically an industry in itself: 296 units were produced for the USAF, and American allies adopted it as a primary defense fighter, boosting Starfighter production to more than 750 units. The Federal Republic of Germany, the Netherlands, Belgium, Italy, Canada, and Japan selected F-104s for their defense forces. Most significant for international aviation progress, however, were the joint aircraft and engine production programs established to build F-104s in Europe, Canada, and Japan. These programs, together with General Electric's J79 jet-engine production, are credited with reestablishing the aviation industries of Germany, the Netherlands, Belgium, and Italy, industries devastated during World War II. A four-nation manufacturing consortium was established in Europe; Canada and Japan each produced their own aircraft. The NATO consortium produced more than 1,800; Canada and Japan produced another 550.

From the Skunk Works came two other precedent-setting aircraft, the super-spy U-2, first flown in August 1955, and the Mach 3 SR-71/YF-12A. The true mission of the U-2 was unexpectedly revealed in 1960 when Francis Gary Powers was shot down over the Soviet Union, forcing President Eisenhower eventually to admit that U-2s had long been photographing Russian military installations. A growth version of the U-2, the TR-1, was returned to production in 1982 at USAF request. An SR-71 Blackbird flying at more than 80,000 feet can map 100,000 square miles of the earth's surface per hour and has flown from New York to London in some 116 minutes.

Lockheed's years under Robert and Courtlandt Gross were marked by brilliant achievement. Robert died in September 1961 and was succeeded as chairman by Courtlandt; Daniel J. Haughton was named president (later to be chairman and CEO). Bob Gross had taken Lockheed from bankruptcy to 1961 revenues of $1.44 billion and a work force of 70,250. Just before his death Courtlandt described Robert's decision-making during those growth years.

*The fact of the case is that not only I, but several of the other peons, didn't have any idea why Robert did many of the things he did, we never could figure it out. You see, Robert gave birth to about 50 ideas a week, of which 49 were about as effective as a foul tip into the visiting team's dugout, but the 50th was a screaming home run all the way from Harvard Square, Cambridge, Mass., to Turkey Crossing, Burbank, California. That is the way things were and no one that I have ever talked to can figure out how Robert got that 50th hit.*

Roy Anderson, Lockheed's current chairman and chief executive officer, said, "We at Lockheed are the shadow of Robert Gross . . ."

In 1965 Lockheed, in what was uniformly believed to be a stepping stone for the next generation of jetliners, won its $1.9-billion bid to build the USAF C-5A Galaxy. Instead the program was plagued by cost overruns (the total project cost exceeded $5 billion), design problems, and contract snags arising from the then-new Department of Defense Total Package Procurement system. Despite all this, the C-5 remains the top U.S. military heavy transport, and Lockheed recently reopened production to build 50 C-5Bs with potential revenues of approximately $8 billion. C-5s, along with C-130s and C-141s, are built at Lockheed's Marietta plant.

47

During the 1960s Lockheed attempted to enter the helicopter business with its AH-56A Cheyenne, but the program was cancelled in 1972 because of conflict within the Defense Department and performance difficulties with the helicopter.

Ordered by American Airlines in June 1955 and later by other carriers, Lockheed's L-188 Electra became the first U.S.-built turboprop airliner, but was quickly overtaken in the marketplace by the advent of pure-jet transports. Early in its career, design problems led to two mysterious fatal Electra crashes and the imposition of speed restrictions by the Federal Aviation Administration. In a heroic test program, Lockheed engineers and pilots identified the problem: engine-induced harmonic vibration leading to catastrophic wing flutter. With modifications, including the rebuilding at company expense of aircraft already delivered, the airplane was given a clean bill of health and became extremely popular with pilots, who praised its outstanding performance. Only 170 Electras were built, far too few to make it profitable, but the design gave birth to the P-3 Orion long-range antisubmarine patrol aircraft, nearly 600 of which have been delivered to the U.S. Navy and several allied nations. The S-3A Viking twin-jet, advanced carrier-based antisubmarine aircraft continues Lockheed's primacy in this specialized defense role.

The Electra experience caused Lockheed to skip the competition for the first generation of pure-jet airliners. That market went to Boeing's 707 and the Douglas DC-8. But when, in 1963, the U.S. government announced a competition for a U.S. supersonic transport (SST), Lockheed was ready. The company wound up in a runoff of its L-2000 SST against Boeing's 2707. On December 31, 1966, Boeing was declared the winner, in spite of the fact that the Seattle designers subsequently abandoned their complicated swing-wing concept in favor of a design remarkably similar to Lockheed's double delta. Once again, Lockheed had apparently missed the next step in civil transports. As it turned out, a U.S. SST was never built.

The next opportunity to reenter the civil marketplace came when U.S. carriers, led by American Airlines, established specifications for a 250-passenger, wide-bodied jetliner of less capacity and range than the giant 747 whose great size was economical only in high-density, long-haul markets. Lockheed's original design was twin-engined, but airline preferences ultimately resulted in a three-engine design, the L-1011 TriStar.

The program began badly when in February 1968 Lockheed's L-1011 lost the initial marketing round to Douglas in Long Beach as American ordered DC-10s. However, only six weeks later a unique consortium was assembled to announce the largest-ever kickoff order for an airliner. TWA, Eastern, and British Air Holdings Ltd. placed orders and options for 144 L-1011s. Key to Lockheed's success was its decision to power the L-1011 with Rolls-Royce RB.211 turbofan engines and to tie Rolls and the British government into the financial package. The Air Holdings Ltd. order capped the complex financial arrangement with Rolls and Westminster.

The L-1011 triumph was short-lived. In early 1971 Rolls-Royce announced that it could not fulfill its contract to deliver the RB.211 and placed itself in the hands of a receiver. Because of massive financial commitments to the TriStar program, and the C-5 snags, Lockheed in turn found itself on the verge of bankruptcy. Led by Dan Haughton, who shuttled between Los Angeles and London, Lockheed management worked diligently with British financial interests, the British government, and airline customers to resuscitate Rolls-Royce. Prime Minister James Callaghan's government stipulated that Lockheed's finances must be guaranteed by Washington. Thus, in 1971 began one of the most controversial industry-government efforts in U.S. history. Although the request to the U.S. government was only to guarantee up to $250 million in commercial loans to Lockheed, the proposal generated powerful opposition within the aviation and business communities. The Emergency Loan Guarantee Act was finally passed in August 1971 and signed by President Nixon. Lockheed was saved, the British government was assured, Rolls-Royce Aero Engines was nationalized, and the TriStar program was able to move forward.

Production delays, competition from American and European rivals, and the sluggish world airline market in the late 1970s ultimately forced cancellation of the L-1011 TriStar program. The last of 250 L-1011s, a -500 model for TAP Air Portugal, rolled from the Palmdale assembly line in September 1983.

In the mid-1970s Lockheed became embroiled, along with some 400 other U.S. corporations, in what was euphemized as "overseas payments problems" stemming from questionable offshore marketing practices. In early 1976 Robert Haack was named chairman, with a specific charge to improve the tarnished image of the firm. By September 1977 the company's health was much improved. Haack was succeeded by Roy Anderson as chairman and CEO; Lawrence O. Kitchen became president and chief operating officer.

Haack, Anderson, Kitchen, and the rest of the team managing today's Lockheed were dedicated to a strong financial and technical return of Lockheed to its former stature. One executive noted: "Our people...fought back with fierce determination, with pride, with unselfish dedication to an entity they believed in." In 1974 the company was worth about $50 million. In late 1982 stock-market value of the company was approximately $1.4 billion. In 1983 Lockheed sales were $6.5 billion, with net earnings of $263 million and a funded backlog of $7.7 billion. Employment in 1983 totaled 71,800 men and women, more than 15,000 of them engineers and scientists.

## DOUGLAS AIRCRAFT: BUILDER OF AIRLINERS FOR THE WORLD

During the 1920s, with Don Douglas heading a veteran team in Santa Monica, Douglas Aircraft became the largest single supplier of aircraft to America's military services.

Despite the Depression, Douglas was comparatively healthy. The finanical community, however, remained cautious about advancing credit to airplane builders, believing with some justification that they were unable to project future business. Nonetheless, with the help of investment banker Richard Millar, chairman of the financial committee of the Douglas board, Douglas was able to secure through Security First National Bank the first revolving credit for any aircraft manufacturing company in the United States — persuasive evidence of the unusual confidence Douglas had earned among California financiers.

Douglas had achieved fiscal respectability as a maker of military aircraft, but even the most sanguine banker could hardly have foreseen the company's coming fortunes.

On August 2, 1932, Transcontinental and Western Air's vice-president of operations Jack Frye sent a now-famous two-paragraph letter to Douglas and other manufacturers, defining specifications and requesting bids to build "ten or more trimotor transport airplanes." The closing sentence asked: "How long would it take to turn out the first plane for service tests?"

TWA had requested bids on this new transport to gain a leg up on competitor United Airlines, which had kicked off Boeing's twin-engine 247 transport with an order for 60 planes. Because United was a part of the United Aircraft and Transport empire that also included Boeing, it was clear to the rest of the industry that the UAL order would be filled before deliveries to any other potential buyer. TWA had acted promptly to establish a competitive situation.

Frye's letter arrived on Monday, August 5, and Douglas took it home with him, mulling over its challenge until 2 a.m. Assembling his design, engineering, and production chiefs the next morning, Douglas read the letter aloud to what may have been the most talented team ever gathered at one airframer.

The company's chief engineer was James "Dutch" Kindelberger, whose assistant was Arthur E. Raymond. Stress analysis was done by J. Lee Atwood, and other seasoned staff members included Jack Northrop, Harry Wetzel, Ed Burton, and Fred Herman. To augment this group were distinguished aeronautical engineers from the California Institute of Technology—

Clark B. Millikan, Arthur L. Klein, and W.B. Oswald.

Although TWA had asked for three engines, Kindelberger and Douglas believed they could build a twin-engine plane with performance and passenger capacity superior to any trimotor or Boeing's 247; over the next weeks the group refined their thinking to incorporate a formidable array of imaginative design features in their ultimate proposal to TWA. As it turned out, the answer to the final question posed in Jack Frye's letter was 11 months. The Douglas answer to TWA's solicitation flew on July 1, 1933—and it was far more airplane than Jack Frye and his colleagues had envisioned.

Designated the DC-1, the six-ton transport exceeded the airline's specifications and featured more powerful engines, retractable landing gear, and wing flaps that allowed landing speeds to 60 mph and greater payloads. Its spacious cabin was unprecedentedly quiet, the result of innovative work by acoustics engineer Stephen J. Zand.

On September 20, 1932, TWA announced its selection of the DC-1 at a unit cost of $58,000, without engines. The DC-1 was only a prototype; TWA's initial order for 25 aircraft became the DC-2—slightly larger and able to accommodate 14 passengers.

When the DC-1 rolled out of the hangar at Clover Field in June 1933, one airline pilot said: "Too big, it won't fly." But it did. On September 20, 1933, the only DC-1 ever built demonstrated its capabilities on the most challenging of TWA's transcontinental routes, from Winslow, Arizona, over the mountains to Albuquerque, New Mexico, flying with one engine shut down (a capability TWA consultant Charles Lindbergh had insisted upon) and passing en route a TWA Ford Trimotor that had departed from Winslow Airport well ahead of it.

In addition to pioneering an entire generation of transport aircraft, the DC-1 prototype left another mark on aviation history. In a footnote to the federal government's heavy-handed grappling with aeronautical policy, in February 1934 all civilian airmail contracts were cancelled and turned over to the Army while Postmaster

General James A. Farley strove to unring the bell of his predecessor Walter Folger Brown's 1930 "Spoils Conferences." Jack Frye invited his enthusiastic compatriot Eddie Rickenbacker of Eastern Air Transport to join in demonstrating civil aviation's capabilities in the DC-1. The night before cancellation of the airmail contracts took effect, Frye and Rickenbacker flew the sleek Douglas ship with a full load of mail from Burbank, California, to Newark, New Jersey. Despite winter flying conditions, they made only two refueling stops, covering the continent in a record-setting 13 hours and four minutes. A New York newspaper reported: "This plane has made obsolete all other air transport equipment in this country or any other."

Air transport's revolution only began with the DC-2, however. In midsummer 1934 C.R. Smith, president of American Airways, called from New York. Douglas wisely interrupted his board meeting to take Smith's call. American had already ordered DC-2s; this time Smith wanted a fast sleeper airplane to serve his transcontinental route. Although Douglas was at first reluctant to even consider development of a new airplane because of the DC-2's popularity, Smith informally committed himself to buy 20 of a new plane.

At the board meeting finance committee chairman Millar posed two questions: How did American plan to pay for the new aircraft, and how many did Douglas think might be sold? To the first question, Doug answered: "I haven't the remotest idea." As to the second, with C.R. Smith's promise of 20 orders in hand, Doug confidently estimated that they could sell "as many as 75 airplanes." He was low by more than 10,000.

The airplane, the Douglas Sleeper Transport (DST), provided 14 berths and entered service with American in June 1936. But it wasn't as the DST that this airplane would gain fame. It was obvious at the outset that this growth version of the DC aircraft could carry more passengers, 21 versus 14 in the DC-2.

On December 17, 1935, the first Douglas DC-3 lifted from the runway at Clover Field, Santa Monica. One writer later opined: "With the

DC-3 the airframe revolution was complete." Air travel and airlines would never again be the same. As C.R. Smith characterized it: "It was the first airplane which could make money just by hauling passengers." Within two years Douglas Aircraft had sold 803 DC-3s and the airplane was carrying 95 percent of America's civil traffic. The DC-3 became the favorite airplane of at least two generations of pilots. It was, as pilot-writer Ernest Gann noted, "an amiable cow that was forgiving of the most clumsy pilot." Until the advent of the jets in the 1950s, the DC-3 would remain the standard against which all civil aircraft would be measured. In its military dress—C-47 Skytrain for the Army Air Corps, R4D for the Navy, and Dakota for the British Royal Air Force—more than 10,000 Douglas-made DC-3s were credited with changing the course of World War II.

The DC-3 was the foundation upon which Douglas would build transport successors. Design of the DC-4, the first Douglas four-engine transport, was begun in 1938. Soon after the DC-4 announcement, 40 orders had been received from U.S. airlines for delivery in 1942. However, war in Europe and the events of December 7, 1941, changed all that. The U.S. Army Air Corps commandeered the airline orders, eventually taking delivery on more than 1,100 C-54 Skymasters (the DC-4's Air Corps designation). It was R5D in the Navy. An Air Force C-54, nicknamed "The Sacred Cow," became the first Presidential aircraft; it only carried Franklin D. Roosevelt twice, but was used on diplomatic missions.

In November 1946 Douglas delivered to American and United simultaneously the first DC-6s and was working on the even more advanced DC-7, to debut in May 1953. The ultimate refinement of the Douglas reciprocating engine transport was the DC-7C, known as the "Seven Seas" on U.S. domestic and international routes worldwide. Douglas produced more than 1,000 of the DC-6 and -7 series, splendid machines which, with Lockheed's Constellations and Boeing's Stratocruisers, reigned over a golden age of piston-driven airliners and brought true nonstop service to every major city-pair in the world.

But piston-engined they were, and their fate was soon heralded by a high-pitched shriek rapidly becoming commonplace at military bases around the globe. The turbojet engine, born during World War II, first proved its absolute superiority over all previous power plants in fighter and attack aircraft, then swept propellers from the wings of big, multi-engined bombers. Transports were next, and the baton of leadership among commercial aircraft builders was about to pass from Santa Monica, Long Beach, and Burbank to the Northwest.

With its Air Force B-47s operational since 1947, and drawings for the leviathan B-52 circulating among its engineers, by the mid-1950s the Boeing Company of Seattle had accumulated more large jet aircraft experience than any company in the world. And its president, William M. Allen, launched his company into the jet transport business, shrewdly anticipating that Boeing's designs could be adapted to commercial as well as military service.

While Britain's ill-fated De Havilland Comet of 1949 had inaugurated scheduled airline jet service in 1952, the graceful ship was ahead of technology's limits, and in early 1954 two catastrophic accidents revealed fatal design flaws. While the cause—premature metal fatigue leading to explosive fuselage decompression—was found through dogged investigative work, and subsequent models of the Comet performed admirably, Britain's brief jetliner lead was lost. And airline executives now eyed jets with reservation and even apprehension.

The first buyer for the 707 type was the United States Air Force, which ordered 29 KC-135 tankers in March 1955. The impact of that order reverberated in Southern California, for at a stroke Boeing took a colossal step toward command of the world civil jet transport market.

In early June Douglas Aircraft announced its entry in the race—the DC-8. Douglas possessed extensive military jet aircraft experience; its studies of aircraft using turbojet engines had begun in 1945. In 1952 the company established a Special Project Office, a quiet in-house effort to explore jet-powered transports. The decision to go public with the DC-8 was triggered by two factors: the Boeing KC-135 order, and the prodding of Pan American World Airways executives, who had ordered the Comet, then witnessed its demise. Pan Am, in turn, relished the advantages of a buyer's market in which two or more manufacturers competed for its business, as well as for that of other airlines. A major hurdle for Douglas was the already flying 707 prototype. But that could be a competitive advantage: the engineers in Long Beach could learn much from Boeing's experience, and the Douglas sales staff had a "rubber airplane" still flexible to customer wishes.

Douglas engineers went swiftly to work and designed a machine with several features that exceeded those of the Boeing airplane, particularly better landing and take-off characteristics and greater range, although as it turned out the 707 consistently cruised 20 mph faster than the DC-8. Knowledge, experience, and plain old "feel" for airline requirements paid off, and in October 1955 Pan Am placed the first airline order for this new generation of jet transports. For both manufacturers, relative size of the order seemed significant: Pan Am signed for 25 DC-8s and 20 707s. Twelve days later United Airlines contracted for 30 DC-8s. A major factor in early airline preference for the DC-8 was its wider and longer fuselage with its resultant greater passenger seating capacity. By the end of 1955 Douglas had signed four U.S. and six overseas airline customers.

The DC-8 was rolled out in April 1958 and first flown May 30th, and it entered service with United and Delta on September 18, 1959. Meanwhile, Boeing had acted quickly to adapt its 707 to airline demands, announcing a larger and longer range variant, the Intercontinental. For months the sales lead changed from California to Washington, but by late 1957 the trend that has continued well into the 1980s was established: Boeing orders stood at 145, Douglas at 124 (556 DC-8s would be built before production ended in 1972). On October 26, 1958, a Pan Am 707 inaugurated U.S. scheduled passenger jet service with a New York-Paris flight.

With the DC-8 and 707 having revolutionized aviation and the world's travel patterns over the relatively long hauls for which they were designed, planners focused on jet aircraft for short-to-medium length routes not economical for the big jets.

Spurred by engineer and salesman Jackson R. McGowen, Douglas Aircraft Company in 1963 announced its twin-engine DC-9 program, to be headed by John Brizendine (both men would serve as Douglas presidents), and in May Delta Air Lines placed the launch order for 15. Particularly attractive to airline customers was the plane's two-man flight deck. (Boeing's 727 then required three—pilot, first officer, flight engineer.) The DC-9 first flew in February 1965 and entered airline service in December. By the end of 1982 Douglas had delivered 976 DC-9s in several variants. A much refined growth version—first named the Super 80, renamed the MD-80 in 1983 when the company changed the "DC" designation scheme to "MD"—with improved fuel economy and low noise characteristics, by mid-1984 had generated more than 440 orders and options.

In 1970 Boeing's wide-bodied 747 entered service. But the huge airplane's capacity (400 or more passengers) and range limited its economic operation to high-density long-stage routes. Remaining to be filled by a current-technology airplane was an important niche: the medium-stage route with moderate traffic density. Many such markets are served by airports incapable of handling the giant 747. The Europeans, recognizing the potential market and anxious to break the virtual monopoly enjoyed by American airframe manufacturers worldwide for many years, had begun development of the A300 Airbus, a state-of-the-art twin-engine wide-body. Created by a consortium of European firms led by the French, Germans, and British, the Airbus was slow to gain acceptance. American Airlines began to push Douglas and Lockheed for a wide-body airplane that could economically serve the New York-Chicago market and remain within aircraft size and noise restrictions in effect at New York's La Guardia Airport. Both Lockheed and Douglas proposed three-engine aircraft: Lockheed the L-1011, Douglas the DC-10.

The race for airline orders began again, renewing a ritual of airframe builders. The cost of developing a new jetliner approaches billons of dollars, routinely exceeding the total net worth of the firms involved. One executive neatly summarized the process: "You bet your company." John Newhouse chronicled the events summarized here in a series of *New Yorker Magazine* pieces (later published in book format) whose title reflects the attitude taken by some of the airframe executives who call their industry's mammoth risk-taking "The Sporty Game."

In the midst of apparent success with its DC-8 and DC-9 production, but trying to launch a completely new aircraft program, Douglas was beset by massive financial problems which led in 1967 to one of the most significant mergers in the history of U.S. aviation: the venerable Douglas Aircraft Company was purchased by McDonnell Aircraft Corporation of St. Louis, creating the McDonnell Douglas Corporation (MDC).

McDonnell Aircraft was founded in 1939 by James S. McDonnell, known by his industry colleagues as "Mr. Mac." Following a pattern established during the 1920s which saw the military services each "adopt" manufacturers into their respective "stables," McDonnell was generally known as a Navy firm. Its greatest success, however, came with the multi-service F-4 Phantom II jet; more than 5,000 were built between 1958 and 1979. Seeking to broaden its market base into the civil sector, McDonnell found ailing but prestigious Douglas an attractive merger candidate.

In February 1968 American Airlines announced its decision to purchase DC-10s; United Airlines followed a month later. Lockheed promptly countered with its L-1011 deal with the British government, Rolls-Royce, Eastern Airlines, TWA, and Air Holdings. This division of an airline market soon to be assaulted by a world oil crisis and stagnant demand doomed both airplanes to production runs well below their break-even points.

Confidence in the DC-10 was later eroded by several disastrous crashes, the first related to cargo door latch failures, a later one to operator maintenance procedures. Reversing the practice of adapting military airplanes for commercial applications (Boeing's B-377 Stratocruiser was adapted from World War II's B-29, and the 707 derived much from the B-47 and was designed in parallel with the KC-135), the company reworked the DC-10 into the KC-10—a tanker for in-flight refueling operations. The 60 units initially ordered by the Air Force are valued at nearly $3 billion.

Douglas had built a firm foundation with military planes, having produced an amazing array of military aircraft from the 1920s on, first under the design and engineering tutelage of Douglas himself, then Kindelberger, Northrop, the famed Ed Heinemann, and Leo Devlin. In the 1920s, with the World Cruisers, the company began its relationship with the Navy, including delivery of the T2D torpedo bomber that had gone to sea with the newly commissioned carrier USS *Lexington*, followed by the TBD Devastator with its three-man crew. Douglas in the 1930s experimented with flying boats, producing the P3D and DF-151. Douglas' first fighter for the Navy was the XFD-1, built in 1933.

Jack Northrop rejoined Douglas in 1932, this time in a partnership that established the Northrop Corporation as a Douglas subsidiary in El Segundo concentrating on military aircraft development. By 1934 the division had more than 1,000 employees and was producing the A-17 attack aircraft for the Army Air Corps. Its most famous early aircraft was the BT-1, which ultimately evolved into the SBD Dauntless that became the backbone of the U.S. Navy during the early days of World War II in the Pacific. The Navy's Chief of the Bureau of Aeronautics later said of the SBD, "It has sunk more enemy combatant tonnage than all other branches of the service."

When Northrop left in 1938 to form the present Northrop Corporation, the organization became the Douglas El Segundo division, and by the summer of 1939 Douglas had delivered more than 1,500 aircraft to the U.S. Army and an additional 300 to the U.S. Navy and Coast

Guard. Such production was soon to swell by an order of magnitude as World War II required President Franklin D. Roosevelt to call on the aircraft industry to produce 50,000 units per year. Part of a capacity increase program of herculean proportions, construction was begun in 1940 of the Long Beach facility, with units rolling off the line two years later. Long Beach during the war years produced the A-20B, the B-17F, the C-47A (4,285 were produced at Long Beach alone), and the A-26B (which once reached a production high of 108 per month).

Douglas expanded further with plants at Tulsa and Oklahoma City, Oklahoma, and Chicago, Illinois. At Santa Monica in March 1944 aircraft production reached a rate of 322 per month, more than 10 aircraft every day. At peak wartime production Douglas had 160,000 employees and an engineering staff of 5,301 and produced 29,385 aircraft.

In 1946 the company delivered 127 airplanes, three plants were closed, employment dropped to 27,000. Production of DC-4s and a handful of military deliveries helped to maintain Douglas. A contract for the AD Skyraider helped too, eventually implementing production of 3,180 units in 28 different configurations. In conjunction with the National Advisory Committee for Aeronautics (NACA), the company commenced work in jet propulsion and high performance aerodynamics with the D-558 Skystreak.

In one intriguing post-World War II sidelight, General Arnold asked Donald Douglas if his company would provide a base for, and operate, Project RAND (the name derives from "research and development"). Originally financed by the Army Air Force, the project was designed to assure peacetime cooperation between the civilian scientific community and the military on national security research projects. In 1948 the program was spun off from Douglas as the . RAND Corporation, an independent, not-for-profit institution.

The Navy AD had become "bread-and-butter" production, and at Long Beach the giant C-124 cargo transport was in production for the USAF, later to be succeeded by the C-133. The first

Douglas operational military jet was the F3D Skyknight, which on November 2, 1952, became the first Allied jet airplane to make a confirmed kill of an enemy fighter in a night intercept. Under test was the A2D and A3D, to become the USN's heaviest, most powerful carrier-based attack bomber.

One of the Ed Heinemann team's triumphs was the Navy F4D Skyray jet interceptor, which won the famed Collier trophy for 1953, shared that year with Dutch Kindelberger for North American's F-100 fighter. Kindelberger had been a teacher and friend of Ed Heinemann during their early Douglas days, and the delta-wing Skyray had evolved from the work of Heinemann and Northrop in the late 1930s at Douglas El Segundo.

General Electric leased the prototype XF-4D from the Navy, modifying it in 1955 to test GE's Mach 2 J79 turbojet engine at Edwards Air Force Base. The engine went on to power Lockheed's Starfighter, Convair's Hustler, North American's Vigilante, and McDonnell's Phantom. It was the first time an engine manufacturer had flight tested an engine in advance of the aircraft manufacturer.

Douglas attack aircraft were the backbone of U.S. Naval aviation for more than four decades because the company's designers understood Navy requirements. As Ed Heinemann recalled, "Early on, both Donald Douglas and Jack Northrop told me it would be more difficult to build aircraft for the Navy than the Army . . . [Doug told me] . . . 'Remember, the Navy operates in the dynamic, hardhitting environment of the carrier. They ask more from their pilots and their planes. It follows that the designer has to give more if he wants the Navy's business.'"

In 1982 prospects at Long Beach began to rise. The company devised creative financing arrangements for its Super 80 jetliner, garnering major new orders from Pacific Southwest, American, TWA, and Alitalia Airlines. Orders were in hand for KC-10 tankers, and the next generation of civil transports was under study. The "DC" designation, a 50-year tradition, ended when the last DC-10 left the Long Beach factory, after which the company's new airliners bear the prefix "MD" to reflect the combination of McDonnell and Douglas. The first aircraft so designated is the MD-80, formerly the DC-9 Super 80.

## NORTH AMERICAN "GOES WEST"

North American Aviation, today Rockwell International, began as an Eastern holding company created by Clement M. Keys, a former *Wall Street Journal* editor who entered aviation when he purchased Curtiss Aeroplane and Motor Company. North American Aviation (NAA) was established in 1928 as a Delaware corporation. When it finally took off as an aircraft company in 1934, it was headed by men whose aviation roots had been solidly planted in California.

The original NAA envisioned by Keys reflected a trend of the period—the assembling of diverse companies into giant amalgamations. The first major manufacturer under the NAA blanket was Curtiss-Wright Corporation, followed by Curtiss-Robertson Airplane Manufacturing Company, Curtiss-Caproni Corporation, Travel Air of Wichita, Moth Aircraft, and Keystone Aircraft. NAA later owned a majority of Pitcairn Aviation, Inc. (reorganized as Eastern Air Transport in 1930, later to become Eastern Airlines), Sperry Gyroscope Company, Ford Instrument Company, Aviation Corporation of California, Berliner-Joyce Aircraft Company, General Aviation Manufacturing Corporation, and minority interests in Transcontinental Air Transport, Western Air Express, and Douglas Aircraft. By 1934 its Douglas holdings had been divested.

North American Aviation came into the General Motors orbit through General Aviation Manufacturing Corporation (GAMC), organized by General Motors to handle its aviation activities. When North American acquired GAMC through stock trades, General Motors ended up holding a 29-percent interest in North American Aviation.

Rent by the Air Mail Act of 1934 that prohibited a corporation from holding interests in both aircraft production and airmail operation, the tangled web of the NAA holding company unraveled, and the aircraft and airline units were separated, with NAA as a manufacturer remaining a part of General Aviation Corporation. NAA chairman Ernest R. Breech, later president of Ford and TWA, recruited Dutch Kindelberger as president and general manager, wooing him away from Douglas in Santa Monica. Kindelberger brought two key members of his engineering team, Lee Atwood and J.S. "Stan" Smithson.

On January 1, 1935, NAA became an active aircraft manufacturing operation, but prospects appeared bleak, and Kindelberger doubted that the collected holdings and plants could be molded into an efficient operation. But he knew the advantages of West Coast aircraft manufacturing and soon proposed moving the entire company to California, contingent upon receipt of an order from the U.S. Army for a new aircraft under development, the NA-16 basic trainer. In April 1935 a prototype flew to Wright Field for Army evaluation, and NAA was awarded its first military contract, for 42 NA-16s. Kindelberger promptly leased a 20-acre site at Los Angeles Municipal Airport at $600 annual rent.

Although Kindelberger had some difficulty persuading a few of his key workers to move west ("They were under the impression there were hostile Indians west of Pittsburgh"), about 75 of his original crew came to California to start up the Inglewood plant, which was occupied in January 1936 with 250 employees working on the N-16, now designated the BT-9. A contract for 40 additional BT-9s followed. The BT-9 became the AT-6 Texan, one of America's, and Britain's (as the Harvard), most durable training aircraft.

Kindelberger and Atwood knew that a company could not survive on trainers alone, and they had been working on a military observation aircraft whose roots went back to pre-California days. The Army Air Corps in 1936 awarded a contract for O-47s, whose success established NAA as a fully competent producer of advanced tactical military aircraft. O-47 and BT-9 production provided a modest foundation, but a foundation nonetheless. In 1938-1939 the company developed the BT-14 and the famed SNJ trainer in which many Allied pilots first gained serious flight experience.

In the 26 months between the outbreak of the European war and Pearl Harbor, NAA increased production from 70 to 325 units per month, employment rose from 3,400 to 23,000, and factory space went from 425,000 square feet to almost 2.5 million square feet. NAA's production alone was approximately 70 percent more than the entire U.S. aviation industry had produced in 1939. A week *before* Pearl Harbor, Kindelberger said in a speech made only one year after President Roosevelt called for 50,000 aircraft per year: "So much has been accomplished in that time that it seems impossible, as one looks back, that the American aircraft industry has been able to do as much in that period as Germany did in five years, and it is only the beginning."

The NAA team concentrated on requirements to meet the growing threat of war in Europe. On its own, NAA, with Air Corps encouragement, began design of a medium-sized bomber, the A-40, which grew into the B-25 Mitchell bomber ordered by the U.S. Army Air Corps in 1939. Although the Mitchell served with U.S. forces in every theater of operations and was used by British, Russian, Netherlands East Indies, and Chinese air arms, it is best remembered for carrying the famed Doolittle Raiders on their 30 seconds over Tokyo. In an unprecedentedly daring exercise, Air Corps B-25 Mitchells, with Col. Jimmy Doolittle flying lead, were launched from the deck of the carrier *Hornet*.

The plane that became America's best-known fighter, the P-51 Mustang, was born as a result of British interests. Great Britain wanted NAA to build Curtiss P-40s for the Royal Air Force. When that request came in February 1940, Atwood believed NAA could design and produce a superior aircraft in essentially the same time it would take to tool up for P-40 production. The British reluctantly agreed; in April 1940 a contract was awarded NAA for 320 aircraft, not to exceed a unit cost of $40,000. The engineering and design team went to work, and

a frantic 127 days later, on October 26, 1940, the first P-51 Mustang was flight tested. Originally powered by Allison engines, nearly 800 were delivered to British and U.S. air forces. But the unsupercharged Allison engine could not deliver adequate range or high-altitude performance.

The answer was Rolls-Royce Merlin engines for the P-51. The Merlin-powered Mustang reached a record flight speed of 445 mph at 28,000 feet. It was called "the most aero-dynamically perfect pursuit plane in existence" during World War II. By mid-1945 NAA had delivered a total of 14,487 P-51s to Allied air forces. Today, privately owned, exquisitely restored P-51s are often star performers in U.S. and international air shows.

From January 1939 through September 1945, North American Aviation produced 42,683 military aircraft, some 10,000 more than its closest competitor, Convair. This represented 14 percent of all aircraft produced by U.S. manufacturers during the war.

NAA knew of the first American jet, the XP-59, when it first flew at Muroc Air Base October 2, 1942. Kindelberger, who had the added advantage of having personally observed a portion of the German buildup, noted that "... a jet fighter is almost as far removed from a P-40 as a P-40 was from the pusher biplane ... flown from the sands of Kitty Hawk." Nonetheless, the company in the latter years of the war plunged in to produce the Navy FJ-4 Fury jet fighter, which first flew in 1946. In early 1947 the company's B-45 Tornado became the USAF's first multi-jet bomber and was the only plane with atomic weapons delivery capability serving NATO forces through most of the 1950s. In 1948 General Motors divested its interest in North American, Kindelberger became chairman of the board, and Atwood became president.

In 1945 NAA had initiated studies of a high-performance jet fighter, and soon discovered that the study airplane would encounter severe aerodynamic problems as it approached the speed of sound. The answer came from the wartime work of German scientists: swept-back wings. The North American F-86 Sabrejet was born, the first of the truly high-performance, swept-wing, turbojet-powered tactical aircraft. First flight was in 1947, and by September 1948 an F-86 had established a new world speed record of 671 mph.

With the introduction of Russian-built MiG-15s in Korea, it was obvious to military planners and to Kindelberger, who observed that "it takes a jet to stop a jet," that high-performance aircraft were badly needed by Allied forces. Inglewood geared up, and Sabrejet growth versions, F-86Es and -Fs, were rushed into combat. The result was striking: in aerial combat, 802 MiGs were downed; only 58 Sabrejets were lost, a ratio favoring the F-86s by nearly 14 to 1. North American produced variants of the F-86 for nearly 10 years, delivering more than 6,000, some being produced under license in Italy, Japan, Austria, and Canada.

At the height of preparations for Korea, NAA leased the Naval Industrial Reserve Aircraft plant in Columbus, Ohio, which became the Columbus Division, producing T-6 trainers, the Navy's FJ-2 version of the Sabrejet, and eventually the A-5 Vigilante. In the Inglewood shops, work had long before begun on an advanced plane that would be the F-100 Super Sabre, the vanguard of America's "Century Series" fighter aircraft, the majority of which would originate in California. The supersonic Super Sabre promptly set a new world speed record of 755 mph.

North American's X-15 provided training for early astronauts and space explorers such as NASA's Joe Walker, USAF Captain Bob White, and NAA's Scott Crossfield. The X-15 and its engineering achievements provided a solid foundation for North American Rockwell's major role in NASA's space program.

An element of NAA's aircraft diversification was development of the T-39 Sabreliner, a utility trainer and support plane for the military and an executive jet for the civil sector. Two projects in the late 1950s seemed to assure North American's future for the next several decades— Air Force contracts for development of the Mach 3 B-70 Valkyrie, and the F-108 Rapier. The B-70 was projected as the nation's next-generation strategic bomber, to replace B-52s;

the F-108 was to be the next-generation long-range interceptor. The F-108 was cancelled by the Air Force in 1959; the B-70 was cut back to two prototypes and the program ultimately cancelled in 1968. It appeared the company had involuntarily withdrawn from the military combat aircraft business.

In the early 1960s NAA concentrated on space-oriented activities at its Downey plant. However, in 1967 North American Aviation, Inc., merged with Rockwell-Standard Corporation to become North American Rockwell Corporation. The legendary Col. Willard S. Rockwell was named chairman of the board; in February 1973 the company was renamed Rockwell International Corporation; North American Aviation's former operations became North American Aerospace. In 1971 Robert Anderson became president of the company, succeeding Lee Atwood, who remained a board member and senior consultant until 1978. Rockwell's (née North American's) extensive experience in large, high-performance aircraft paid dividends when the company was awarded a contract by the USAF for the new B-1 bomber. However, the next generation strategic aircraft was embroiled in a political morass and was cancelled, except for minimal research and development, during the defense cutbacks under President Jimmy Carter in the late 1970s. Nonetheless, Rockwell continued work, much of it on its own, to hold together a cadre of technologists in the strong belief that the United States must replace its strategic defense force sometime within the balance of this century. In 1982 that perseverance was rewarded with reinstitution by the government of what is known as the B-1B program. Rockwell is testing derivatives of its original B-1 and should ultimately produce the B-1B as the USAF strategic bomber.

In the course of its more than 50-year history the company fostered several intriguing combinations. Most notable, of course, was the Kindelberger-Atwood team, about which the American Institute of Management in the 1950s said:

*The growth and success of North American Aviation*

*refutes the statements of some commentators that engineers are seldom good managers—Messrs. Kindelberger and Atwood deserve special compliment on the manner in which they have kept the company healthy through hectic wartime growth and drastic retrenchment.*

The most fortuitous and far-reaching combination, however, was that which resulted in the present company itself, the joining of North American with Rockwell Standard with its substantial share of two American industries, aerospace and autos.

## ANOTHER CONGLOMERATE: CONVAIR AND GENERAL DYNAMICS

A company with roots as complex as North American Rockwell's is the California manufacturer best known during its halcyon days of civil and military aircraft production as Convair. Today a division of General Dynamics Corporation, Convair traces its origin to Reuben Fleet's Consolidated Aircraft Corporation and Gerard "Jerry" Vultee's Airplane Development Corporation, later Vultee Aircraft. There are even ties to today's AVCO Corporation. AVCO was the acronym used for many years for Aviation Corporation, founded in 1929 when W. Averill Harriman and Lehman Brothers underwrote the first stock issue. AVCO's initial management included Pan American Airways founder Juan Trippe and Sherman Fairchild, a name still known in aircraft manufacturing circles.

In 1931 Aviation Corporation became associated with Cord Corporation, formed in 1929 by E.L. Cord as a holding corporation for his automobile, aircraft, and engine companies, including Auburn, Cord, and Duesenberg automobile companies, Stinson Airplane Company of Detroit, and Lycoming Manufacturing Company (maker of aircraft engines) of Williamsport, Pennsylvania.

AVCO and Cord in late 1932 bought Jerry Vultee's Airplane Development Corporation, the company Cord had helped Vultee found earlier in Glendale, California. Vultee was graduated from Throop Technical Institute (later named

Caltech) in the early 1920s, then worked with the Ford Motor Company as a sales promotion engineer before joining Douglas in 1925, then Lockheed in 1927, where he worked directly with Jack Northrop.

Consolidated Aircraft Corporation was created in May 1923 by Major Reuben H. Fleet, a World War I pilot who had received his training in 1917 at North Island and was later a military airmail pilot and air service contracting officer at McCook Field, Dayton, Ohio. Fleet combined the postwar remnants of two nearly defunct companies, Dayton Wright and Gallaudet Corporation (where he had been general manager), and founded Consolidated with $25,000 cash of his own and his sister's money. Consolidated began in Rhode Island, moving in 1924 to Buffalo, New York. In Buffalo Fleet and his designers created the Consolidated "Fleet," a smaller version of its military trainer for commercial use, and the Fleetster, an eight-passenger, high-wing monoplane with a metal monocoque fuselage. During this period too the company became known for its flying boats, the Consolidated Admiral and Commodore, used by Pan American in the Caribbean.

In January 1934 six P2Ys demonstrated the capabilities of long-range aircraft and the Navy's ability to quickly mobilize and move to offshore locations. In late 1933 the Navy P2Ys, beginning on the East Coast, flew to the Panama Canal Zone, then north via Mexico to San Diego. From San Diego the flying boats winged to San Francisco where, on January 10, 1934, they took off from the Bay and flew to Hawaii—2,408 miles of formation flying in approximately 25 hours.

Most famous of Consolidated's flying boats was the PBY Catalina, whose design was conceived in Consolidated's Buffalo facilities but whose production began in San Diego. Long plagued with adverse weather conditions while attempting test flights of flying boats in Lake Erie and the Niagara River, and dissatisfied with less than adequate factory facilities, Reuben Fleet in 1934 selected a factory site on San Diego Harbor adjacent to Lindbergh Field. It became one of America's busiest aircraft production facilities, beginning operations in the summer of 1935 after the move of 157 carloads of machinery, equipment, and materials and 311 employees.

With Consolidated's move to San Diego following by only a few months North American's move to Los Angeles, the companies joined Douglas and its Northrop Division, Lockheed, Ryan, and Vultee to make Southern California the undisputed center of aircraft manufacturing in the United States.

That period in 1934-1935 was the turning point in the shift of America's aircraft manufacturing center from east to west. By 1937 California was the leading producer of aircraft products, totaling $51.9 million annually versus a distant $15.5 million for second-place New York. Only eight years earlier, in 1929, comparable figures were New York, $17.2 million, California, $4.9 million.

Consolidated and the Navy celebrated the company's move to San Diego with an order for 60 PBY Catalina flying boats, the first model flying in October 1936 from San Diego Harbor. Consolidated abandoned the civil transport flying boat business to Martin, who developed the famed M-130 China Clipper, and to Boeing, whose B-314 Clippers were the ultimate U.S. development of the flying boat concept. The superior economics of the four-engine land planes developed just prior to the war soon made the big boats obsolete.

Consolidated's San Diego move had one other signficant affect. Lawrence D. Bell, who had started with Martin in Los Angeles and later joined Consolidated in 1928, resigned his position as Consolidated's vice-president and general manager to found Bell Aircraft in Buffalo, taking over the vacated Consolidated facilities.

By 1939 Consolidated, responding to an Air Corps request to submit designs for a heavy bomber to outperform the on-line B-17, proposed an aircraft that became the XB-24. Chief of the Army Air Corps "Hap" Arnold asked for a new bomber that would "fly the skin off" any rivals. The result was the B-24 Liberator bomber, designed and ready for production in

just nine months. More than 18,000 Liberators, including many at Ford's Willow Run, Michigan, plant, were produced. During the first production year (1940) employment at Consolidated's San Diego plant went from 3,000 to more than 13,000. By early 1941 Liberator bombers with British Royal Air Force markings were being ferried from San Diego to England.

Meanwhile, Jerry Vultee, with orders from Turkey, Brazil, the Soviet Union, and China for 76 complete aircraft and additional parts for 29 V-11 attack bombers, moved his company from Glendale to Downey, California. Despite international success, Vultee had sold no V-11s to the U.S. Vultee, an experienced pilot, flew his own plane to Washington to add personal emphasis to the sales effort. On the return trip his ship crashed on Mount Wilson in a snowstorm, killing the 38-year-old Vultee and his wife—a sad loss of a California aviation pioneer whose passing would reverberate through the industry for years.

Without its founder, with only a small backlog of orders, and a less-than-effective production capability, Vultee was apparently foundering. Parent Aviation Corporation sought new management. For Vultee's president, AVCO selected Richard Millar, then on Douglas Aircraft and Maddux Airlines boards and confidant to Don Douglas and Jack Northrop. Millar moved quickly to strengthen the company's management, engineering, and production capabilities. By August 1939 Vultee had been awarded an Army contract for 300 BT-13 Valiant basic trainers; 11,000 would eventually be built. In 1940-1941 Vultee produced the A-31 and A-35 Vengeance dive bombers first designed for Great Britain and later ordered by the U.S.

In 1940 Vultee Aircraft Corporation absorbed another AVCO subsidiary, Stinson Aircraft, and its Michigan operations. In 1940 Vultee/AVCO opened a Nashville, Tennessee, production facility to meet production demands. In less than a year during 1940-1941, Vultee had quadrupled in size. Delivery demands called for new production techniques, and Vultee installed fully powered assembly lines, the first successful use of mass production techniques in the airframe industry.

In San Diego, problems were brewing. Fleet had always operated Consolidated under one-man control, but wartime pressures soon proved the impracticability of this management strategy for a major aircraft manufacturer. Consolidated's military customers became concerned. As a result of the B-24's initial operational success, the War Department outlined an ambitious program to accelerate production of the plane—a cooperative effort amongst several major U.S. companies. Production facilities were financed and built by the War Department for Ford Motor Company at Willow Run, Michigan, and for Douglas at Tulsa, Oklahoma, and the giant Plant 36 at Fort Worth, Texas, as part of Consolidated's facilities. Even recognizing the massive challenges facing him, Fleet was reluctant to relinquish control of the company he had formed 13 years before.

Operating under a state of national emergency, the military services and government acted to save Consolidated and, hopefully, to save face for Fleet. A number of corporate suitors were encouraged. The powerful Victor Emanuel had taken over AVCO's presidency and moved quickly to purchase Fleet's shares in Consolidated, despite the fact that, in his own words, "We knew nothing about big airplanes." In December 1941 AVCO, through its Vultee subsidiary, bought Fleet's 440,000 shares (34 percent) of Consolidated Aircraft for $10,945,000.

Vultee's Millar handled the sale. Having worked closely with Fleet, Millar remembers him as a dramatic showman. When the deal had finally been resolved, the principals, their bankers, and their attorneys assembled to close the sale. At the appointed hour everyone was present except Fleet. Finally, 45 minutes late, he arrived. His eyes moist, he explained he'd just had lunch with "his boys" and was having second thoughts about his decision to sell. As Fleet expanded on his reluctance and his personal nostalgia, Millar slowly but perceptibly inched away the $10.9 million check that had been prominently placed in front of Fleet's spot

at the conference table. Fleet's eyes followed the check. Before it went beyond arm's length, Fleet reached out and took the check, noting that "a deal is a deal."

Victor Emanuel brought in two experienced Republic Steel production executives, placing Harry Woodhead at Vultee and Tom Girdler at Consolidated. In March 1942 the companies officially merged to become Consolidated Vultee Aircraft Corporation, later Convair.

Economic history records occasional interaction between the aviation and automotive industries. During the 1930s Ford's association with Bill Stout led not only to some airline ventures, but the worthy Ford Tri-motor, the "Tin Goose." Rolls-Royce engines have long powered aircraft. Packard, Ford, Cord, General Motors, and individual divisions of automakers appear tangentially to the industry, most frequently to meet demands of wartime production, sometimes in attempts to diversify. But the experience of the two industries during World War II, when it was hoped that Detroit's mass-production capabilities might be adapted to airframe building, was more a study in contrast than a blending of assets.

Ford's saga of building B-24s at its Willow Run plant illustrates the differences between the two industries. In late 1939 Ford management evaluated possible production of military aircraft. Those in the company advocating the move were led by Henry's son, Edsel, and senior manager Charles Sorenson. In July 1940 Ford rejected a Douglas invitation to participate in the building of 2,500 planes. In December the government suggested that Ford look into B-24 production. Even before the company seriously assessed aircraft production, Henry Ford advised Sorenson, "Those planes will never be used for fighting. Before you can build them, the war will be over."

In January 1941 Edsel Ford, his sons Henry and Benson, and Sorenson went to San Diego to investigate Consolidated's operations. Sorenson said: "I liked neither what I saw nor what I heard." In analyzing the situation and making a comparison between the two industries, Sorenson wrote: "The work of putting together a four-engine bomber was many times more complicated than assembling a four-cylinder automobile, but what I saw reminded me of nearly 35 years previously when we were making Model N Fords . . . here was a custom-made plane put together as a tailor would cut and fit a suit of clothes.''

Sorenson proposed a detailed plan utilizing automated automobile production methods, construction of a giant new facility in which to do this, and a projected production rate of one bomber per *hour*. That compared with Consolidated's target schedule, not yet met, of one bomber per *day*. Fleet, pointing out the pitfalls of leaping into massive aircraft production in one fell swoop, proposed that Ford make components for Consolidated to assemble. Sorenson responded: ''We'll make the complete plane or nothing.''

The result was that the U.S. government underwrote construction of the Willow Run plant, Consolidated licensed Ford to build Liberators, and production was split between complete aircraft and ''knockdown'' assemblies that Consolidated and Douglas would complete. In operation, Ford found that mass producing a big bomber was even more difficult than it had originally appeared. Sorenson was correct in his opinion that Consolidated's production methods were inadequate to meet wartime requirements. During most of the the production program, Consolidated and Ford bickered, reflecting divergent production approaches. Each company learned, but never fully adopted, the other's production techniques.

By mid-1942 Convair had established a subcontractor system to feed Liberator components into San Diego through a collection point in Santa Ana. Other Southern California airframe manufacturers, particularly Lockheed, adopted similar subcontracting systems.

Between July 1, 1940, and August 31, 1945, Convair, second only to North American, produced 30,903 aircraft. The immediate postwar years were turbulent for Consolidated Vultee. Parent AVCO worked seriously at diversification. At Vultee there was an effort at plastic-and-aluminum homes and at San Diego

they tried building flying autos. AVCO purchased ACF-Brill Motors Company of Philadelphia (transit buses) and its subsidiary, Hall-Scott Motor Car Company of Berkeley.

At San Diego the company took a giant step to enter the civil transport business with design of the Convair-Liner, a twin-engine, medium-range airliner. A program that would later save the entire company, the giant B-36 inter-continental bomber, was in development at Convair's Fort Worth division. Convair management had astutely judged market requirements for a commercial airliner, essentially a DC-3 replacement; but development cost overruns on the Convair-Liner, problems in production start-up, and the difficulties of financing for airline customers led to a long and costly delay before first delivery of the airplane. In 1947 Convair reported a net loss of $16 million. To the surprise of the financial community, Floyd B. Odlum (who later married Jacqueline Cochran), president of Atlas Corporation investment company, acquired AVCO's holdings in Convair through purchase and trade agreements. AVCO later bought back from Convair its interest in the Nashville plant and ACF-Brill properties.

Odlum immediately brought to San Diego LaMotte T. Cohu, then president of TWA and former general manager of Northrop Aircraft. Odlum and Cohu set Convair on a recovery course. The Convair-Liner was developed into the highly successful 240, 340, 440 series of civil transports, beating the competing Martin 2-0-2 for the short-to-medium range airline route market. More than 1,000 of the 240-440s were built, including C-121 military transports and T-29 navigator trainers for the Air Force. In a most controversial decision, Convair's B-36 was selected as the USAF's next-generation strategic bomber over Northrop's B-49 Flying Wing, which had already been ordered into production.

By 1949 Convair once again was profitable. Odlum's Atlas Corporation began looking for a buyer for Convair. Talks were held with Lockheed, but Bob Gross felt the asking price too high; Curtiss-Wright showed only modest interest. Not until 1953 did Odlum find a suitor, and another aviation conglomerate was on its way to being assembled.

John Jay Hopkins had originally formed General Dynamics Corporation around his Electric Boat Company, America's foremost submarine builder. General Dynamics already owned Canadair, a leading Canadian aircraft manufacturer. In May 1956 Odlum and Hopkins completed negotiations, and Atlas Corporation's 17-percent interest in Convair was sold to General Dynamics. It made a powerful combination: at the time Convair was America's eighth-largest defense contractor.

Convair entered the jet age with two major military programs: the F-102 Delta Dagger all-weather interceptor at San Diego, and the B-58 Hustler bomber at Fort Worth—both sophisticated delta-wing, supersonic planes. The F-102 inaugurated Richard T. Whitcomb's area rule ("Coke bottle") concept in fuselage design for supersonic flight; the Hustler was billed as the first Mach 2 bomber. Although technologically advanced, only a few Hustlers were produced for a brief service life. The F-102 and its higher-performing sister F-106 Delta Dart, however, became the mainstay of the Air Defense Command during the 1950s-1960s.

Convair was a wholly owned segment of New York-headquartered General Dynamics, but San Diego management enjoyed considerable autonomy. Under the leadership of former USAF General Joseph T. McNarney with John V. (Jack) Naish serving as his executive vice-president, the powerful division in 1956 generated three dollars of every four of General Dynamics sales. But Convair was about to enter a twilight zone.

The company's dark hour began optimistically enough when Howard Hughes sought a medium-range jetliner for his most cherished property, Trans World Airlines. Convair undertook a design that, after repeated name changes, emerged as the 880. The first metal was cut with firm orders for only 40 aircraft—10 from Delta, 30 from Hughes/TWA—partly because Convair was anxious to enter the high-stakes jet transport market, having already

prepared plans for a plane (the Model 18) that some experts believed could have rivaled the 707 had it been in competition early enough. But work on the 880 soon snarled in the unending design changes and long waits for decisions and approvals common to Hughes' unorthodox work style. And, strange as it must have seemed to the San Diegans, TWA's quixotic owner was caught in a cash bind. His airline desperately needed a fleet of big jets to remain competitive in both international and domestic markets where Pan Am and American 707s were drubbing TWA's obsolete Connies. Unwilling to commit himself to long-term financing with outside lenders, Hughes encountered increasing resistance from his TWA board and the banks in a confrontation that would ultimately wrest the airline from his control. Convair payments from TWA were delayed as internal costs soared, and *Fortune* magazine quoted one Convair executive as saying, "Hughes wanted to keep [the 880] from TWA's competitors. So people who might have bought the 880 if we had been allowed to sell it to them bought the DC-8 or the 707 instead." Only fifty-five 880s were built. Next, a variant of Convair's airframe, called the 990 and designed as the world's fastest jetliner, was added. But it complicated matters when only 31 units were sold (to American Airlines and Swissair) after the first examples failed to perform as predicted . Both variants went into service behind schedule, and prospective customers went elsewhere. Bad came to worse, and the 880/990 program caused parent General Dynamics to lose a single-year record $425 million on the jetliners: Convair was permanently out of the jetliner business.

But the stumble was atypical, and on the strength of its diversified operations in the 1960s and 1970s, General Dynamics (the Convair name is little-used) prospered with military and aerospace programs, including the Atlas Missile program in San Diego.

FRED ROHR GIVES NEW MEANING TO SUBCONTRACTING
Fred H. Rohr, a gifted metalsmith and production planner, conceived the notion of

providing component units and assemblies to primary airframe manufacturers while working for Claude Ryan and William Boeing, where he had contributed to the *Spirit of St. Louis* and Boeing's Model 277. His hands-on experience during the industry's transition from the cloth-and-wood airplanes of the 1920s to metal construction complemented his vision and skills ideally. One day in the mid-1930s Rohr was working overtime in Boeing's Seattle plant, fitting cowl panels to an engine. Claire Egtvedt, then chairman of Boeing, was touring the plant and stopped to watch Rohr work. Egtvedt said: "Fred, you ought to go into business for yourself. You could make and fit the necessary parts around an engine and then sell the whole assembly as a package, a power package." When war loomed later in the decade, Rohr was ready to implement just such a concept.

In 1940 Reuben Fleet urgently needed competent subcontractors for his rapidly building Consolidated production line. When Fred Rohr established his company in San Diego that summer, Fleet demonstrated his confidence by purchasing 25,000 shares of stock. Rohr's first big contract came from Consolidated for design and installation of Sperry bombsights on six LB-30s, the British version of the B-24 heavy bomber.

Burt Raynes, who succeeded Rohr as head of the company, recalled the excitement of 1940: "On our way to the Consolidated plant, Fred asked me if I thought I could handle a job of designing and installing the automatic pilot and controls system. His enthusiasm was so intense that really I never had an opportunity to reply, and two hours later, after a conference with Consolidated engineers and officials, representatives of the Sperry Company, and a delegation from the British government, we had the job."

Following the Sperry work, Rohr won a Consolidated contract to manufacture what became its specialty, ready-to-install airplane power packages. This subcontract, for 200 shipsets of nacelles with engines for PB2Y3 flying boats, was the industry's first of its kind. Similar contracts soon came from Lockheed for nacelles for Hudson bombers. Today's Rohr Industries has designed and built power packages, nacelles, thrust reversers, and other major components for the majority of civil transports and military aircraft, a list that virtually chronicles the progress of aviation since the founding of the company in 1940.

Fred Rohr believed strongly that if the necessary production tools or techniques did not exist, machines and systems must be created to meet the requirements. Among contributions from Rohr teams are a special drophammer for aircraft manufacture, sound suppression techniques for jet engines, thrust reversers, automated material handling and storage systems, forming presses, honeycomb construction advances, five-axis tooling mills, and brazing and welding techniques for both aviation and space applications. From its beginning in 1940, Fred Rohr's San Diego company has become the leading subcontractor to the aviation industry and has grown some 400-fold.

THE ANOMALOUS HOWARD HUGHES
While California's great aeronautical figures were each unique, for the most part their careers follow a pattern parallel to aviation itself, moving from solitary or small group contributions to ensemble achievement. Sooner or later the genius of Martin, Douglas, Lockheed, Northrop, and their peers emerged in large factory complexes integrating the skills and devotion of many people. But alone among that company of giants is Howard Hughes, a man who gave his very considerable talent to aviation and to the world always from a curious and oddly disturbing remove that grew over the years until at his death in 1976 isolation defined the man himself. If much of his life remains enigmatic, Hughes' lifelong devotion to aviation may be his least mysterious quality. California aeronautics would certainly be the poorer had this imaginative and compelling man not passed this way.

With vast income from an inherited business, Howard Hughes during a legendary career tried his hand at filmmaking; at airplane design, test, and fabrication; at airline operation; in electronic systems development and manufacture; in airport development and management; in Las Vegas real estate and gaming; and in a web of other interests that may never be unspun.

Howard Robard Hughes, Jr. (called Sonny by his family) was born on Christmas Eve, 1905, in Houston, Texas. His father, Big Howard, a Harvard-educated lawyer-turned-entrepreneur, founded the Sharp-Hughes Tool Company in 1908 (partner Walter Sharp died not long afterward and the elder Hughes acquired full ownership) and patented a rotary drill bit that enabled proliferating oil companies and wildcatters to penetrate the Texas shale and reach previously inaccessible crude far below. The bits, their patents, and their leasing themselves became gushers, and the family never again wanted for money. Sonny's interests were science, machines, and mathematics. In the extensive home machine shop his father provided, the teenager motorized his bicycle with an ordinary storage battery and auto starter motor, and taught himself to play the ukulele and saxophone.

After the boy's elementary education in Houston, Massachusetts, and Ojai, California, the elder Hughes arranged for special classes at the California Institute of Technology to prepare Sonny for entrance to Rice Institute. While at prep school in 1920, young Howard won a bet with his father on the Harvard-Yale shell races, the senior Hughes having agreed to buy the boy anything he chose. What Sonny wanted was a flight in a flying boat he'd seen. Shouting questions at the pilot all the time they were airborne, he gave himself his first flying lesson during that signal flight. Evidence suggests that in the years to come Hughes' happiest hours would be spent in cockpits, preferably those he'd had a hand in creating.

During Howard's second semester at Rice in 1924, Big Howard died of a heart attack. At age 18 Howard Hughes persuaded the Houston probate judge to invoke a Texas statute permitting courts to grant adult status to minors, and so immediately claimed his three-quarter

interest in Hughes Tool Company, which he soon made complete by buying his relatives' holdings.

With an estimated annual income of $2 million, Hughes set out for Hollywood in 1925 with his new bride, Ella, a daughter of Houston's distinguished Rice family. His objective: movie fame. He wasted no time entering the producers' ranks. Of his first films, one was a flop, the other a modest success, the third gained an Oscar.

Then Hughes discovered he could combine his two great passions, movies and flying. He had learned to fly in 1925, repeatedly enrolling for lessons at different airports and not telling subsequent instructors about his prior training. And then he saw *Wings*, the aviation film that won the first Academy Award for Best Picture. In their authoritative book, *Stunt Flying in the Movies*, Jim and Maxine Greenwood narrate the inevitable:

*Hughes saw* Wings *shortly after it premiered in 1927 at the Biltmore Theatre in Los Angeles. In fact, during the picture's run there he returned to see it several times, mentally noting specific details at each showing. Even at the tender age of 22, Howard Hughes was convinced he could make a better World War I picture than* Wings.

With an investment of $4 million and three years of filming, Hughes produced *Hell's Angels*, one of the most ambitious aviation films ever made. (Among the unimpressed was Ella, who wearied of waiting four years for a husband too busy to come home, returned to Houston, a divorce, and a $1.25-million settlement.) Starring the soon-to-be legendary Jean Harlow, *Hell's Angels* premiered at Grauman's Chinese Theatre in Hollywood on May 27, 1930. Having nearly completed the film while sound-track technology was making its debut, Hughes converted it to sound before final release, a process requiring reshooting of much footage. For his Great War flying epic, Hughes used 37 airplanes and their pilots, searching U.S. and European fields to locate authentic machines. A Sikorsky S-29, to be disguised as a German Gotha bomber, was purchased from aviation adventurer and record-setter Roscoe Turner and was purposely crashed in a battle scene filmed over the San Fernando Valley. Hughes' realistic recreation of aerial battles, the addition of the sound track, and elaborate promotion paid off. The film ultimately grossed more than $7 million, surprising industry skeptics.

He produced only five more movies, including Jane Russell's controversial *The Outlaw*, before setting the silver screen aside and getting to the serious business of airplanes, but his dedication to perfection before and during the making of *Hell's Angels* and his consummate interest in aviation virtually define Howard Hughes' public life from his 25th year.

With his racing victory in a Boeing 100 (a plane he'd ordered before setting out on a rambling flight eastward from Burbank with his newly acquired associate Glenn Odekirk in the summer of 1932) at an All-American Air Meet in Miami in January 1934, Hughes began a seemingly endless series of aeronautical innovations and "firsts." Among the innovations was this very Boeing, actually a civilian version of the Army Air Corps P-12 pursuit fighter (Navy designation, F4B-1) — doubtless in 1932 the only military fighter owned by a private citizen. Preparing the plane for the race, Hughes made so many modifications that Glenn casually suggested that next time Howard should build his plane from scratch.

That, of course, is precisely what the man who knew what he wanted did in 1935. The H-1 Racer, secretly created in a Glendale hangar with Odekirk, fledgling aeronautical engineer Dick Palmer, and a 16-man support crew implementing Hughes' ideas, embodied such advances as power-driven retractable landing gear, flush rivets, split flaps, and drooping ailerons. Flashing across the Santa Ana sky on its first trial, it set a new world speed record as Hughes pushed the H-1 to 352 mph. In January 1937 he flew the H-1 from Burbank to Newark in seven hours, 28 minutes, at an average speed of 332 mph, to break his own record set the year before when he had flown a Northrop Gamma from Burbank to New York.

Next came international records. In 1938, with a specially equipped Lockheed Model 14, Hughes set a round-the-world record of three days, 19 hours, and 17 minutes. The ship was fitted with avionics including three separate radio transmitters, an automatic pilot, and systems redundancy typical of Hughes' attention to detail and safety. Speaking at New York City Hall the day after his return, Hughes said: "The airplane was fast because . . . young men trained mostly at the California Institute of Technology, working in a factory in California, put in two hundred thousand hours of concentrated thought to develop [it]." Prior to choosing the speedy Lockheed, Hughes in 1936 had bought from Transcontinental and Western Air their prototype Douglas DC-1. Four years later a meeting with TWA president Jack Frye would lead to Hughes' acquisition of the air carrier and the birth of Kelly Johnson's beautiful Lockheed Constellation.

To facilitate administration, Howard now formalized his aviation interests by calling the Glendale operation the Hughes Aircraft Company (initially operated as a division of the Tool Company). From this Glendale cadre late in World War II came Hughes' next project at the leading edge of technology. Hughes and his organization created the XF-11, originally derived from their DX-2 experimental aircraft. The XF-11 had twin boom fuselages, one for each of its two 3,000 h.p. piston engines which drove two four-blade, 17-foot diameter counter-rotating propellers. A short fuselage in between housed cockpit and avionics platform; it was designed as a strategic photo reconnaissance plane. The airplane had a sea-level speed of more than 400 mph and very nearly cost Hughes his life during its maiden flight on a Sunday morning in July 1946. Shortly after takeoff from Culver City, the machine abruptly shuddered and pitched to the right as the airspeed fell. Unable to identify the cause of the problem, and rapidly losing control, Hughes headed the crippled airplane toward the only clear spot he could see, the Los Angeles Country Club golf course. He didn't get that far, and the airplane smashed into a Beverly Hills home. The critically injured Hughes was pulled from the wreck by a Marine sergeant visiting nearby and was hospitalized for months. Recovering consciousness two days later, he narrated his analysis of the crash to Odekirk: the rear starboard propeller must have gone into reverse pitch, he theorized; investigation confirmed his suspicion. Following his release from the hospital, Hughes ordered the second XF-11 adapted to single-rotation propellers, but despite Hughes' heroic efforts, the aircraft never sold.

Each Hughes achievement, however, was in part a prelude to the ultimate expression of the genius of this multifaceted eccentric, the airplane for which he is best known, the H-4 *Hercules*. Like others in the Hughes line, only one was built; and it remains today the world's largest airplane. The *Hercules* for more than 35 years has been called the "Spruce Goose," although it's made mostly of birch with some poplar and a good deal of balsa wood, and was shrouded in mystery and intrigue for many years. H-4 technical and statistical superlatives abound, beginning with dimensions: a wing span of 319.92 feet, 124 feet greater than a 747's and capable of sheltering a DC-10 beneath each wing.

In 1942, when Nazi submarines in one month sank 300,000 tons of Allied shipping, industrialist Henry J. Kaiser proposed that the United States build gigantic flying boats to transport men and materiel to the war theaters. When he took his concept to the War Production Board, Kaiser was authorized to go ahead with the planning of such a transport as long as it did not use essential metal. Kaiser, experienced in Liberty Ship construction, turned to Howard Hughes because of his work with revolutionary aircraft and long-distance flying.

The Kaiser-Hughes Corporation was founded in 1942, receiving U.S. government contracts to build three Flying Boats, designated HK-1 (Hughes-Kaiser, first aircraft). The connection was dissolved when it became apparent that Kaiser's expertise in ship construction was little help on the Flying Boat and the shipyards were unsuitable or unavailable in any case.

With Hughes Aircraft funds a plant was built at Culver City, facilities that eventually served both Hughes Aircraft Company and Hughes Helicopters.

Despite grave personal difficulties—injuries in plane crashes in 1943 and 1946 and a nervous breakdown in 1945—Hughes pressed forward with the Flying Boat. But when the war in Europe ended in 1945, the H-4 was still unfinished. Although there was heavy pressure in Washington to terminate the contract, Hughes managed to get an agreement for continued development and construction of one Flying Boat (instead of three) for the original $18 million contract figure, and invested an additional $7 million of his own money.

By mid-1946 giant components of the H-4 were ready to be moved from Culver City to Terminal Island, Long Beach, for final assembly and flight test. In order to transport the massive components along the 28-mile route, some 2,300 power and phone lines had to be moved or cut and then restored. The transfer took two days and cost $55,000. Schools were recessed so children could watch. Spectators lined the entire route.

Although the Flying Boat was nearing completion in 1947, Hughes was once again called to testify before a U.S. Senate committee investigating war contracts. The chairman of the Senate Investigating Committee was Maine Republican Owen Brewster, who fared second-best in several skirmishes with Hughes during the fractious hearings. With good effect, an angry Hughes told the committee about his airplane: "I put the sweat of my life into this thing. I have my reputation rolled up in it, and I have stated that if it was a failure I probably will leave this country and never come back, and I mean it."

On a grey Sunday morning, November 2, 1947, with Hughes in the left seat, the airplane was eased into the waters of Long Beach Harbor. There were two high-speed taxi tests, one with a bevy of reporters. Then, at 1:40 p.m., Hughes advanced the throttles of the eight 3,000 h.p. engines for a third taxi run. As the great hull skimmed along the harbor waters and moved up on the step, to the amazement of the crew on board and one lone reporter from a Long Beach radio station, Hughes unexpectedly lifted the H-4 into the air, and the behemoth roared steadily and relentlessly along about 70 feet above the calm harbor for a mile or so before its builder's gentle hand let it settle easily in a satisfying hiss upon the ocean. None among the thousands who watched from afar, nor among the crew on board, could know the mighty ship would fly only that once.

In typical Hughes style, the flight had been made without official clearance and had not been scheduled for the original test program. Interviewing Hughes afterward, the startled radio reporter asked if it had been an intentional first flight. Hughes responded: "Certainly. I like to make surprises. It felt so buoyant and good, I just pulled it up."

From that day in 1947 until October 1980, the dream boat was hidden away in a humidity-controlled $1.75-million hangar on Terminal Island. Round-the-clock guards and a crew of 300 kept the H-4 ready to fly at any time with only three months of preparation. The guards were reduced to about 35 in the mid-1960s and finally to five in 1976.

For a time, the ship's future was bleak, with one proposal being made to cut it up for piecemeal display in museums around the country. But farsighted efforts by the Aero Club of Southern California created a far more satisfactory outcome. Under lease to the Wrather Corporation, the *Hercules* today is handsomely displayed beneath the world's largest geodesic dome adjacent to the retired Cunard liner, *Queen Mary*, close by Long Beach Harbor.

The Flying Boat was not Howard Hughes' final aircraft construction effort. In 1953 his company developed the giant XH-17 Flying Crane helicopter. Designed for the U.S. military as a heavy lift test vehicle, the XH-17 successfully proved the Flying Crane concept with its ability to lift more than 50,000 pounds using a pressure-jet system from two jet engines ducted to the tips of the 130-foot diameter main rotor blades. In 1957, at the opposite end of the spectrum, Hughes Helicopters' first commercial helicopter, the lightweight, low-cost 269-A,

established a world endurance record of more than 101 hours.

In 1964 the Hughes 300 was selected as the U.S. Army's primary trainer. As the TH-55A, it has been used to train more than 30,000 U.S. Army pilots and has become the standard trainer for many other nations. The Army OH-6A followed in 1966, setting 23 world records for speed, distance, and altitude. Hughes 500 series helicopters, fastest in their class and able to lift one ton, are used for civil and industrial applications; in military garb, they are the 500MD Defenders. In 1983 Hughes Helicopters flew the first production version of the Army AH-64 Apache advanced attack helicopter, the product that promised profitability for the first time in the company's history.

In 1953 the complex interrelationships of Hughes Tool and its Aircraft Division began to be sorted out. The Howard Hughes Medical Institute was created and received all stock of the newly organized Hughes Aircraft Company in exchange for the Aircraft Division assests, which had been contributed to the institute by Hughes Tool Company. In subsequent action, Hughes Helicopters was created as a subsidiary of SUMMA Corporation, the business entity of which Howard Hughes maintained control until his death. In early 1984 SUMMA announced that Hughes Helicopters had been purchased by the McDonnell Douglas Corporation for $470 million.

By 1948 Hughes Aircraft Company was drifting and dwindling as its staff sought meaningful work elsewhere. But Glenn Odekirk suggested to Hughes that electronics were a fertile field for development, and ultimately Hughes invited an old acquaintance, retired Air Force General Harold L. George, to head up a research-oriented company concentrating on such esoteric projects as electronic guidance and advanced airborne search radar. George agreed, and in a kind of industrial tour de force, Hughes set about hiring a management and engineering team of dizzying competence. Granted almost unlimited funds, a liberal charter, and a conducive atmosphere in which to work was a team of some 100 scientists and engineers headed by a who's who of modern aerospace achievement: Charles B. "Tex" Thornton, Ira Eaker, Simon Ramo, Dean Wooldridge. While these giants moved on to build their own companies, their early days with Hughes are among the most productive in post-World War II American industry. Hughes Aircraft Company, although a private corporation wholly owned by the Howard Hughes Medical Institute, is a vast complex of electronics systems research, development, and production capabilities dedicated to advanced technology for space, military, and industrial applications. Despite the Hughes Aircraft name, the company no longer has any connection with airplane development or production.

In the last significantly aviation-related phase of his career, Hughes conceived a grandiose future for Las Vegas, Nevada, a central element of which was the transformation of McCarran Field into an intercontinental airport hub to be served by ocean-leaping supersonic liners and a regional airline that would link domestic points. To that end, he moved his headquarters to Las Vegas and swiftly generated a literal frenzy of speculation among the local citizens. Francis T. Fox, then general manager of the Los Angeles Department of Airports, was hired as Hughes Director of Aviation to oversee both the airport program and the acquisition of what would become Hughes Airwest—the mercurial aerophile's last airline.

It seemed a fitting, if poignant, conclusion to his complex life that on April 5, 1976, a frail and aging Howard Hughes died aboard a small jet airplane carrying him from Acapulco, Mexico, to Houston, the city of his birth.

## JACK NORTHROP FOUNDS A FOURTH COMPANY

Because of Jack Northrop's close early associations with Allan and Malcolm Loughead, Donald Douglas, Claude Ryan, and others, the roots of Northrop Corporation run wide and deep in the industry. Northrop completed his six-year contract with Douglas in 1938, and in March 1939 chartered a company that would concentrate on research and development of

advanced aircraft technologies and his concept of the ultimate clean airplane—the Flying Wing. By June, as corporate financing and legal preliminaries neared completion, designers were already at work on the N-1M Flying Wing.

In 1929 test pilot Eddie Bellande had flown Northrop's first Avion Flying Wing. Now the veteran test pilot, TWA captain, and personal friend again influenced Jack Northrop's destiny when he introduced Northrop to TWA director LaMotte T. Cohu. Able and farsighted, Cohu would succeed Jack Frye as TWA president in 1947 and would later become president of American Airlines and American Aircraft and Engine. Recognizing that every U.S. aircraft manufacturer would soon become involved in military production, he convinced Northrop the new company should prepare to manufacture as well as design and develop military aircraft.

In early 1939 Northrop Aircraft was incorporated with John K. Northrop as president and chief engineer, Cohu as chairman of the board and general manager, and Bellande a member of the board of directors. Prior to September groundbreaking at Northrop's present location in Hawthorne, the company set up headquarters in the Hotel Hawthorne, nicknamed the "Yellow Peril" and better known for hosting ladies of pleasure than aero moguls.

With Northrop and his engineering staff immersed in aircraft design, Cohu sought the corporation's first business. In early 1940 Consolidated's Fleet, well aware of Northrop's reputation, awarded the company a subcontract to build PBY-5 tail sections and eventually engine cowlings and seat installations. The next month brought Arctic explorer-pilot Bernt Balchen, who had earlier flown Northrop-designed airplanes, to the factory. With him was the Norwegian Buying Commission, in the U.S. to seek suppliers. Soon the company had a welcome contract from the Norwegian government to design and build 24 seaplane patrol bombers—the N-3PB—Northrop's first production aircraft.

That the company's first aircraft order should come from a foreign government was apt: Northrop Corporation remains a leading supplier of military aircraft to America's allies. The British awarded Northrop a production contract for 200 Vultee-designed V-72 Vengeance dive bombers, and Boeing subcontracted a portion of its B-17 Flying Fortress to the young Hawthorne organization.

Production work did not hinder innovation: the company earned a Navy contract to study a gas turbine engine and propeller combination, the turboprop; and the first true all-wing airplane, the N-1M, was under development. Only a year old, the company had made giant strides. Asked to identify his position in those vibrant days, Jack Northrop revealed his priorities when he replied, "I was chief engineer and president."

Northrop's engineering team under Walt Cerny was at work on the N-1M. Early Wing designs were reviewed at the Guggenheim Aeronautical Laboratory at the California Institute of Technology with the lab's preeminent director, Theodore Von Kármán, and his associate, William R. Sears, who would become chief of aerodynamics for the company in 1942. First flown in July 1940, the tailless, 39-foot span N-1M was designed so pilot, twin engines, and retractable landing gear were all enclosed within the wing. To allow elimination of the empennage, Northrop twisted his wings so the angle of attack at the tips was smaller than at center span, thus supplying the same aerodynamic forces as a tail. Wing panels were adjustable on the ground for sweep and dihedral, allowing efficient assessment of various flight regimes.

Von Kármán's judgement of Northrop is revealing of both men. In his autobiography, Von Kármán wrote:

*He had an intuitive grasp of aviation and he produced some great and beautiful aircraft designs. One of the best of them was the Flying Wing . . . Northrop always was one idea ahead of everyone else . . . a gentle, generous, and talented man with great daring.*

In 1942, amidst the turmoil of wartime production, infant Northrop Aircraft suddenly was America's 13th-largest airframe manufacturer, with a substantial base of subcontracting and licensed manufacturing.

On December 7, 1940, Jack Northrop had submitted a preliminary design for a prototype night fighter derived from observations made by U.S. officers during the Battle of Britain. In January 1941, under a $1,367,000 Army Air Corps contract for two airplanes, work began on the Northrop XP-61 Black Widow, one of the war's best-kept secrets. The two-engine, twin-boom, heavily armed, and radar-equipped interceptor served in the European and Pacific theaters from mid-1944, helping to clear the skies of nighttime enemy bombers. By war's end the company had produced nearly 1,100 airplanes, more than 1,300 tail surfaces for flying boats, and nearly 45,000 cowlings and 25,000 nacelles for B-17s.

The program that established Northrop in its own right was the development of a bomber version of Jack Northrop's Flying Wing, kicked off late in 1941 following a visit by Assistant Secretary of War Robert Lovett and Army Air Corps Major General Oliver P. Echols. Working with these defense planners Northrop submitted to the Air Corps at Wright Field preliminary designs for what was to become the XB-35 Flying Wing. Recognizing the long lead time involved with this revolutionary design, defense planners anticipated operational service in 1945-1950.

Although the N-1M had flown in 1940, this machine would be substantially larger. So the decision was made in 1942 to build the N-9M prototypes approximately one-third the size of the XB-35. The first N-9M flight came on December 27, 1942, at Hawthorne. Although one prototype was lost in flight test, the remaining three N-9Ms flew from Muroc Army Air Base for more than three years, giving military pilots experience with all-wing aircraft flight characteristics. (Only two Northrop Wings have survived in any form. An N-1M is at the NASM's Silver Hill, Maryland, facility, and the second prototype N-9M is in the custody of the Air Museum-Planes of Fame at Chino, California, and is now being restored to flying condition.)

The company during the war also worked on development and flight test of 12 experimental planes applying the flying wing concept, including the JB-10 "buzz bombs"; America's first military rocket plane, the MX-324 Rocket Wing; the first prone-pilot interceptor, the XP-79 Flying Ram; and the XP-56.

The big wing, however, remained the focus of company management and U.S. military planners. The piston-powered XB-35 first flew from the Hawthorne facility to Muroc Army Air Base in June 1946. And even as the propeller-driven version was built and tested, Northrop engineers were readying the basic airframe design for installation of eight turbojet engines to create the YB-49, which made its maiden flight in October 1947, again from Northrop Field— what is now Hawthorne Municipal Airport. Few who beheld the stately progress of the Flying Wing as it swept across Southern California skies will forget its startlingly graceful presence. He and Sears, wrote Von Kármán, "used to get up and drive to the desert at dawn to watch the tests [of the Flying Wing]. As the wing flew over the flat land like a great bird, it seemed to me that I was participating in the birth of aviation all over again."

Early Wing aerodynamic instability problems were quickly rectified with a Minneapolis Honeywell Electronics autopilot system nicknamed "Little Herbert." Air Force project officers called the YB-49s that had gone into flight test the "cleanest, most trouble-free and most ready to fly new bombers ever received from Air Force contractors." The commander of the 8th Air Force called it, "the fastest bomber I have ever flown . . . a fine ship with a real future."

Although Northrop, program officers, and pilots had no way of knowing it then, the Flying Wing had no future at all with the Air Force. The giant B-36, then being developed by Consolidated Vultee at the government plant in Fort Worth, Texas, would shortly be selected as the nation's next strategic bomber. Even though some experts hailed the Wing as one of the most advanced designs since the Wright Flyer, and YB-49 performance surpassed that of the B-36,

the Air Force ordered the Wing program cancelled and the 11 units already built scrapped. Ironically, recognizing the company could not possibly meet production requirements for the Wing at Hawthorne, Northrop had earlier contracted with Consolidated Vultee to build YB-49s in Fort Worth. More than 30 years afterward the program's termination remains a controversy.

Jack Northrop believed the Flying Wing concept would ultimately become a reality. His continued belief was well-founded. In 1979 NASA Administrator Robert A. Frosch wrote to Northrop, saying, in part:

*Our studies of technology needs for potential future large cargo/logistics aircraft have led us to investigations of span-loaded configurations during which we have, in effect, rediscovered the flying wing . . . Our analyses confirmed your much earlier convictions as to the load-carrying and efficiency advantages of this design approach, and studies performed for us by the major manufacturers of large airplanes have further corroborated these findings.*

The cancellation of the Flying Wing was a severe setback to Northrop Aircraft Incorporated, but after V-J Day the company had resumed its peacetime efforts with two programs: an Air Force order for 175 F-15A Reporters (which did not materialize), and work from United Air Lines converting surplus C-47 and C-54 transports to civil airliners. The company tried the civilian market with a rugged three-engine transport designed for unimproved airports, but just as the deluge of surplus Jennies had swamped the Loughead's Northrop-designed S-1 in 1919, auction-block Skytrains and Commandos preempted the market for Northrop's N-23 Pioneer in 1947. The prototype never went into production, but did give rise to the military C-125 Raider (25 were produced), a small airborne assault and rescue aircraft for the USAF.

In March 1946 Northrop entered the missile business with an Air Force contract to develop America's first intercontinental bombing missile, the SM-62 Snark, whose inertial guidance system was a preliminary step toward leadership in the manufacture of guidance systems. Simultaneously, design and engineering teams had been at work on a new all-weather interceptor, resulting in May 1946 in two prototypes of the XP-89, later to become the F-89 Scorpion. More than 1,000 Scorpions built by Northrop served with Air Defense forces until 1969.

The year 1952 was pivotal for Northrop Aircraft. The company acquired Radioplane Company of Van Nuys, a leading manufacturer of target drone systems. Its president, Whitley C. Collins, became a member of the Northrop board of directors, eventually to be elected president of Northrop. Radioplane is now Northrop Ventura Division, a leading producer of pilotless aero vehicles—drones.

Then in late 1952 came an event that was to drastically alter the company's course. A disheartened Jack Northrop, his innate enthusiasm drained by events surrounding the cancellation and wanton destruction of his personal dream, the Flying Wing, severed all connections with the last company he founded. Not until the late 1970s, when he was named a director emeritus, was Jack Northrop again associated with the company he began.

In 1953 Thomas V. Jones, then on the staff of the RAND Corporation and with experience in air transport planning and economics, joined the company as assistant to chief engineer William Ballhaus (later president of Beckman Instruments and Northrop board member). Jones succeeded Collins as president in 1959 and set a course for the company distinctly apart from other aircraft manufacturers. The first objective was to become the world's leading producer of high-performance tactical fighters, particularly to meet defense requirements of nations that could not afford the high-cost weapons systems then being developed for the U.S. military. The second objective was modest diversification and a solid position as subcontractor for at least one major civil aircraft program.

Jones' philosophy was to use technology to simplify rather than complicate. He encouraged

development of projects with company funds and recognition of a product's real cost over its full life span—a concept Jones called "life cost." Typifying Northrop policy was the N-156 prototype, a lightweight, high-performance, relatively low-cost fighter conceived to counter what Jones saw as a questionable trend toward ever more complex technology. An October 1961 *Time* magazine cover story said, "It is Jones who has done most to bring economy and simplicity to the intricate and expensive field of aerospace."

Production of the N-156 came when the Air Force chose a derivative—the T-38 Talon—as its primary advanced jet trainer. The T-38 was first flown in 1959 and produced until 1972. More than 1,100 units were built for the USAF, NASA, USN, and the Federal Republic of Germany. Jacqueline Cochran flew a T-38 to six new flight records in 1961, and from 1974 to 1982 the Air Force Thunderbird demonstration team performed in Talons. Simultaneously, Northrop continued development of the N-156F Freedom Fighter, and in 1962 the Department of Defense selected the N-156F as tactical fighter for favored nations under the U.S. Military Assistance Program (MAP). The F-5 subsequently became a frontline fighter for five nations. Soon Norway, Spain, and Canada bought F-5s; the aircraft was supplied to the Netherlands and Venezuela through the Canadian production program. Higher-performance models—F-5E and F-5F Tiger IIs—were developed, and by 1983, 30 countries were flying F-5s; and nearly 3,000 of the T-38/F-5 family had been produced at Hawthorne, El Segundo, and Palmdale and 700 more under license or co-production agreements abroad.

In 1966, again with corporate funds for facilities and tooling, the company collaborated with Boeing on the 747. With a kickoff order worth $450 million for 201 shipsets, Northrop began building the 153-foot-long main fuselage section of the widebody airliner, and production on 747, 747SP, and freighter cargo doors continues in the 1980s.

With the F-5 international success, Tom Jones set a new goal for his team: develop a more advanced successor. By 1967 the company created the P530 Cobra, intended as an F-5 follow-on and, in its YF-17 configuration, a major competitor in the USAF lightweight fighter competition with General Dynamics' YF-16. Under the Air Combat Fighter (ACF) "fly before buy" concept, two prototypes were built by each company for a flyoff to win the "contract of the century," so called because a consortium including Belgium, The Netherlands, Norway, and Denmark announced it would select a NATO fighter based on the U.S. choice. The U.S. Navy also sought a versatile aircraft to complement its larger F-14s. The triple order could easily exceed 3,000 airplanes and approach production volume not seen since World War II.

In early 1975 the USAF, however, with an eye to engine commonality with its own F-15, selected General Dynamics' F-16 for its air combat fighter requirements. Less than four months later the Navy selected the McDonnell Douglas-Northrop YF-17 (redesignated F/A-18 Hornet) to meet its fighter and attack requirements into the 21st century. The most devastating blow to Northrop's business plans, however, came when the NATO consortium selected the aircraft they believed would be operational with U.S. forces—the F-16.

General Dynamics, without fighter production since the F-106, was now back in military aviation with the largest single potential of any aircraft program since the Second World War. Northrop had become a subcontractor (to McDonnell Douglas) for an aircraft it had originally designed and developed. The carrier-suitable F-18 went into service for the Marine Corps at El Toro, California, in early 1983 and will eventually replace the F-4s and A-7s in USN/USMC service.

The fiscal jury has not yet returned a verdict on the company's F-20 Tigershark, a fighter designed for the international market. More than $600 million has been invested in the plane which made its maiden flight in August 1982 and for which Jones envisions a possible 300 sales orders from the dozen nations considering the Tigershark and an ultimate market of perhaps 1,000 units. So far, with three airplanes built and in the test program, no firm

sales have materialized.

Despite setbacks, the company continues to evoke Jack Northrop-Tom Jones design and business principles. Northrop has found, however, that some of these concepts take longer than others to bear fruit. Fortunately, corporate results had not been predicated solely upon being prime contractor for the F-18 or on sales of the F-20. In 1983 Northrop profits for the first time in its history topped $100 million, principally as a result of its expanding electronics business combined with research and development on what industry analysts have called the nation's next-generation defense system, the super-secret Stealth bomber.

*Above: Lockheed Chairman Daniel J. Haughton shuttled between Los Angeles and Britain to negotiate finances that would permit the TriStar (and Lockheed itself) to survive the Rolls-Royce bankruptcy. Courtesy, CALAC*

*Opposite: Over Muroc Dry Lake near the end of 1944, Lockheed test pilot Tony LeVier flew Lockheed's XP-80A, a Kelly Johnson design that became the first operational USAF jet fighter. Courtesy, EAFBHO*

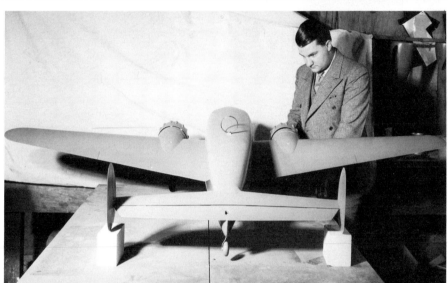

*Reaching 152 mph in a takeoff roll of 5,200 feet, Lockheed's L-1011 TriStar wide-bodied airliner lifts off the Palmdale runway for an unprecedentedly lengthy 2.5-hour-long maiden flight on November 16, 1970. H.B. "Hank" Dees was in the left-hand seat. Courtesy, CALAC*

*Kelly Johnson examines a Lockheed Model 12 Electra Junior in October 1935. Two years before, while a technician at the University of Michigan, he had urged the double tail for the Model 10 to improve lateral control and was hired to begin his extraordinary half-century with Lockheed. Courtesy, CALAC*

*Above: Donald Douglas (left) confers in 1959 with two men whose skills accelerated his company's rise to greatness: Arthur E. Raymond (center), principal architect of the DC-1 and chief engineer for subsequent DC airplanes through the DC-8, and Edward H. Heinemann, preeminent conceiver of combat aircraft, particularly for the U.S. Navy. Courtesy, MD*

*Right: Shown here after rollout at the Douglas Santa Monica plant in June 1933, the DC-1 prototype presaged reliable and economical air transport worldwide. No single machine challenges "Old 300" as the most important airplane in commercial aviation history. Courtesy, Gordon Williams*

*Left: Flying past its parent company's pyramid headquarters building in San Francisco in 1983 is a Transamerica Airlines stretched Douglas Super 70 DC-8, newly re-engined with CFM56 turbofans. The advanced technology engines dramatically extend the useful life of the nearly 20-year-old DC-8 airframes. Courtesy, Transamerica Airlines*

*Right: Prototypes of North American's F-100 Super Sabre, the first jet fighter to sustain supersonic speed in level flight, flew in 1953. When production ended in 1959, 2,249 units had been built for the USAF. The F-100F two-seat training version is shown here. Courtesy, Rockwell International (RI)*

*Left: The first of two North American XB-70 Valkyries, laden with innovative technology later applied to other planes, lifts off on its maiden flight in September 1964. Conceived as a strategic bomber, but made obsolete by missile technology even before it flew, the XB-70 attained a speed of Mach 2.85 and an altitude of 68,000 feet. Courtesy, RI*

*Below: North American's F-86 Sabrejet was the first truly high-performance, swept-wing, turbojet-powered tactical aircraft. It first flew in 1947. More than 6,000 F-86s were produced over a decade. Courtesy, RI*

*Bottom: North American's James H. "Dutch" Kindelberger and Lee Atwood (right), whose aero engineering skills were matched by their outstanding management talent, are pictured with NAA chief engineer Ray Rice (left) reviewing plans for the F-86 Sabre in the early 1950s. Courtesy, RI*

More than 18,000 of Consolidated's B-24 Liberators were produced during WWII at San Diego, Ford's Willow Run plant, and Fort Worth, Texas. The B-24 design was ready for production nine months after "Hap" Arnold ordered a bomber to "fly the skin off" its rivals. Courtesy, General Dynamics (GD)

Reuben Fleet (shown here about two years before his death in 1975) began Consolidated Aircraft Corporation in 1923 with $25,000. He earned his wings at North Island in 1917, was an airmail pilot, and led the Air Mail Service's Army operation when airmail service began in 1918. Courtesy, San Diego Aero-Space Museum

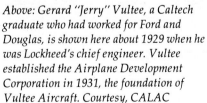

Above: Gerard "Jerry" Vultee, a Caltech graduate who had worked for Ford and Douglas, is shown here about 1929 when he was Lockheed's chief engineer. Vultee established the Airplane Development Corporation in 1931, the foundation of Vultee Aircraft. Courtesy, CALAC

Right: Convair's F-106 Delta Dart, which was designed in the 1950s for primary defense against Soviet manned bomber attack, remained the fastest single-engine fighter in the world (Mach 2.4 plus) from 1956 until retirement some 25 years later. Courtesy, GD

*Top: The XF-11, created by the newly formed Hughes Aircraft Corporation late in WWII as a strategic photo reconnaissance plane, had 3,000-hp engines and a level-flight speed of 400 mph. Pictured about 1949 is the second prototype. Courtesy, EAFBHO*

*Above: The 1953 Hughes XH-17 Flying Crane helicopter was designed for the military as a heavy-lift test vehicle. Using a pressurejet system from two turbine engines ducted to the tips of the 130-foot diameter main rotor blades, it lifted more than 50,000 pounds. Courtesy, R.E. Falk*

*Right: Howard Hughes' 200-ton Hercules flying boat, conceived during WWII as a troop transport impervious to submarine attack, was completed too late for wartime duty. The all-wood masterpiece is now displayed alongside Long Beach Harbor in a fine museum setting. Courtesy, Wrather Port Properties*

Photographed at the height of wartime output is the Burbank production line for Lockheed P-38 Lightning fighters. Ten thousand were produced by the war's end. In the Pacific the plane's twin-engine security was valued during long over-water flights, and Lightnings downed more Japanese aircraft than any other fighters. Courtesy, CALAC

This 1947 view from the right-hand side of the jet-powered Northrop YB-49 Flying Wing's cockpit shows the raised controls (left) for the pilot, whose view was through the plane's left-hand bubble canopy. The copilot's windows (right) were set into the wing's leading edge. Courtesy, NC

At a 1978 gathering industry colleagues honored 83-year-old John K. Northrop (left). Here he is shown with Richard Millar, former Northrop chairman, Vultee president, and board member at Douglas Aircraft and Maddux Airlines. Courtesy, NC

Northrop's P-61 Black Widow night fighter was the young company's first major production airplane. From 1942 until 1946, 726 units were built. Early models, painted glossy black with red serial numbers, carried three-man crews. Courtesy, NC

After their introduction with the RAF in 1941, North American P-51 Mustangs were fitted with Packard-built Rolls-Royce Merlin engines. They became one of WWII's great fighters, combining a 440 mph speed at 30,000 feet with an 800-mile plus range. The Los Angeles production line is shown about 1944. Courtesy, RI

CHAPTER FIVE

# EDUCATION, RESEARCH, AND TESTING

Every schoolboy knows an aviation highlight or hero or two—the Wrights at Kitty Hawk, Lindbergh across the Atlantic, Yaeger over the Mojave, Armstrong on the moon. But some turning points are little known, some heroes too little praised. One such protracted moment was aviation's transition from cottage craft to scientific discipline and integrated industry, beginning shortly after the First World War. The heroes were scientists, academicians, test pilots, and a few visionaries like Daniel and Harry Guggenheim.

In 1922, for all the nation's proliferating aero ventures, only five American colleges had programs in aeronautical engineering: the Massachusetts Institute of Technology (MIT), the California Institute of Technology (Caltech or CIT), the University of Michigan, the University of Washington, and Stanford University. Jerome Hunsaker, later to earn distinction with the Navy, NACA, and Bell Laboratories, had begun the nation's pioneer aero engineering course at MIT following the first aero instruction ever offered there—a series of lectures given by Albert Merrill in 1913. Other courses were assembled elsewhere from mechanical engineering programs, urged by a few persistent students and faculty members. The tinder sparked to life in 1922 at New York University when Alexander Klemin and Collins Bliss arranged to offer elementary aerodynamics as an alternative to the electrical engineering option for mechanical engineering seniors. The following year they introduced a four-course program of aerodynamics and airplane, propeller, and airship design. Dean Charles Snow of the College of Engineering approved the three-year experiment with Klemin as an associate professor of aeronautical engineering but insisted that financial support must come from outside sources. When all the program's graduates promptly found jobs, Chancellor Elmer Brown decided to make NYU's commitment to aeronautical engineering permanent with funding of $500,000 for staff and facilities.

A committee to seek public subscription of the money was formed in March 1925, and among the members, because of his friendship with Alexander Klemin, was Harry Guggenheim, whose family had amassed a substantial fortune from various domestic and foreign mining and related industrial enterprises. Three months later Harry Guggenheim's father, Daniel, endowed three professorial chairs, a laboratory, and other research facilities—the nucleus of NYU's Daniel Guggenheim School of Aeronautics. And that was the beginning.

By year's end the Guggenheims had announced plans to support aviation development nationwide, and the Daniel Guggenheim Fund for the Promotion of Aeronautics, with Harry as president, came into being in January 1926. Major provisos of the fund included allocation of $2.5 million to promote aeronautical education in universities, colleges, secondary schools, and for the general public; to assist in the extension of aeronautical science; and to further the development of the commercial airplane as a regular means of transport for goods and passengers. Work would be in the civil sector only, not duplicate existing efforts nor infringe on government activity, and be complete projects.

In his introduction to Reginald Cleveland's 1942 history of the Guggenheim Fund, Robert Millikan wrote:

*I will comment upon but one element . . . worth to the United States many times the whole cost of the funds expended. That element consisted in the choice by the far-sighted directors of the fund of university centers as the keys to their promotional effort. It was very penetrating insight that realized at that time when the so-called practical man was in the driver's seat that the days of the enthusiastic inventor, the born mechanic, the daring son of Daedalus as the chief agent in aeronautical progress, were gone. All honor and glory to him. But the problem of perfecting commercial aeronautical transportation, by making each pound of fuel carry a given load the maximum possible number of miles, of insuring the maximum of safety and of the reliability of air travel, that required fundamental knowledge and analytical power in the field of both fluid and solid mechanics such as was to be found in general only in the university atmosphere.*

In his moving account of the Guggenheims' gifts to aviation, *Legacy of Flight,* historian Richard Hallion recounts the trustees' review of aeronautics "west of Michigan" particularly at Caltech, Stanford, and the University of Washington. Western aviation concerns would increase, they believed, and proper educational facilities would stimulate this increase and furnish the growing industry with well-trained engineers. Their foresight was superb.

GALCIT, AN AERONAUTICAL CAMELOT
In Pasadena, California, Throop Polytechnic Institute, founded in 1891 by Amos Throop, built its first wind tunnel in 1917. Three faculty members—Albert Merrill (a largely self-taught inventor), Harry Bateman, and Richard Tollman (physicists by training)—offered a few aeronautics courses between 1918 and 1926.

Robert A. Millikan came from the University of Chicago in 1921 to be chairman of the Executive Council at Caltech (Throop Institute's name from 1920) and set out to increase the school's national stature. (His 1923 Nobel Prize

in physics was a felicitous touch.) By December 1925 Millikan was discussing plans for an aeronautical lab at Pasadena with General John J. Carty who had worked with the Guggenheims at NYU. Learning of the fund's plans, Millikan lost no time in urging the trustees to consider Caltech, emphasizing the school's excellent reputation in physics, Southern California's clear interest in aviation, and the proximity of manufacturers, particularly Donald Douglas. Douglas wrote to Millikan in December 1925: "We find innumerable cases where if facilities were handy for test and research work, we would avail ourselves of them. As it is now we do not do as much of such work as we should as it is cumbersome because of distance and other obstacles to have it done at existing Eastern laboratories."

From Palo Alto in May 1926 Stanford President Ray Lyman Wilbur submitted his university's proposal for a grant for research instrumentation and staffing to include an aerodynamicist, a materials physicist, and a structural engineer. Stanford professor William F. Durand (whose many important contributions included definitive studies of propeller theory and design and the start of an exhaustive aero encyclopedia) was also a trustee. At their June meeting the fund board approved grants of $305,000 to CIT for the construction of a laboratory and the establishment of a graduate school of aeronautics, and $195,000 to Stanford. Ultimately the fund would finance six major university aeronautical programs—the four already named, plus programs at the University of Michigan and the Georgia Institute of Technology. By the mid-20th century, almost all American senior aeronautical engineers were graduates of these six schools.

The Caltech-Guggenheim complex consisted of two components: the research-oriented Guggenheim Aeronautical Laboratory at the California Institute of Technology (GALCIT) and the Daniel Guggenheim School of Aeronautics devoted to aeronautical education, both housed in a single building completed in 1928. Popular usage applied GALCIT to the institution as a whole, which would swiftly rise to world eminence because of a group of remarkable thinkers and doers. Already on campus were Harry Bateman, Clark B. Millikan (Robert's son, recently arrived from Yale), Merrill, and Arthur L. "Maj" Klein. Their restive minds were already teeming with fresh ideas about the applications of mathematics and physics to their burgeoning discipline of aeronautics. Robert Millikan and Harry Guggenheim agreed on a central scheme to achieve GALCIT's potential: put at its center a world-class scientist who would both guide the institution and attract the best faculty and students by his presence. Millikan knew exactly whom he wanted: a professor at the Technische Hochschule at Aachen, Germany, one of Europe's two most outstanding aeronautical scientists, with "a rare combination of exceptional theoretical grasp with practical insight into, and a physical approach to, the problems of aeronautics." In 1928 negotiations were complete, and Millikan's offer of a permanent position at Caltech was accepted in 1929. So began one of history's great scientific collaborations—it would last for 35 dazzlingly productive years—when GALCIT opened its doors and its heart to Theodore Von Kármán.

During its first 10 years GALCIT concentrated on structural research and aerodynamics, and formed a partnership with the Douglas Aircraft Company in Santa Monica in 1928 when Robert Millikan approached Douglas to see if he could supply anyone to teach prospective staff members at the lab the practical side of aircraft design. Arthur E. Raymond, then Douglas' assistant chief engineer, wrote in his autobiography, "So I started teaching Saturdays and continued until 1934 when Kindelberger left to form North American and I succeeded him as Chief Engineer. In 1932, Caltech graduate W. Bailey Oswald went to Douglas as the firm's chief aerodynamicist, a position he held . . . into the 1950s." In Raymond's first Saturday class were Clark Millikan, Klein, Ernest Sechler, Bateman, and Merrill. One project of the group was the *Dill Pickle*, a stubby little biplane with an articulated lower wing intended to increase stability at low speeds. Said Raymond, "it crashed softly." The relationship was a fine

source of talented men for Douglas—one student was Bailey Oswald, whom Raymond recruited to head up aerodynamicists working on the DC-1. Maj Klein began a part-time consulting assignment at Santa Monica in 1932, going to one-half time in 1937.

The immediate result was that most California-built military or commercial airplanes for many years were designed on the basis of wind-tunnel tests carried out at GALCIT. The DC-1 may not have been typical, but its story sheds light on the symbiosis between industry and academe. Under Kármán's twinkling eye, Oswald, Klein, and Clark Millikan put a 1/11 scale model through 200 test runs, three wings, and six different flap configurations in the 200 mph tunnel in the fall and winter of 1932. Maj Klein and Millikan had been experimenting with fillets (the curved panels used to fair intersections of aircraft structure surfaces) as proposed by Kármán on the Northrop Alpha's engine cowling. In 1932 the DC-1 wind tunnel test model exhibited turbulence-induced buffeting and the CIT team decided to try the fillets on the intersection between wing and fuselage of the model. Kármán tells of the satisfaction he found in climbing into the tunnel's section to smooth in the putty used to form the fillets. Soon they had eliminated the buffet and added 30 mph to the plane's speed.

Caltech's wind tunnels were a powerful resource for the school and industry. With its 1,000 hp fan, capable of simulating air speeds from 30 mph to 200 mph, the 10-foot unit operated 17-hour days seven days a week during World War II.

GALCIT was alive with ideas, crackling with energy and discipline which illuminated the contemporary personal and professional writings of Kármán, Millikan, and the others. The willingness to try new things abounded. Typical is the evolution of Frank J. Malina's rocketry research, which broke important ground for all his successors. In 1936 Malina approached Kármán and asked permission to conduct a few experiments, and was authorized to work with small quantities of liquid rocket propellant in the GALCIT building (with no university funding) until a misfire in the basement sent clouds of oxidant through the building one weekend and the experimenters round with oily rags on Monday to wipe off the rust from the building's iron fittings. Kármán banished the rocket crew to an Arroyo Seco location not so sensitive, and the beginnings of the Jet Propulsion Laboratory were in place by 1943.

The results of all this ferment were described by Richard Hallion:

*By 1940, this institution had already earned a major share of the credit in getting American air transport off the ground, and its students, scientists, and engineers, under the able and paternal direction of Theodore Von Kármán, were already investigating the feasibility of flight faster than sound and the potential of the rocket engine. Its wind tunnels ran day and night, testing for hundreds of hours the new products of America's aviation industry, many of which later contributed greatly to Allied air supremacy in the Second World War. Then there was applied research: studying the effects of wing fillets in reducing wing-fuselage aerodynamic interference, examining the behavior of flying wing and tailless aircraft configurations, developing aircraft instrumentation and test procedures, measuring the stall characteristics of highly tapered wings, and analyzing the flow of air around bridges and wind-run electrical generators, to name just a few of the topics examined.*

Clark Millikan succeeded to the GALCIT directorship in 1949, earning great respect from his own faculty colleagues and the international aviation fraternity for his teaching, research, and leadership. During his professional life, all of which was spent at GALCIT, Millikan remained dedicated to the partnerships between the schools, industry, and government. Speaking to the Royal Aeronautical Society in 1957, he said:

*During recent years the aeronautical industry has begun increasingly to demonstrate an awareness of its responsibility for the training of young engineers and scientists and for the encouragement of the basic sciences which underlie its technical progress. Most of the major companies now have fellowship programs in connection with institutions offering aeronautical curricula. There have also been significant contributions to colleges in support of special educational projects and facilities such as wind tunnels, special laboratory facilities, libraries, and so on.*

In no small measure the support of academe Millikan applauded was due to the efforts of farsighted administrators like himself.

GALCIT's contributions to every phase of aeronautics since 1928 continue under Director Hans W. Liepmann. They are beyond conventional valuation; it suffices to acknowledge great and lasting achievement.

UNIVERSITY OF SOUTHERN CALIFORNIA
The focused theoretical and scientific direction carefully chosen by the Millikans, Kármán, and their team in Pasadena was contrasted by the direction chosen on South Hoover Street.

The University of Southern California's involvement with aviation dates from the late 1920s, with the earliest courses offered in the Department of Trade and Transport of the College of Commerce. Under the leadership of Earl W. Hill, the university's commercial program emphasized an eclectic balance of aero-related disciplines—manufacturing, air transport, the government, airport operators, and technology. Early students were enthusiastic enough to found at USC the first chapter of a national aviation fraternity, Alpha Eta Rho, in April 1929.

As the federal government increasingly participated in aviation matters after the passage of the Civil Aeronautics Act in 1938, colleges sometimes became almost inadvertent partners. Launched experimentally in 1938, the federal Civilian Pilot Training Program was intended to increase the nation's pilot pool, and a five-year plan was enacted by Congress in 1939. The CPTP, drawing upon USC, Stanford, the University of California (at both Berkeley and Los Angeles), and Pasadena City College, trained pilots in 50-student classes for elective, non-

degree credit. During 1940 the College of
Engineering was asked to participate under the
leadership of Professor Sydney F. Duncan of the
Mechanical Engineering Department, and a 40 x
60-foot building was built on campus behind the
Engineering Building. It was immediately
labeled "The Hangar," filled as it was with spare
airplane parts. Actual flying was done under
contract at Gardena Valley Airport at Redondo
Beach Boulevard and Western with Piper Cubs.
The CPTP trained some 70,000 pilots for the
military before its termination in 1942.

The university's commitment to the scientific
aspect of aviation came more cautiously, initially
facing conservative resistance from the school's
central administration, although USC's first
engineering degree was awarded in 1908, and
the College of Engineering organized in 1928.
Robert Vivian, then dean of the School of
Engineering, in his account of USC's engineering
history tells of discussing possible research
contracts during World War II with a university
trustee who was also the dean of the medical
school. USC, said the trustee, should "teach only
engineering courses and leave the research to
Caltech." But Vivian was not so easily
dissuaded, and in later years Caltech men would
significantly affect the university's direction.
Zohrab Kaprielian arrived in 1957 after three
years at CIT, eventually rising to become USC's
chief academic officer. Alfred Ingersoll also
brought some of the spirit of Pasadena with him
when he became Engineering School dean in
1960 at the age of 40. The first significant
research contract came from Lockheed in 1944,
allocating $10,000 to assay spot welding of
aluminum alloy, under Professor Duncan's
direction. Soon NACA and Office of Naval
Research grants followed.

It was at USC that Roy Marquardt, a 1942
graduate from CIT who had begun his
exploration of ramjets at Northrop Aircraft,
continued his highly successful work with
advanced propulsion systems. Under
Marquardt, the university arranged to build a
large engine test cell at Kaiser Steel Company's
Fontana plant near San Bernardino, where spare
capacity from the blast furnace blowers made a

convenient air supply. After much loud testing
and two unscheduled explosions, the local
farmers complained that their chickens had
stopped laying, and Marquardt and his team
were asked to move. Marquardt went on to form
his own successful company.

The next major step came with the influx of
engineering student applicants in 1945, and for
the next five years a boom of returning GIs
strained the resources of faculty and plant alike.
One brief program was centered up the coast
where USC's College of Aeronautics operated
from 1946 to 1950 at Hancock Field in Santa
Maria Airport. The College of Aeronautics had
been founded in 1928 by Captain Allan Hancock
as Hancock Foundation College of Aeronautics.
During the Second World War, the site became
one of America's nine "Little Randolphs" (so-
named after the Army's famed Texas airfield
used for pilot training) and hosted the training
of 8,400 aviation cadets of the Army Air Force.
At the site the university offered pilot training,
lower division engineering courses, and special
programs like the 1947 "Short Course for
Airport Managers and Airport Owners" in
cooperation with the Civil Aeronautics
Authority. The college thrived briefly on a
steady flow of GI Bill students, using several
inherited surplus aircraft and a few planes
bought for advanced pilot training, but in 1950
the engineering faculty returned to the main
campus in Los Angeles, the aero staff moved on,
and the site was eventually subdivided into
residential parcels.

But at University Park in Los Angeles the
years saw imaginative development, typified by
the 1948 School of Engineering decision to accept
36 career military officers into a two-year
program leading to the Master of Science degree
in Aeronautics & Guided Missiles. Next came a
Cooperative Engineering Program for the MS,
chiefly concerned with electronics engineering,
in collaboration with the Hughes Aircraft
Company. In a matching funds program, the
Hughes organization subsidized needed
equipment and facilities not otherwise practical
for the school to acquire. The Aerospace
Engineering Department was formed in 1964,

with the Jet Propulsion Laboratory's John Laufer heading the new unit. Undergraduate aeronautics classes were added, the masters' curriculum upgraded, and a doctoral program initiated; the first USC aeronautics PhD was awarded in 1966.

Under the impetus of increasing concern about flight safety in the Air Force, the USAF Inspector General sought development of suitable training programs. In part because of its proximity to the Directorate of Flight Safety Research at Norton Air Force Base near San Bernardino, USC was selected in September 1952 to establish a training center where Flying Safety Officers could be trained in scientific accident investigation techniques and related disciplines. Subsequent joint studies with manufacturers, airlines, and other government agencies were the basis in March 1953 of an initial safety curriculum. The first 16-week program included elements of aeronautical engineering, aviation physiology, aircraft accident prevention, and educational principles and techniques. Programs were broadened to include students in the private sector, and off-campus locations were utilized, particularly at military bases in the United States and even overseas. Soon the operation was named the Aerospace Safety Division, then the Institute of Aerospace Safety and Management, then the Institute of Safety and Systems Management. Graduate courses were added in 1970, baccalaureate offerings in 1975; by 1983 some 20,000 students had participated in the program.

NORTHROP UNIVERSITY
Northrop Aeronautical Institute was formed in 1942 to provide technical training for Northrop Aircraft personnel, and Jack Northrop enlisted the aid of technical educator James L. McKinley in designing a suitable engineering and technical curriculum. At war's end, the great wave of returning veterans and vastly expanded aeronautical industry assured good demand for every available classroom and laboratory slot, and the institute opened for public enrollment in 1946 with a two-year engineering certificate program and a shorter technical program.

Separating from the parent corporation and moving to its current Inglewood site in 1953 after merging with California Flyers School of Aeronautics, the Institute broadened its academic base to offer the Bachelor of Science degree. The school changed its name to Northrop Institute of Technology in 1959, achieved nonprofit status, and further broadened its course offerings to earn accreditation from the Western Association of Schools and Colleges in 1960. Expanding well beyond aeronautics, the school added curricula in business and management, and graduate programs. After opening a School of Law in 1972, the board of trustees in 1975 changed the school's name to Northrop University.

CLAREMONT'S BATES AERONAUTICS PROGRAM
Unique among California's aviation education programs is that of the Bates Aeronautics Program at Claremont's Harvey Mudd College. Made possible by a foundation established in 1960 by Isabel Bates and implemented at Mudd in 1962, this program is a four-semester, co-curricular sequence of classroom studies and flight training available only to a small number of participants each year. It is built upon the premise that "the privilege of flight and the investigation of the aeronautical sciences" enhance a student's work in the sciences, the humanities, and personal growth, and it focuses on personal values and their relation to the skills and attitudes demanded of the responsible airman. Two Cessna 172s are owned and operated by the foundation for students in the program.

Classroom and flight instruction are given by the same instructor, part of the program's precepts that "analytic capability, judgement, and positive action based on logical integrated thought can be developed through the use of the airplane as a tool in the flight environment [and] results are most likely to occur under the leadership of an instructor who is constantly aware of the responses of the student . . . and is able to provide strong direction and guidance."

From its inception, the Bates program has

been administered by Harvey Mudd instructor Iris Critchell, who not only designed the curriculum and teaches regularly, but who for more than two decades has shared her home and family with her students as part of the value orientation upon which the program's philosophy is built.

GENERAL AVIATION EDUCATION
Since the 1920s most airports large enough to support even a modest fixed base operator or two have boasted a flight school of some sort. From the independent licensed instructor with an Airman's Information Manual and a Piper Cub to a full-blown military contract student production line operated during the Second World War, flight training has represented a large proportion of aviation education. Flight training may be offered independently or as part of some broader educational undertaking, from a community college associate degree program to a baccalaureate engineering curriculum.

Mount San Antonio College (Mt. SAC) in Walnut exemplifies the approach to post-secondary aero training adopted by several of California's 107 community colleges in recent years, in which aviation programs and courses are administered through an aeronautics and transportation department within an industrial studies division. Courses range from employment-oriented air transportation surveys and advanced flight training on the one hand to aircraft maintenance technology and flight control basics on the other. Reduced-rate flying clubs insure economical flight costs for students, and Mount San Antonio College, like other colleges across the nation, maintains a student flying team that participates in contests sponsored by the National Intercollegiate Flying Association.

At war's end in 1945, challenges for those who would nourish their fresh taste for aviation were many and tough—as would-be airline operators and others soon knew well. One young nurse who'd been forced by airline rules of the day to give up her San Francisco-based air hostess job when she married, and who ran an emergency dispensary at the Army Air Force base where her

husband was on wartime duty, took flying lessons on weekends in hopes of joining Jacqueline Cochran's corps of women flyers. Peace came before her call to arms, and in 1946 Marsha Toy found herself in Los Angeles hoping somehow to return to the aviation community she enjoyed so much.

Reflecting on how difficult she had found obtaining her first airline job 10 years earlier, Toy decided to offer a series of classes for young women aspiring to airline careers. After working with several partners and developing her curriculum and sales strategy, she was ready to look for a well-located classroom when an acquaintance offered her space on the mezzanine of the Hollywood Roosevelt Hotel. It was there that the Marsha Toy Air Hostess School began in 1946—where a young woman could spend $150 and six weeks and learn what she needed to know to land a position with an airline. With their instructor's energetic training—and her old airline's welcome to women already trained—Toy's graduates were often on the job the Monday after their last class.

What worked with stewardesses could work with ticket agents, reservationists, and cargo clerks, she reasoned, and Toy soon enlisted more instructors. She expanded her system, by then called Airline Schools Pacific, into a chain of 14 schools in California and communities outside the state. Having sold all but one unit (a school in Hollywood now known as Academy Pacific), Toy believes that a small proprietary school can swiftly and economically adapt training programs to the constantly changing airline and travel industry more effectively than large, traditional educational institutions.

THE WORLD'S BEST-KNOWN FLIGHT TEST CENTER
If a threshold of creativity was crossed after 1927 at the drafting table, in the classroom, the laboratory, and the wind tunnel, aviation's next great challenges would be faced from 1947 onward by relentlessly inquiring and courageous scientists and airmen collaborating in the air above and on the ground of what would become Edwards Air Force Base.

Most visitors approach California's Mojave Desert from the south via the Antelope Valley Freeway through the San Gabriel Mountains, or by air from Los Angeles over the San Gabriels. Seen from the 8,000-foot altitude needed to clear the mountains, the Mojave Desert and its aviation encampments compel the eye and stir the imagination. Shimmering in the elusive distance are the Palmdale and Mojave airports, Edwards and George Air Force Bases, and just visible on the northern horizon, the Navy's China Lake installation. Here beneath crystalline skies is California's high desert, dominated by Rosamond and Rogers dry lakes.

The flattest of landforms (Rosamond's curvature is a mere 18 inches in 30,000 feet), the desolate dry lakes appear from the air as serene seas amidst the abruptly tortuous mountains of the surrounding desert. Rogers Dry Lake covers 44 square miles and is crisscrossed by seven man-marked landing paths. One 15,000-foot runway, extended by 9,000 feet of lake bed, provides 4-1/2 miles of landing surface. High above the desert nearly limitless visibility aids flight maneuvering, observation, and aerial photography, although pollution from the Los Angeles Basin has recently begun to degrade air quality. The region is sufficiently remote that aircraft maneuvers and jet noise disturb no neighbors.

The Mojave has been a center of aeronautical achievement since October 2, 1942, when America's first jet—the Bell XP-59A Airacomet— made its first flight from makeshift facilities at Muroc Field. The vast lake beds had served military aviation since 1933 when the Army Air Corps first used Rogers Dry Lake as a bombing range. The lake name was a corruption of Rodriguez, and the name Muroc comes from the frustration of a family of settlers who arrived in 1910. Clifford and Effie Corum wanted to give their new town the family name, but both the post office and the Santa Fe Railroad objected, saying there were places with too-similar names. But backward, the name passed bureaucratic muster. The 301,000-acre installation itself was renamed Edwards Air Force Base in 1950 to honor Captain Glen W. Edwards, the Air Force

test pilot killed in a crash of a YB-49 Flying Wing in June 1948.

Because most military activity was classified, it was some time before the public began to learn of the epochal events above Muroc Air Force Base. In 1947 Captain Charles (Chuck) Yeager broke what some experts had long believed to be the impenetrable "sound barrier," flying the Bell X-1, the first in a long line of rocket-powered research vehicles tested at Edwards that sped aviation technological progress. The very next week, tests began on Northrop's Flying Wing. Of the X-series research vehicles, the X-15 (first flight, September 17, 1959, with Scott Crossfield at the controls) was especially important. First, the aircraft was more complex by an order of magnitude in purpose, design, and operation than its predecessors. The project's support staff from NASA and the Air Force—including 12 civilian and military pilots—was as large as the combined groups for all earlier rocket plane programs. The teams, the systems they developed, and the prodigious collection of flight and operational data were of incalculable value for later projects, especially the United States space programs. The three X-15s built by North American made 199 flights over nine years at Edwards and set altitude (354,200 feet) and speed (4,520 mph) records still standing in 1983.

Edwards hosts diverse operations and programs, among them the USAF Test Pilot School, the USAF Rocket Propulsion Laboratory, the Army's Engineering Flight Activity, Air Force Test and Evaluation Squadrons, and Military Airlift Command weather and rescue services. The Air Force Communications Service provides the extensive base and long-range communications, navigational aids, air traffic control, and communications engineering and installation support required for advanced technology testing.

Next to the USAF Flight Test Center itself, the best-known Edwards tenant is NASA's Hugh L. Dryden Flight Research Center. Most of the agency's Space Transportation System (shuttle orbiter) programs have been tested here, and the shuttles themselves are assembled at Rockwell's nearby Palmdale facility. The center also manages the Utah Test and Training Range, including testing of remotely piloted vehicles (RPVs).

Most U.S. corporations engaged in aircraft and engine development and production maintain tenant facilities at Edwards and conduct their own test programs in close cooperation with the military and civilian agencies charged with contract management of America's aviation and space programs.

## AERONAUTICAL MUSEUMS

California's aviation interest has been nourished in recent years by dozens of aviation museums and libraries around the state, from modest collections at community colleges, civil airfields, and military bases to elaborate exhibitions. As important to every museum as its collection and professional staff is the nourishment of community roots: museums thrive on the skills, energy, and devotion of their volunteers and the affection and interest of their communities at large. Nowhere are these truths better proven than in the bustling enterprise known as the San Diego Aero-Space Museum, which first opened in Balboa Park on February 15, 1963, after two years of preparation under the guiding spirit of its first president, Preston M. "Sandy" Fleet, son of Consolidated Aircraft Company's founder, Reuben Fleet.

From the first, the museum has focused on flight-worthy aircraft, both originals and faithful replicas. Early examples, displayed in the Food and Beverage Building adjacent to the San Diego Zoo, included two Montgomery gliders, the San Diego-built *Wee Bee* and *Queen Bee*, and a fine reproduction of Glenn Curtiss' A-1 Hydro-aeroplane. Space in the building and initial financial support were provided with the aid of Mayor Charles C. Dail as a result of the efforts of Fleet, Captain Norval R. Richardson, Andy Borthwick, Claude Ryan, and Joe Jessop. By 1965 growth required bigger quarters, and the collection was moved to Balboa Park's Electric Building. For the next 13 years prized pieces were added, among them a Japanese Zero fighter raised from ocean depths, a lovingly recreated *Spirit of St. Louis*, and a Curtiss Jenny.

Then in February 1978 an arsonist's match reduced most of the treasures to ash and charred fragments, and the laborious task of recreating the irreplaceable began. Browsing through today's galleries in the beautifully refurbished Ford Building, with aircraft restoration workshops humming in the basement and scholars perusing a meticulously catalogued collection of books and other materials in the second-floor library, the visitor may enjoy vintage and modern aircraft arrayed in dramatic, informative settings exquisitely conceived and executed. After the fire, community support, a dedicated staff, and the untiring work of hundreds of knowledgeable volunteers have seen the museum returned to its well-earned place as California's preeminent aero museum.

## THE AIR MUSEUM "PLANES OF FAME"

Dedicated to restoring historic aircraft to flying condition, Edward Maloney's Air Museum first opened its doors in 1957 at Claremont, California, displaying just six aircraft. Now headquartered at Chino Airport, the collection includes more than 50 airplanes, many of them flying at air shows and in Hollywood productions. Maloney's spotless Republic P-47 Thunderbolt, North American P-51 Mustang, and Vought F4U Corsair aircraft highlight the museum's World War II group, and one of only two extant Northrop Flying Wings is presently being restored to flying status by volunteers working under the museum staff's direction.

## MOVIELAND OF THE AIR MUSEUM

The remarkable careers of pilots and entrepreneurs Albert Paul Mantz and Frank Tallman met in 1961 when the two men combined their collections of vintage aircraft under the banner of Tallmantz Aviation Incorporated. Two years later they opened their Movieland of the Air Museum at the Orange County (now John Wayne) Airport, with Spads, Fokkers, Camels, Nieuports, and Mailwings arrayed before movie-like sets that delighted visitors to the huge hangar. Both men earned great distinction as movie stunt pilots, and their collection included much-photographed aerial veterans of such films as *Catch-22, It's a Mad . . . World, Lafayette Escadrille,* and *Twilight Zone.* After Mantz' death while filming *Flight of the Phoenix* in 1965, Tallman continued operating the museum in parallel with the company's film work until his own death. In early 1984 when owner Frank Pines was unsuccessful in locating a buyer interested in continuing the museum's operation, the future of the 40 or so remaining airplanes was clouded.

## A GRAND DESIGN

Attractive as they are, few would agree that the museum and library facilities in California are commensurate with the state's epic aviation history. To remedy this long-acknowledged disparity, the Southern California Historical Aviation Foundation has begun laying the groundwork for a major aerospace museum, library, and aircraft restoration center—the

California Air Museum—to be located in the Los Angeles basin. Using a centennial celebration of John Montgomery's 1883 San Diego glider success as the occasion to announce the proposed museum, foundation president Donald G. Page cited the results of an extensive federal survey that indicate such a museum may be expected to attract millions of visitors each year. Plans include multiple wings with space to exhibit up to 100 aircraft, restoration facilities, classrooms, and a spacious auditorium. An aerospace library will provide resources for scholarly research in aviation history and related disciplines.

Teaching, researching, testing—the foundations upon which aviation, as all significant achievement, is built—are a rich part of California's aeronautical past and present. They are certainly the guarantee of its greatness tomorrow.

*Shown in 1969 are Tony LeVier (left) and Herman "Fish" Salmon, who began their Lockheed careers ferrying Hudson bombers at the start of WWII and ultimately earned reputations among the industry's greatest test pilots. Courtesy, CALAC*

*Historian Richard Hallion calls these aircraft "the seven most important experimental designs of the early 1950s." Displayed in 1953 at Edwards around the Douglas X-3, clockwise from top left are the Convair XF-92A, Bell X-5, Douglas D-558-2, Northrop X-4, Bell X-1A, and Douglas D-558-1. Courtesy EAFBHO*

In the GALCIT 10-foot wind tunnel during 1932-1933 the Douglas DC-1's aerodynamics were refined by an array of prodigious intelligences, including those of Clark B. Millikan (left) and Arthur L. "Maj" Klein. Courtesy, Caltech Archives

Caltech's Cooperative Wind Tunnel (CWT), sponsored by five airframe builders, opened in 1945. It featured pressure levels from one-tenth to four atmospheres, an eight and one-half by twelve foot test section, 12,000 hp electric fans able to generate supersonic wind velocities, elaborate force measuring devices, and automatic reduction and recording of data. Courtesy, Caltech Archives

The January 1947 ground breaking for JPL's wind tunnel drew a heady crowd: (from left) GALCIT professor (later director) Clark B. Millikan; Allen E. Puckett, GALCIT professor and later chairman of Hughes Aircraft; Louis Dunn; Caltech president Lee A. DuBridge; Major General Everett S. Hughes, USAF; GALCIT director Theodore Von Kármán; and Robert A. Millikan, Nobel laureate and the original driving animus behind Caltech's seminal involvement with aeronautics. Courtesy, Caltech Archives

Clark B. Millikan, GALCIT director from 1949 until his death in 1966, was an accomplished researcher, admired teacher, and an enormously effective promoter of cooperation between the academic and industrial communities. This portrait was made in 1958. Courtesy, Caltech Archives

Lawrence Bell (left), president of Bell Aircraft Corporation, posed with Major Charles Yaeger and the newest Bell supersonic airplane, the X-1A, in December 1953 at Edwards Air Force Base. Courtesy, EAFBHO

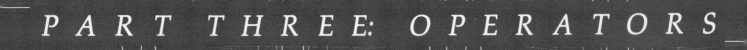

*The Western Air Express Model Air Line, sponsored by the Guggenheim Fund in 1928, captured the public imagination with its speedy and reliable service between Los Angeles and San Francisco. The* Los Angeles Times *front page featured this Gale cartoon two days after service began on May 26, 1928. Courtesy, Western Airlines*

# CHAPTER SIX

# MILITARY AVIATION

Even as the earliest hesitant and frail aircraft struggled into the sky, the powerful military potential of aircraft swiftly became a compelling impetus to aviation development. The military potential of the airplane was, in the minds of a number of imaginative men, far more significant than the mere thrill and exhilaration of flight which so captivated the general public.

The military establishment, a primary factor in aviation's meteoric growth, began its partnership with the airplane in 1898 when the government funded Dr. Samuel Langley's development of a full-size version of his Aerodrome. The project was abandoned in some embarrassment after the underpowered machine fouled its catapult launching mechanism during two trials in October and December 1903 and plunged ignominiously into the Potomac. The Army bought its first Wright airplane in 1908, and the Navy's first aircraft purchase, from Glenn Curtiss, was made in 1911. Never looking back, the "military-industrial complex" soon became arguably aviation's single most influential institution. John Rae summarizes the reality succinctly:

*The story of the American aircraft industry presents a unique intertwining of business, politics, and technology. The industry has depended for its existence on one major customer, the United States government.*

Early military support came largely from younger officers and civilian administrators who foresaw a need to create a base for the development of aeronautical technology and manufacture. Such men allied themselves with the emerging group of builders energetically tackling the technical and financial hurdles of an infant enterprise (during 1914 sixteen American private firms built just 49 aircraft) while most of the senior establishment remained skeptical during the technical, administrative, and political controversies that occupied the services and federal authorities for decades.

Congress established the National Advisory Committee for Aeronautics (NACA) in 1915 to support basic aeronautical research, while the development of operational aircraft was essentially left to private industry.

The same favorable weather and geography that drew pioneer aeroplane builders and daring pilots also attracted military aviation to California. The growing nucleus of manufacturing itself helped to lure Navy and Army aviation to Pacific shores.

By 1911 there was considerable interest in Naval aviation. A number of military experts recognized the potential for aircraft that could operate in a maritime environment. In November 1910 a civilian pilot, Eugene B. Ely, flew a Curtiss biplane from a specially built platform installed on the cruiser *Birmingham*. Then, only two months later, on January 18, 1911, Ely made Naval aviation history as the first aviator to land his aeroplane aboard a ship. He flew from Selfridge Field, San Francisco, to San Francisco Bay, landing his Curtiss aboard the cruiser *Pennsylvania*. Following an hour's turnaround time, Ely took off from the *Pennsylvania*, returning to land ashore. He had completed the first takeoff and landing mission from a Naval vessel, precursing modern carrier operations.

Only a month later the *Pennsylvania* was in San Diego harbor. Curtiss, who by this time had set up operations at North Island, flew near the cruiser, taxied his hydroaeroplane (Curtiss' term) alongside the ship, and was hoisted on board with the boat crane. The Curtiss aircraft was later lowered again into San Diego Harbor, took off and returned to land, demonstrating once more the compatibility of aircraft with Naval operations. An interested spectator at this amphibious aircraft operation was Navy Lt. Theodore G. Ellyson, the first military pilot to be graduated from Curtiss' flying school at North Island and entered in Navy records as Naval Aviation Pilot Number 1. To the same Curtiss school, the U.S. Army sent Signal Corps officers who would become the Army's first pilots.

## GOLDEN STATE LEADERSHIP IN MILITARY AVIATION

World War I's enormous impact on American aviation derived in part from the crash program that resulted in production of nearly 14,000 airplanes from April 6, 1917, to November 1, 1919. Curtiss far outproduced others with 4,010 aircraft, including some built under license in California. The next-largest producer was Dayton-Wright with 3,506, and far down the list was California's Glenn Martin whose plant produced 10 airplanes for the war effort.

Although the airframe industry had not fully discovered the advantages of California climate and geography, airplane designers knew about California-built engines. Hall-Scott, the San Francisco-based company that had pioneered the design of engines specifically for aircraft, built 1,255 engines during the war, surpassed only by the producers of the Wright engine and automobile manufacturers such as Packard, General Motors, Willys-Overland, Lincoln, and Ford.

With the Armistice in November 1918, America's nascent aviation industry was halted in its traces. Contracts totaling $100 million were cancelled without warning or notice, and aircraft production in the United States dropped from a wartime peak of 14,000 in 1918 to a low of 263 in 1922.

Most important to California, the First World War provided further impetus to the development of flying schools at San Diego. The first-ever Military Aviation School with three Army and one Navy officer students opened there in January 1912 under Glenn Curtiss' tutelage. In 1913 the Army consolidated its aviation training, then part of the Signal Corps, at North Island, San Diego. The Army's installation was ultimately called Rockwell Field, for Lieutenant Louis C. Rockwell, 10th Infantry, who fatally crashed in September 1912. In 1913 Rockwell Field was designated the "Signal Corps Aviation School."

In May 1917, as America entered the Great War, a joint Army/Navy Board said: "The Board is of the opinion that North Island, San Diego, California, is the best location in this country for the establishment of a joint Army and Navy Aviation Station for the primary training of pilots . . ."

Because a dispute continued over legal ownership of the land, including requisite compensation to a number of claimants, the 65th Congress of the United States passed an act "Authorizing the President to take possession, on behalf of the United States, for use as sites for permanent aviation stations for the Army and Navy, and for aviation school purposes, of the whole of North Island in the harbor of San Diego, California, and for other purposes."

In 1917 North Island, San Diego, was officially recognized as the primary training site for U.S. military aviation pilots.

To the surprise of no one, rivalries between the two services resulted in intriguing feats of annoyance. The Army, in Thomas Morse "Scouts," delighted in flying in formation, then buzzing the slower Navy seaplanes. To counter, Navy pilots were usually able to turn their aircraft in such a way that the small "Scouts" were caught in the wake of the big Liberty-powered Navy ships. The result was a scattering of the Army formation.

One of the first officers assigned to the Army's Rockwell Field was Major H.H. "Hap" Arnold, who would become Chief of Staff for the U.S. Army Air Corps' successful worldwide effort in

World War II. Arnold is sometimes called the "Father of the U.S. Air Force." In addition to Arnold, other military aviators trained at North Island who went on to great fame included Army officers J.H. "Jimmy" Doolittle and Major Carl "Tooey" Spaatz.

The end of World War I was celebrated in San Diego with a two-hour demonstration of maneuvering and a flyover of 212 Army and Navy aircraft. The aeroplanes cavorted at altitudes ranging from 600 to 3,000 feet. At one point during the air exhibition, all 212 aircraft flew in a "V" formation over San Diego. Major Spaatz and Lt. Doolittle were among the pilots in this flawless massive formation and celebration.

MILITARY AVIATION AND THE NORTH
Although San Diego, its North Island, and the harbor played a significant role in early military and civil aviation, so too did the San Francisco area, where for the first time live bombs were dropped from an aircraft on a target. Two types of bombs had actually been developed by the pilots—Lieutenants Myron S. Crissy and Philip O. Parmalee. One bomb was designed to be set off by the concussion of landing; the other contained a time fuse set in advance to detonate after a predetermined number of seconds. History records only that they apparently worked.

World altitude, speed, and distance records were set by California-built airplanes, flown by California-trained pilots, on flights that frequently began or ended in San Diego, Los Angeles, San Francisco, or Oakland. Beginning with the first around-the-world flight in Douglas World Cruisers in 1924, pilots including Arnold, Doolittle, Spaatz, Eaker, and Yeager established ever higher standards for military airplane performance, all in a context of growing national awareness.

SAN DIEGO'S NORTH ISLAND
Beginning in 1910 as the first U.S. government flight training facility and retaining permanent status after the drastic military cutbacks at the war's end, by the middle 1920s North Island was one of two Naval stations (the other, Hampton Roads, Virginia) to provide flight instruction (by then incorporated into the regular curriculum) for U.S. Naval Academy midshipmen.

By the late 1920s the first Navy aircraft carriers, USS *Saratoga* and USS *Lexington*, had anchored at San Diego. Pilots from the carrier USS *Langley* and from North Island were among those flying 125 Navy aircraft along with 126 Army, 11 Marine, and 210 civilian planes participating in the 1928 National Air Races and Aeronautical Exposition at Mines Field, Los Angeles. Aerial photography, popular with photojournalists and Hollywood cameramen of the day, captured Navy biplanes, pursuit, and fighter aircraft in precise formations over San Diego Harbor and evoked the glamor of Naval aviation of that period. In 1931 Marine Corps "Flying Leathernecks" joined their Navy airmen in the skies above Navy aircraft carriers, and by 1935 four flattops—*Lexington*, *Langley*, *Ranger*, and *Saratoga*—were based at North Island.

From its inception North Island hosted men and aircraft of both Army and Navy, the Army at Rockwell Field, the Navy at NAS North Island. The natural rivalry between the two services generated not a few informal confrontations. The skies over San Diego Harbor became crowded, and traffic patterns congested. In 1935, after 18 years of joint operation and years of effort to make North Island a one-service air base, the Army Air Corps evacuated Rockwell Field as part of a trade involving air operations at Pearl Harbor; Anacostia, Maryland; and Sunnyvale, California. Army Air Corps operations were moved to Sunnyvale, and North Island finally became all-Navy.

From 1938 it was obvious to most San Diego observers that the Pacific Fleet was preparing for war. Maneuvers were held between San Diego and Hawaii; battleships, carriers, and cruisers were continually active around North Island. And the Fleet Marine Force (FMF) was now headquartered at the base.

On Sunday morning, December 7, 1941, San Diegans and North Islanders in particular, even more than most U.S. citizens, were galvanized to action. The great carriers on which Naval aviation depended were fortunately dispersed that day, *Yorktown, Wasp,* and *Ranger* in the Atlantic, *Lexington* at sea southeast of Midway Island. *Enterprise* was 200 miles west of Pearl Harbor with Admiral W.F. "Bull" Halsey aboard. At North Island, the *Saratoga,* just out of dry dock, was taking on a new load of aircraft and sailed for Hawaii the morning of December 8. Within two weeks, one quarter of North Island's stock of aeronautical spares was en route to mid-Pacific Navy bases, and three shifts labored ceaselessly to service, repair, and promptly return every available aircraft to operational duty.

At the peak of war buildup in 1943, the teeming base was the hub for massive supply, service, and support functions for the entire Pacific theater, including newly established Marine Corps Air Stations at El Toro, El Centro, and Kearney Mesa. USN Auxiliary Air Stations were swiftly established at other California locations—Ream Field, Salton Sea, Holtville, San Clemente, Huntington Beach, and the Coast Guard Air Station, San Diego.

By war's end North Island had processed, serviced, supported, or shipped every aircraft type in the Navy and Marine Corps inventory. On V-J day in 1945 there were 2,538 aircraft at North Island awaiting tranportation to combat zones.

## IMPACT OF WORLD WAR AND THE COMING OF PEACE

San Diego's herculean wartime efforts reflected those of the nation at large and illustrate the enormous impact of federal, particularly military, spending in California. Historian Walton Bean describes the phenomenon:

*In the period including the fiscal years from 1940 to 1946 the federal government spent 360 billion dollars within the continental United States. Of this sum, it spent about 35 billion in the state of California. It would be almost impossible to exaggerate and it is difficult even to comprehend the full effects of these unprecedented expenditures in stimulating economic expansion. Every previous element in the state's economic history was dwarfed in comparison. . . .In the single wartime fiscal year 1945 the federal government spent more than 8-1/2 billion dollars in California alone. This was more than 10% of all federal expenditures within the United States; and California's population in 1945 was only 7% of the nation's.*

By 1945 this massive influx of dollars more than tripled prewar personal income in California. And aircraft accounted for nearly 60 percent of the money that the federal government spent under prime contracts for goods manufactured in California during the war. Bean further illustrates:

*The wartime expansion of aircraft manufacturing compressed 40 years of normal industrial progress into 40 months. In 1933, all the airframe factories in Southern California together employed only about 1,000 people. In November 1943 they employed 280,300.*

By 1965 North Island was once again gearing up for wartime service and support, this time for the Vietnam conflict. A technique developed at North Island during the early Vietnam escalation was the "cocooning" of aircraft for overseas shipment. Army helicopters, then later Navy and Marine aircraft, were sprayed with plastic that dried to form a "total wrap," permitting transport above deck on a wide variety of ships going to Southeast Asia.

The nature of the Vietnam conflict, a ground-based jungle guerrilla war combined with military aviation support, dictated once again that North Island-based ships, aircraft, and aviators would be heavily involved in combat. Like so much of America, San Diego and North Island were deeply scarred by Vietnam.

From its initial 1911 achievement in training Naval Aviator No. 1, North Island's growth has been synonymous with the growth of Naval aviation. In the words of Rear Admiral R.B. Moore, Commander, Fleet Air, San Diego, "There is little wonder that Naval aviation grew from infancy to maturity here. The weather is wonderful for aircraft operations, there are plenty of operating areas and the people in the local community—the most civic minded to be found anywhere—have always been great friends of the Navy."

## NAVAL AVIATION MOVES NORTH

Although the first demonstration of an aircraft landing aboard a ship had been made in 1911 in San Francisco Bay, and Naval aviation in California had traditionally been concentrated at North Island, aeronautical roots in Northern California run deep.

Fittingly, the Navy's first base at Sunnyvale (now Moffett Field) was devoted not to airplane but to lighter-than-air craft operations at its establishment in the early 1930s. Encouraged by German dirigible successes, Navy leaders had successfully advocated development of "dreadnoughts of the sky", resulting in the delivery during 1923-1924 of the USS *Shenandoah* and *Los Angeles*. They led the way for two even grander dirigibles, the *Akron* and the *Macon*, sister ships nearly three times the size of the *Los Angeles* and twice the size of Germany's *Graf Zeppelin* then in transatlantic passenger sevice.

New Jersey's Lakehurst Naval Air Station was chosen as the home base for the *Akron* and a search begun for a suitable West Coast domicile for the *Macon*. A three-year effort by civic leaders in the Bay Area culminated in February 1931 when President Herbert Hoover signed a bill authorizing the purchase of 1,000 acres of farmland near Sunnyvale to house the *Macon* and its support operations. Officially commissioned on April 12, 1933, Sunnyvale Naval Air Station was but eight days old when the *Akron* and 73 of its complement of 76 were lost during a storm off the New Jersey coast. Among the dead was Rear Admiral William A. Moffett, Chief of the Navy's Bureau of Aeronautics and champion of lighter-than-air craft: in 1942 Sunnyvale was renamed Moffett Field.

Arriving in California in October 1933, *Macon* performed the role of a "flying aircraft carrier" with five Curtiss F9C-2 Sparrowhawk fighter planes that could be launched in flight and retrieved by an ingenious trapeze device; but its career was short-lived. After 16 months of patrolling, scouting, and supporting the Pacific

Fleet, in February 1935 during fleet exercises the *Macon* went down in a storm off Point Sur. Two of its 81-man crew were lost.

Among the few lasting monuments to the brief heyday of the once-proud dirigibles is Moffett Field's imposing "Hangar One." Designed to house *Macon*, the gracefully arched structure encloses eight acres and is so large, and its vaulted roof so high, that fog sometimes forms near the ceiling. Designated a Naval Historical Monument in the early 1950s, Hangar One remains in service today, dwarfing the dozens of Lockheed Orions arrayed beneath its anachronistic splendor.

Following the loss of the *Macon*, Moffett Field in October 1935 was allocated to the Army Air Corps as a part of the trade that made North Island all-Navy and moved the Army from Rockwell Field to Moffett. In 1940 it became the West Coast Air Corps Training Center, a major location for AAC cadet training. Moffett's best-known graduate is actor Jimmy Stewart, who arrived in March 1942. In 1942 the Navy once again took over Moffett as a base for blimps used in coastal antisubmarine work. In 1947 Moffett turned to heavier-than-air craft as the West Coast's largest Naval air transport base and that year hosted its first jet plane. By 1961 the population growth of Santa Clara Valley made jet traffic an unwelcome neighbor: jet operations were moved to Naval Air Stations Lemoore and Miramar.

With the departure of jets Moffett concentrated full time on its role as the West Coast's major antisubmarine warfare (ASW) base. The station accommodates the Navy's largest fleet of Lockheed P-3 Orion ASW aircraft and has become the center of ASW operations and intelligence for the entire Pacific and Far East.

## NAVAL AVIATION EXPANDS IN SAN DIEGO

Although Miramar didn't become a Naval Air Station until the start of World War II, the site dates to WWI as a military installation. Known as Camp Kearny, it was a U.S. Army Infantry Training Center and was named in honor of General Stephan W. Kearny, who gained fame in

1846 when he played a leading role in wresting areas of California from the Mexican government. The area around NAS Miramar, now heavily industrial, is still known as Kearny Mesa.

Between wars the location was used as a target bombing range and a lighter-than-air craft base. Early in 1942 it became an auxiliary air station to North Island with a portion designated a Marine Corps Air Depot, a supply and staging area for aircraft and crews preparing for combat. At the end of World War II the Marine Depot served as a separation center for more than 25,000 U.S. military personnel. In 1946 the installation was consolidated as Marine Corps Air Station Miramar for Naval and Marine aircraft and units of the Fleet. When the Marine air units moved to El Toro in 1947, the area once again became an auxiliary air station. Miramar was designated a full Naval Air Station in 1952 and became home base for all West Coast Navy fighter squadrons.

## EL TORO: BEAN FIELD BECOMES LEATHERNECK AIR BASE

Orange County's 93,000-acre Irvine Ranch has become in the last decade the focus of what was at its inception the world's largest private community development project. Centered around the University of California's Irvine campus, the development includes residential areas, electronics and other industry facilities, and vast green stretches devoted to recreation. One of its most important earlier uses, however, came during World War II in 1942-1943 when what is now Marine Corps Air Station El Toro was carved from one of the Ranch's extensive bean fields.

Commissioned on St. Patrick's Day, 1942, El Toro occupies some 5,700 acres and includes El Toro and the Marine Corps Air Station (Helicopter) at nearby Tustin. Because the base straddles the Santa Ana Freeway, Marine helicopters and fighter aircraft are familiar if dramatic sights to Orange County residents and commuters and travelers.

El Toro's first commander, the man charged with building the base, Colonel Theodore B.

Millard, arrived at his temporary headquarters at the construction site in the fall of 1942 and promptly received a telephone call from his first sergeant in the town of El Toro, three miles away. The sergeant reported that 30 enlisted men had arrived and needed transportation to the site. With no government transport available, Colonel Millard climbed into his own automobile and shuttled the entire initial station complement to the base.

During World War II El Toro was known as a "flyer factory," expanding from its original mission to a full-size Marine Air Wing. At the time El Toro was called the "Times Square" of Western aviation, with more planes landing and taking off there than from any other West Coast base. Nearly shut down during the postwar military cutback, with the advent of the Korean conflict in 1950 El Toro expanded to become the permanent home for the Third Marine Aircraft Wing and Marine Aircraft Group 46.

Among the base's unusual recent assignments were its role as the arrival and departure point for President Richard Nixon's trips to the Western White House at San Clemente and in 1975 as the disembarkation point for "Operation New Arrival," in which some 50,000 Vietnamese refugees arrived in America following the end of U.S. involvement in Southeast Asia.

In early 1983 the first F-18 Hornet fighter aircraft, the vanguard of a new generation of fighter and attack airplanes produced by McDonnell Douglas and Northrop, went into operational service at MCAS El Toro.

## NAVY MOVES INTO CALIFORNIA'S CENTRAL VALLEY

Responding to the Navy's need for a major base for jet operations serving the Pacific Fleet, a 1957 survey concluded that a location near Fresno in California's Central Valley would be ideal; and Congress appropriated more than $10 million to acquire some 20,000 acres with an easement for an additional 12,000 acres of land. NAS Lemoore was commissioned in July 1961 as the master training center for carrier-based squadrons of the Pacific Fleet and headquarters for the Light Attack Squadrons in the Pacific.

## POINT MUGU IS MISSILE DRONE HEADQUARTERS

Originally established as Port Hueneme Naval Base and used by the famed World War II USN Construction Battalions (Seabees), when the Navy began studying and developing pilotless aircraft (drones) immediately following World War II Naval Air Facility Point Mugu was established in 1945 as a satellite of Naval Air Station Mojave. From pilotless aircraft and drones came the Navy's initial missile efforts, and the first launch of a Navy missile occurred in January 1946 when a LOON was fired from Point Mugu. In 1946 the Naval Air Missile Test Center was formally commissioned.

Point Mugu has become the Navy's Pacific Missile Range headquarters for various recoverable drones used as target and observation aircraft and weapons firing support, and houses transport aircraft and helicopters for the Pacific Missile Range as well as for the Navy's study efforts in Antarctica. Navy crews supporting the U.S. National Science Foundation work in Antarctica are based at Point Mugu, deploying each year from the station to the South Pole from October to March.

## TRENCH WARFARE TRIGGERS NEW AIR BASE SITE

Paralleling San Diego's pride of place in Naval aviation, the Army's (later the U.S. Air Force's) oldest permanent West Coast air installation is March Air Force Base, a 640-acre site carved from the expansive Hendricks ranch in the Moreno Valley near Riverside, California.

In 1917, with British, French, and American infantry forces holed up in the cold and muddy trenches of France in what appeared to be a stalemate, U.S. military tacticians looked to air warfare as one way of ending the conflict. War Department strategists decreed the establishment of more than 20 new airfields for training pilots in the hope that they could bring the war to a swift conclusion.

Frank Miller, owner of Riverside's famed Mission Inn, led efforts of the local chamber of commerce to locate a base near Riverside. Named for the town once located there and its small surviving railroad station, Alessandro Flying Strip began to be used in 1917 by Army aviators on cross-country flights from Rockwell Field. In February 1918 Congress approved the site for a "Wing Cavalry Post"; the first aircraft to officially use the site was a fabric-covered DH-4, settling on the dirt strip nestled among wheat, barley, and rye fields. Its pilot was there to survey the new location. On March 1, 1918, the field was officially dedicated and renamed March Field in honor of Lt. Peyton C. March, who had been killed in an aircraft accident in Texas only one month before.

A four-man work crew, under the direction of Sergeant Charles Garlick, was the first U.S. military contingent stationed at March. Using local mule teams to help level the land, Sergeant Garlick and his men and mules worked rapidly. Troops arrived from Rockwell Field in late April; the first Jenny took off on May 15, 1918, inaugurating March Field's training era.

With the rudimentary, condensed flying school techniques of those early years, some March Field-trained aviators even saw service in the skies over France. When the Armistice was signed November 11, 1918, March Field was no exception to the impact of budget reductions and postwar austerity as American sentiment turned once again to peacetime pursuits. By 1921 permanent staff was drastically reduced; by 1923 March Field was officially shut down, one lonely sergeant remaining as caretaker.

But in 1927 March Field was reopened to continue as an Army Air Corps training base, and the Riverside community briefly entertained visions of March becoming the principal Army flying school. The Army had other ideas, and in a decision to affect each location for more than 50 years, Randolph Field, Texas, was selected as the site for aerial bombardment training while March Field became an operational base for pursuit and bombardment operations. March's location in Southern California near the country's largest concentration of aircraft builders provided special advantages. A number of flight firsts and milestone flight testing in the 1920s and 1930s were accomplished at the field. It was, however, a less immediately conspicuous but epochal activity behind its gates near Riverside that truly distinguished the base. In nearby Los Angeles County the expanding capabilities of a growing community of aircraft manufacturers were accelerated by innovative and sophisticated engineering skills being honed at the California Institute of Technology, the University of Southern California, and other academic centers. Synthesizing the ever-expanding knowledge flowing from such institutions as NACA and the competitive arena of the country's fledgling airlines, California airframe builders were envisioning large airplanes whose range and load capabilities would provide the tools for a revolution in military aviation. And ample evidence suggests that March Field was the smithy of thought in which the aviation strategy that would dominate U.S. military thinking for decades was forged.

The aggressive base commander at March from 1931 to 1936 was Henry H. "Hap" Arnold, later head of America's air armada during World War II and one of aviation's most imaginative leaders. In addition to Arnold, other officers who trained or served at March during the 1930s included Generals Carl "Tooey" Spaatz and Curtis LeMay and Lt. General Ira Eaker. It was these men who earned for March the sobriquet "The West Point of the West," as they conceived and developed the concepts of long-range, high-altitude bombing. The strategy would emerge as an essential factor in the Allied victory in World War II and as the foundation for American defense policy until development of long-range missiles decades later.

By the late 1930s the March Field complex had taken on the look of a military base preparing for conflict; in 1938 it became the West Coast central base for bombing and gunnery training. During this period Muroc Dry Lake, now Edwards Air Force Base, was considered a part of March Field and was used as a bombing training site. In 1940 National Guard units from California and Illinois came to March to begin anti-aircraft artillery training. On a real-estate tract nearly as big as the original March Field, Camp Haan became an anti-aircraft facility and in 1946 was incorporated into March Field.

During World War II, 75,000 troops were assigned to the March Field/Camp Haan complex. In 1941 and 1942 secret tests were conducted there that demonstrated the practicality of jet and rocket assistance for takeoff of propeller-driven aircraft, tests that were a giant step towards the jet age.

Following World War II March became an operational base, integral to the newly formed Tactical Air Command. TAC's best-known unit, the 1st Fighter Wing, flew America's first operational jet fighter, the Lockheed F-80, at March. Although it hosted a fighter operation for three of the postwar years, March in 1949 once again assumed its bomber role as a key base of the USAF Strategic Air Command.

During the Korean conflict, USAF bombardment wings going to the Pacific theater were staged at March, which became a major element of America's deterrent force in 1952 when its propeller-driven B-29s were replaced by new six-jet B-47 jet bombers. In 1963 new eight-jet giant B-52 bombers and their support jet tankers, KC-135s, moved in. From 1964 to 1973 March served as a deployment base for bombers as B-52s and support aircraft flew from there to the Western Pacific during the Vietnam War and became a major reception area for returning American prisoners of war.

Dedicated on November 11, 1978, a large area of the base was transferred to the Veterans Administration for use as a National Veterans Cemetery, and in 1979 the March Field Museum was opened, the start of efforts to preserve the artifacts of March Field/AFB and its role in American military history.

MATHER CLOSELY FOLLOWS MARCH
Officially opened in June 1918, the site for Mather Air Force Base had been selected the previous July when the U.S. government awarded an $18-million contract to a group of Sacramento businessmen for the manufacture of military aircraft. These businessmen converted the Globe Iron Works into an aircraft plant to produce Curtiss Jennies. As a natural extension, the enterprising businessmen successfully campaigned to establish an Army flying school

later. Named for Lieutenant Carl S. Mather, killed in a January 1918 air training accident in Texas, the airfield was an additional location for training World War II aviators.

Like March, Mather in 1923 was deactivated and until 1930 was an aerial forest patrol base, an airmail stop, and a touchdown spot during Charles Lindbergh's national tour with the *Spirit of St. Louis.* Following World War II it became the basic navigation training site for the entire Department of Defense and is now the principal location for USAF advanced navigator training.

McCLELLAN AFB EMERGES FROM A SWAP
As a part of the Army Air Corps/U.S. Navy trade that phased out Army Air operations in San Diego, the Sacramento Air Depot was established in June 1936 when Congress authorized $7 million for construction of the War Department's new Air Repair Depot and Supply Base. The base was dedicated in 1939 and later that year was renamed McClellan Field in honor of Major Hezekiah McClellan, pioneer Alaskan Air Route explorer, who was killed in a flight test aircraft in Ohio.

Like other military installations in California, the Sacramento site was selected as a result of the persuasive efforts of the local chamber of commerce and its secretary-manager, Arthur S. Dudley. Dudley, anticipating the urgent need for the development of U.S. military air power, was instrumental in organizing the National Air Frontier Defense Association in 1934. NAFDA, whose membership included chamber of commerce representatives from across the U.S., helped push legislation through Congress in 1935 that provided for the construction of many new U.S. military bases.

Although it employed only 1,000 employees when dedicated in April 1939, McClellan became an industrial giant during World War II, when it employed more than 18,000 civilians, and more than 7,000 aircraft were processed there for use in the Pacific theater. McClellan operated as a logistics, support, and supply base for Far East operations.

In a top-secret operation, McClellan in 1942 was the site for the modification of 22 B-25 Mitchell light bombers for a task force headed by

Lt. Colonel James H. Doolittle, which carried out the first air raid on the Japanese mainland, bombing Tokyo in April 1942. McClellan workers installed new propellers, 60-gallon fuel tanks (fitted into the original lower gun turret location), and cameras, and provided crew survival equipment and final aircraft inspection. The B-25s and Doolittle-led crews departed McClellan on April 1, 1942, and on April 18, 1942, sixteen B-25s lifted off the deck of the U.S. Navy carrier *Hornet* for the famed Tokyo raid.

Following the war hundreds of aircraft were stored at McClellan, headquarters for the Sacramento Air Materiel Area and a deposition point for war surplus material.

In the 1960s McClellan and SAMA took on new stature as the USAF specialist for space systems logistics support and for maintenance of ground electronics communications. In the 1970s McClellan received systems management responsibility for the USAF's new A-10 close air support aircraft. Although a wide variety of aircraft utilize McClellan as a flying base, its principal tasks are logistics, repair, support, and supply for new electronics, flight controls, and ground communications.

FLYING TO CALIFORNIA'S HIGH DESERT
California aviation, born along coastal plains and mesas, in 1940 reached into the high desert. Following the success of other California communities, the city fathers of Victorville proposed the Victor Valley as a site for a civilian elementary flying school in ideal climatic conditions for flight instruction.

In March 1941, however, the West Coast Army Air Corps Training Center proposed a 2,200-acre site near Victorville for use as an Air Corps Advanced Flying School; it was made an active base in October 1941. Two officers and 14 enlisted men from Mather Field were the first to arrive. By February 1942 the first group of instructors for the training school had reported, and advanced pilot training began in February with the first class of cadets. Cadets graduated after nine weeks of training; a new class began every month.

But in 1943, in sharp contrast to big bomber

flights, aircraft at Victorville suddenly became "silent." Two squadrons of the 63rd Troop Carrier Group began training as glider pilots to fly cargo. Emphasis was placed on towing techniques, spot-landing proficiency, and night flying. It was one of many secret weapons planned for use by Allied forces.

Originally called the Air Corps Advanced Flying School, the base later became the Victorville Army Flying School; then Victorville Army Air Field; later Victorville Air Force Base. In 1950 Victorville AFB was renamed in honor of Brigadier General Harold H. George, Chief of Staff of the Far Eastern Air Forces, who had commanded U.S. Air Corps troops in the Philippines in 1941-1942 and died in 1942 in an aircraft crash at Darwin, Australia.

At war's end, the base was placed on stand-by and assigned to the Air Technical Service Command. Its only mission: store surplus B-29s, AT-7s, and AT-11s.

However, the Korean conflict reactivated George—as a training base for North American F-86s for the first Fighter Interceptor Wing deploying aircraft to Korea. In 1951 George became a Tactical Air Command Base. TAC had acquired jet fighters; the new North American F-100 Super Sabre, the first of the Air Force's "Century Series" fighters, became operational at George in 1954; the Lockheed F-104 Starfighter was added to inventory in 1958. In the early 1960s George became a training base for USAF's McDonnell F-4C Phantom II tactical fighters; later it housed Republic F-105D Thunderchiefs. George was the principal site for USAF's new F-4G Advanced Wild Weasel aircraft and became a major location for the new electronic Air Force, including the use of laser technology for weapons delivery. During the 1970s George's 35th Tactical Fighter Wing and 20th Tactical Fighter Training Squadron were the prime U.S. locations for the training of German Luftwaffe pilots who would fly that nation's F-4 Phantom IIs. Tactical Air Command units based at George are part of America's Worldwide Rapid Deployment Force, and the base has become known as home for "hot" fighter pilots.

## SERENE SAN JOAQUIN VALLEY BECOMES TRAINING SITE

The 1939 fall of Poland was the catalyst that spurred America's preparations for waging aerial warfare. The man who had taken early flight training at Rockwell and who was base commander at March during its major buildup was General H.H. "Hap" Arnold. By 1941 he headed the U.S. Army Air Corps.

Under Arnold's direction, Air Corps training underwent a massive buildup. "It was not unusual to find a training field with dozens of planes flying above it, bulldozers on the ground finishing the earth work, cement mixers turning out concrete runways yet to be built, and men in the open still clearing the brush off what had been grazing land," observed Arnold about the breathless haste of the Army's aviation training.

By early 1941 Air Corps pilot training had jumped to 30,000 a year, 100 times the 1939 level. In recognition of the near certainty of U.S. involvement in the European war, 20 new Air Corps training bases were completed or under construction by December.

Like many other installations, Castle Air Force Base was born in 1941 as a training site. Unlike some new bases elsewhere, however, Merced Army Airfield had distinct geographic advantages, being located in the agricultural heart of the San Joaquin Valley, halfway between the Sierras and the sea. Almost equidistant to the Pacific and High Sierras, the Merced area is called "Gateway to Yosemite."

The first BT-13As arrived at Merced Army Airfield in November, and at the peak of wartime cadet training the flight school graduated 1,000 cadets every five weeks; some 40,000 flying hours were logged each month on 600 training aircraft.

After Brigadier General Frederick W. Castle died over Europe on December 14, 1944, when he stayed at the controls of his flaming B-17 so his crew could escape, Merced Army Airfield was named Castle Air Force Base in his honor.

Castle, deactivated briefly in 1946, the next year became home to the newly named 93rd Bomb Wing, inheriting the proud heritage of the

93rd Bombardment Group of World War II. In 1946 the 93rd was flying B-29s from Castle; it operated B-50Ds beginning in 1949, and by June 1954 was part of the Strategic Air Command and had received B-47s, its first jet bombers. B-52s arrived a year later, KC-135 jet tankers to support B-47s and B-52s came in 1957.

## SUPPLY DEPOT IN THE INLAND EMPIRE

To support the pre-World War II American air buildup, the Army Air Corps recognized the requirement for strategically located supply depots, and civic leaders of San Bernardino envisioned a military complex that would not only support the war effort but also boost the area's economy.

The San Bernardino Air Depot was activated in 1941 to provide support for the buildup of Southern California's military preparedness. Later called the San Bernardino Air Materiel Area, it was located in the heart of what has become known as the Inland Empire.

In 1950 the depot was renamed Norton Air Force Base in honor of Captain Leland F. Norton, a San Bernardino native who was killed in 1944 while flying an A-20 bombing mission in the skies over France. Norton is one of the state's few military installations named for native Californians.

The base remained an Air Force supply center until 1966 when it became home for the 63rd Military Airlift Wing of the USAF's Military Airlift Command. The base mission was changed from supply to flight operations, and Norton was a troop departure point during the Vietnam War. A Lockheed C-141 Starlifter from the 63rd was the first U.S. aircraft to land in Hanoi, North Vietnam, after the ceasefire; it picked up the first group of 40 American prisoners of war. The 63rd also transported returning American troops and displaced Vietnamese following the cease-fire. On the lighter side, the 63rd provided airlift for the famed Bob Hope worldwide Christmas tours during the Southeast Asia years. The original San Bernardino Army Air Force Supply Depot encompassed about 500 acres; Norton AFB now covers 2,438 acres.

## NORTHERN CALIFORNIA WINDS AID AIRFIELD SELECTION

Travis Air Force Base was established in 1942 because the vast surrounding plain and its strong, prevailing winds replicated conditions found on the decks of aircraft carriers. Originally staked out by the Army Corps of Engineers, the site was named Fairfield-Suisun Army Air Corps Field and boasted one short airstrip and a few temporary buildings. The first initial Naval detachment came from Hamilton Air Field, near San Francisco, to open the field. The Navy tenure was short-lived; in 1943 the Army Air Transport Command made the base home for Consolidated Vultee B-24s. Its primary role, however, was as a major aerial port for troops and supplies going to the Pacific. In 1945 Fairfield-Suisun Field became a permanent U.S. Army Air Force installation.

In 1951 Fairfield-Suisun was renamed in honor of Brigadier General Robert F. Travis, then ranking officer at the base, who was killed when his B-29 crashed on takeoff. With the exception of the period from 1949 to 1958, when Travis Air Force Base was assigned to the Strategic Air Command, the base has been a major military airlift site.

Travis is now home base for the 60th Military Airlift Wing (MAW), the first to put in service an operational squadron of Lockheed C-141 Starlifters, which during the Vietnam conflict airlifted wounded, troops, dependents, and high-priority cargo. Travis became home for the David Grant Medical Center, now the second-largest USAF medical facility. In 1973 Travis-based C-141s returned from the Philippines with one of the first groups of returning American POWs, their arrival documented on television and in newspaper coverage. The 143 POWs brought to Travis were treated and debriefed at Grant Medical Center.

In April 1975 the Travis-based 60th MAW assisted in the massive evacuation of thousands of South Vietnamese from their war-torn country to Travis.

A once-tiny airfield located on a prairie now covers more than 6,000 acres and hosts about 9,000 military personnel and 2,400 civilians.

## BEALE AIR FORCE BASE LINKED TO CALIFORNIA HERITAGE

Beale AFB, at least by its name, has close ties to California history. The founder of the U.S. Army Camel Corps, and subsequently the state's largest landholder, General Edward Fitzgerald Beale was a pre-Civil War Annapolis graduate assigned to duty in California under Commodore Stockton at the outset of the Mexican War.

Recognizing California's enormous potential, Beale resigned his Navy commission and was appointed Superintendent of Indian Affairs for California and New Mexico. Later commissioned a brigadier general in the Army, Beale reportedly helped end California's Indian wars. General Beale later became Surveyor-General of California and Nevada, a position in which he was able to accumulate massive California land holdings. President Abraham Lincoln commented about Beale's land acquisition, "Well, I appointed him Surveyor-General out there, and I understand that he is monarch of all he has surveyed."

It seems only fitting that the largest military training site in the West should be named after this California land baron. Opened in October 1942 as Camp Beale, it encompassed more than 86,000 acres of land. During World War II the camp was a personnel replacement depot, a prisoner-of-war encampment, the site of a 1,000-bed hospital and, finally, a West Coast separation center.

Declared surplus by the War Department in 1947, the facility was requisitioned by the newly formed U.S. Air Force as an air base. From 1948 to 1951 Beale AFB was the site of bombardier-navigator training. Beale has a varied history of USAF command use. At various times during the early 1950s it was part of Air Training Command, Continental Air Command, Aviation Engineer Force, and finally the Strategic Air Command.

Under its SAC colors, Beale became home for KC-135 jet tankers and in 1959 was named support base for three Titan missile sites. In the mid-1960s Beale became headquarters for the USAF Strategic Reconnaissance Wing, which mans and maintains the Air Force's fastest aircraft, the Lockheed SR-71, and the famed Lockheed U-2 aircraft as part of USAF reconnaissance activities.

Complementing the reconnaissance aircraft is Beale's massive 10-story phased-array radar used for detection and early warning against sea-launched ballistic missile attacks on the continental United States and to track satellites in earth orbit.

## CALIFORNIA COAST IS USAF MISSILE CENTER

On an angular peninsula 55 miles north of Santa Barbara that forms a portion of California's central coast, the Air Force in 1956 selected an abandoned Army military training ground named Camp Cooke to become the "aerospace center of the United States Air Force." The USAF selected the 98,400-acre wild and isolated promontory, what some have called an "Army ghost town," as home for its fledgling missile program. In 1958 it was renamed Vandenberg Air Force Base in honor of World War II hero General Hoyt S. Vandenberg, the USAF's second chief of staff.

Vandenberg's isolated location and natural land barriers provide an ideal launching site for intercontinental ballistic missiles, and it is the only U.S. military installation launching missiles and satellites. Although Cape Canaveral is better known as a launch site because of the manned space flight program, approximately 50 percent more launches of unmanned satellites into space have been made from Vandenberg. Contrails—white in the day but bizarre scarves of improbable color at dusk—wafted askew by winds over the Pacific are familiar to Californians from San Diego to San Francisco.

Beginning in October 1985 Vandenberg is scheduled to play a major role in the Space Shuttle Program, with as many as 10 launches per year planned during the 1990s. Satellites can be placed in polar orbit more safely from the northern Santa Barbara County site than from Florida's Cape Canaveral, and a 15,000-foot runway already built will allow the shuttle to land as well as take off from the base.

*At San Diego's Western Aviation Progress Exhibition in August 1928, pilots from the carrier USS* Langley *and North Island were among those flying 125 Navy aircraft along with 126 Army, 11 Marine, and 210 civilian planes in a mass flight over the city. A similar armada performed at the National Air Races in Los Angeles the following month. Courtesy, NASM/SI*

*Navy Lieutenant Theodore G. "Spuds" Ellyson was the first military pilot to be graduated from Curtiss' flying school at North Island and "Naval Aviator No. 1." Here he is pictured at the control of a Curtiss plane, probably in 1911. Courtesy, NASM/SI*

*Above: A prolific and ingenious designer and builder, Glenn Curtiss began his career in his native Hammondsport, New York, racing and building motorcycles. In 1911 (about the time this photo was taken) he moved to San Diego, where his work with sea-based aircraft changed Navy history. Courtesy, U.S. Naval Historical Center*

*Right: In this 1911 (probably February) view of Curtiss' North Island, San Diego, base are Curtiss pusher biplanes (center and right foreground), Antoinette monoplanes, and, in the background, the cruiser USS* Pennsylvania, *which Curtiss used to demonstrate the capabilities of his hydroaeroplane. Courtesy, National Air and Space Museum/SI*

The USS Macon *is towed from Moffett Field's monumental Hangar No. 1 late in 1933 by the rail-mounted mooring rig designed for handling the Navy's leviathan airships.* Macon *served as a "flying aircraft carrier" with five Curtiss F9C-2 Sparrowhawk fighter planes that could be launched in flight and retrieved by an ingenious trapeze device. In a February 1935 storm the* Macon *broke up off Point Sur. Courtesy, U.S. Navy, NAS Moffett Field*

*Above: The career of Henry H. "Hap" Arnold, "Father of the U.S. Air Force," paralleled the rise of California aviation, from North Island to his retirement. In this November 1944 photograph at the Burbank plant with a P-38 in the background, General Arnold (right) confers with Lockheed's president Robert Gross (center). Courtesy, CALAC*

*Top: Regarded by experts as one of America's most effective warplanes during WWII was Lockheed's P-38 Lightning (an "H" model is shown in 1943), more than 10,000 of which were built. Courtesy, CALAC*

Ryan Aeronautical was long the leader in the development of non-rotary wing aircraft able to fly vertically and to hover. Two prototype Ryan XV-5A Vertifans, using conventional jet engines for forward flight and ducting for vertical operation, were tested from 1964 through 1966 for the Army. Courtesy, R.E. Falk

Below: Lockheed's F-104 Starfighter set speed and altitude records and was widely adopted by Allied air arms. This March 1954 photograph shows the prototype XF-104 (with F-86 chase plane) on an early flight from Edwards AFB. Courtesy, CALAC

Above: Northrop's supersonic T-38 Talon trainer first flew on April 10, 1959. USAF, USN, NASA, and Federal Republic of Germany orders totaled 1,189 airplanes (most built at Palmdale) through January 31, 1972. Courtesy, NC

# CHAPTER SEVEN

# AIRLINES

If airframe builders and military planners shared attractive cause in choosing California, air transport entrepreneurs within the state, across the nation, and internationally have found the state's geography and demographics irresistible. California's prosperity derives in part from air routes that link the state to the world marketplace. California's thriving metropolitan complexes are distant enough from one another to render intercity surface passenger transport inconvenient and close enough to permit economical air transport in near-perfect flying conditions all year round. In 1982 some two million passengers flew between Los Angeles and San Francisco over the world's most heavily traveled air route—337 air miles measured in minutes by modern jetliners. And because it lies entirely within a single state's borders, this teeming market remained essentially immune from the economic regulation of the federal Civil Aeronautics Board, which for 40 years limited airline management options virtually everywhere else in America.

Hundreds of air carriers, from San Francisco Bay ferries and commuter networks to intercontinental titans, have thrived upon California's tides of commerce. Of those bred in California, some were destined for lasting achievement, but most were bound for a fleeting touch and go. Airlines have found California golden indeed, and they have reciprocated: as California has nourished airlines of nearly every size and kind, so have the carriers contributed mightily to California's prosperity and prestige.

## CONTEXT AND PERSPECTIVE
Airline companies, like the men and women

who build and operate them, reflect their environment and their times. Individual as they appear, airlines everywhere are true creatures of the 20th century, their destiny shaped by government policy for nearly 50 years; thus California's airline story is incomplete without a glimpse of the context of U.S. airline development.

America's airlines began in earnest after World War I when the resources needed to sustain them became accessible, including suitable airplanes, investment capital, a market, and public acceptance. Government participation began when the post office received its first airmail appropriation in 1917—$100,000 for experimental service operated until 1921 between Washington, D.C., and New York. In 1919 Congress funded a transcontinental airmail service between New York and San Francisco (via Cleveland, Chicago, and Omaha). The whole route was operational by May 1920, with flights in the daytime and trains at night taking about 75 hours. By 1921 the trip needed just over 33 hours, the trains having been foregone.

On Secretary of Commerce Herbert Hoover's recommendation, in September 1925 President Coolidge convened the nine-man President's Aircraft Board headed by financier Dwight Morrow to "investigate the entire U.S. military and civilian aeronautical establishment." The board's report led to the Air Commerce Act of 1926, which established the Army Air Corps and the Aeronautics Branch of the Department of Commerce, with the power to license and certificate aircraft and airmen.

The first airplanes of substantial carrying capacity and reliability made their appearance, including William B. Stout's Tri-motor (it became the famed Ford Tin Goose), which first flew on June 11, 1926, and Lindbergh's flight in May 1927 almost overnight persuaded America that flying could be a *practical* part of modern life.

Financial incentive for the private sector came with the Kelly Act of 1925, which funded the carriage of mail, modified by the McNary-Watres Act of 1930 allowing 10-year mail contracts with a space (rather than weight) payment plan—a genuine inducement for airlines to solicit passengers to augment mail income. The Postmaster General was authorized to extend or consolidate routes "in the public interest." In a crucial episode, President Herbert Hoover's Republican Postmaster General Walter Folger Brown met with airmail contractors in his office between May 14 and June 9, 1930—sessions soon dubbed the "Spoils Conferences"—and enforced his notion of the public interest by awarding mail contracts only to carriers whose size and strength he judged adequate for a stable national system of airlines. Five large companies won all but two of twenty-two contracts.

When the Democrats took office in 1933, a probe of the airmail contracts followed, and a Senate Special Committee, chaired by Alabama Democrat Hugo L. Black, used allegations against Brown as the basis for a call to action. With more alacrity than wisdom, Postmaster General James A. Farley and President Franklin D. Roosevelt were persuaded to cancel the extant contracts, which they did on February 19, 1934, and order the Army to fly the mails. Army fliers, ill-prepared for a ferocious winter, operated a reduced mail system with great courage from February to June 1934. Sadly, 10 aviators lost their lives in training and mail flights, but public pressure brought reason to bear: new bid requests were issued to commercial carriers on March 30, 1934.

In April Farley laid down new rules to bidders: airmail contractors were forbidden to hold financial interests in other aviation enterprises, and no company or person involved in the "Spoils Conferences" might bid. However,

company reorganization to expunge the tainted names would suffice as atonement. Thus, American Airways became American Airlines, Eastern Air Transport became Eastern Airlines, and Transcontinental and Western Air became TWA, Inc.

Continued attention to commercial aviation culminated in the Civil Aeronautics Act of 1938, which set the pattern for air transport regulation until 1978. The law's keystone was the five-member Civil Aeronautics Authority (later the Civil Aeronautics Board, or CAB), with broad authority to regulate routes and rates, and market entry and exit of air carriers. The enabling mechanisms included issuance of the Certificate of Public Convenience and Necessity based upon criteria of the public interest, and the requirement that each applicant must be "fit, willing, and able" to perform before designation as a Certificated Carrier.

The suspension of the airmail contracts in 1934 was the watershed from which the board's first carrier certification decisions derived. The post-1934 survivors received Grandfather Routes in 1938 and, with few exceptions, emerged as the Trunk Carriers—one of the historical groupings under which U.S. airlines were categorized until 1980.

Categories relevant to the California story included: *Domestic Trunks* (16 carriers, 10 surviving until 1982); *International & Territorial Air Carriers; Domestic Local Service* (from 1945, an experimental category with 20 carriers awarded three-year certificates later renewed for terms ranging to five years until 1958 when profitably operated awards were made permanent and a "use it or lose it" policy established); *All-Cargo Carriers* (no passengers, no mail—first awarded certificates in 1949); *Helicopter Air Carriers; Supplemental Air Carriers* (a classification created in 1955 to replace *Large Irregular Carriers*—that unruly breed whose very name perplexed the mandarins but who didn't mind their usual label—"the nonskeds").

In October 1980 the board addressed the changed carrier environment created by the Airline Deregulation Act of 1978 and established new categories: *Majors* (operating revenues over

$1 billion annually) — in 1980 there were 12: American, Braniff, Continental, Delta, Eastern, Northwest, Pan American, Republic, Trans World, United, USAir, and Western; *Nationals* (revenues from $75 million to $1 billion) — there were 17, including AirCal, Air Florida, Flying Tiger, World, et al; *Large Regionals* (revenues from $10 million to $74,999,000) — there were 18, including Air Midwest and Golden West; *Medium Regionals* (revenues up to $9,999,000 and operating only aircraft with 60 or fewer seats, or 18,000 lbs or less maximum payload) — there were 25, including McCulloch and Imperial; and the ubiquitous *Other* (primarily charter operators).

Under board control from 1938 to 1977, airline competition was essentially limited to the realm of service. After 1978 virtual freedom of action for market entry and exit and fare setting made price the principal competitive tool for managers, much as it was within California from 1946 until 1965. John Newhouse, describing the complex decisions faced recently by carrier managers, with a nice understatement wrote, "Managing an airline is one of the more inexact sciences." Certainly deregulation changed the rules, and it remains to be seen how the industry in California and elsewhere will cope with its new context. Writing in 1977, Bob Serling surveyed the bewildering disarray of the airline industry and offered this wry assessment: "If we've lost our perspective, we're no different from the fools and madmen who perpetrated the idea in the first place that an airline was a workable proposition."

Because the CAB's federal economic writ never ran to airlines operating wholly within the boundaries of a single state, intrastate airlines in California fall within the jurisdiction of the California State Public Utilities Commission, responsible for "regulation of the transportation of passengers by air within California for [an] orderly, efficient, economical, and healthy intrastate passenger air network." The intrastate phenomenon, shared in kind only by Texas and Florida, is central to California airline history. Economists and politicians since 1946 repeatedly turned to California to validate diverse

assertions about the effects of regulation on airline operations.

THE PIONEERS
*Syd Chaplin Airlines.* Two partners planning a Curtiss aeroplane dealership in Los Angeles became the founders of California's airline industry in 1919. Syd Chaplin and Emory Rogers apparently decided that a seaplane shuttle operation to the popular resort of Santa Catalina Island some 30 miles offshore would enhance their plans. So Rogers journeyed to the Curtiss factory in New York to arrange the dealership and delivery of a jaunty little MF Seagull flying boat, and Chaplin negotiated with the island's owners, the William Wrigley, Jr., family, for landing privileges at the island.

The Wrigleys agreed to landings in St. Catherine's Bay near the island's only town of Avalon, the Seagull arrived via Railway Express, Art Burns was hired as manager and pilot, and mainland waterside terminal space was secured in Wilmington from the Marine Equipment Company. During the first week of July flights began — three round trips each day at a fare of $42.50 return. They painted "Chaplin Air Line" on the Seagull, but the operation was usually simply called Catalina Airlines. At the season's close in mid-September, scheduled service stopped, and the partners went their separate ways. Their tiny enterprise is honored as the first California airline, and the subsequent tale of the Catalina route is intriguing out of all proportion to its diminutive mileage.

*Ryan Airlines.* While Claude Ryan is perhaps best known for innovative airplanes and leadership among manufacturers, his "Los Angeles-San Diego Air Line" was characteristically imaginative and competent, noted in the records as "the first regular airline service year round over U.S. mainland."

In 1924 the 26-year-old Ryan had set up shop at San Diego's Dutch Flats, buying, rebuilding, and reselling airplanes and training pilots. When playboy and financier B. Franklin Mahoney showed up one day to take flying lessons, he wound up a partner and underwriter of expansion; Ryan's biographer William Wagner attributes the airline idea to Mahoney. By March 1925 the pair were operating daily schedules with six war-surplus Standard biplanes that Ryan and his colleague Hawley Bowlus reequipped with 150 hp. Hispano Suiza engines and widened to accommodate five passengers. The operation's first Los Angeles field was at 99th Street and Western Avenue, later moved to Angeles Mesa (now Crenshaw) in Baldwin Hills. Fares began at $14.50 one way and $22.50 round trip, and 5,600 passengers were carried in 1926.

The queen of the fleet was the famed Douglas Cloudster, which Ryan bought for $6,000 and elegantly remodeled into an 11-passenger transport—doubtless the first luxury edition of a Douglas plane. Compared with Ryan's other work, the airline was only a middling financial exercise, and in 1927 the partners concluded that their future lay in manufacturing, not airlines, and discontinued scheduled flights.

*The Beckoning Skies.* After 1927 imagination was the only limit for would-be aero moguls, at least at the start. Nevada Air Lines, for example, flourished from May 1929 until February 1930 by providing rapid transport from the film capital to Reno, Nevada. The idea originated with Lockheed's dapper Carl Squier, and Ray Boggs served as president. If passengers aboard one of the line's four flashy Vegas sought a little glamour for their high-priced ticket, they needed only to peek into the cockpit where they might find Roscoe Turner or even Wiley Post piloting.

Charles F. Wren, owner of Pickwick Stage Systems, tried his hand at airline operations in March 1929 when he began services between Los Angeles and San Diego using Van Nuys-built, three-engine Bach Air Yacht monoplanes. In July San Francisco was added, two months later, Mexico City. By 1930 Wren's routes extended into Central America, but shut down altogether after only a few months.

## MAJOR ENTERPRISES
*Western Air Express.* California's earliest air services did not survive for many reasons—inadequate finances, lack of suitable aircraft, absence of a viable market—but in 1926 conditions were favorable enough to sustain one

fledgling airline beyond infancy. Determination, energy, and offended civic pride in Los Angeles proved sufficient to launch Western Air Express, an enterprise hardy enough to endure trials which grounded a great many others while Western Air Lines perseveres as "the nation's senior carrier."

Dissatisfied with the selection of San Francisco as the Pacific terminus of the country's first transcontinental airmail line in 1920, Los Angeles business leaders were more than receptive when in 1926 Harris M. "Pop" Hanshue proposed to bring direct air service to their city. The energetic Hanshue, then 40 years old and a successful auto dealer, persuaded *Los Angeles Times* publisher Harry Chandler, realtor Bill Garland, and James Talbot of Richfield Oil to join in organizing an airline venture. On July 13, 1925, Western Air Express was incorporated, and by mid-September the company was ready for business, with Hanshue in the cockpit.

In October 1925 the post office awarded the first five contracts to private carriers—Colonial Air Transport, Robertson Aircraft Corporation, Varney Speed Lines, National Air Transport, and Western Air Express, which won the 660-mile Civil Air Mail (CAM) Route 4 between Los Angeles and Salt Lake City. The company swiftly bought six Douglas M-2 mail planes, began training pilots at the Griffith Park National Guard Airport, and set up operations at Vail Field near the main L.A. post office with a 4,000-foot oiled runway and a small hangar and office. Mail service began on April 17, 1926, with one M-2 from each city; the first passenger service began in May. During the first year 730 trips were scheduled, and only nine were cancelled, and on September 30, 1927, Western paid the first dividend to stockholders ever paid by an airline.

In October 1928 Hanshue and Talbot, with several WAE stockholders, capitalized the separate WAE Incorporated in the amount of $5 million and early in 1929 acquired control of Anthony Fokker's American manufacturing company, Atlantic Aircraft. Parent Western continued to grow, adding five four-engine Fokker F-32s and routes stretching to Kansas

City, Missouri, via Amarillo. After acquiring Sacramento's Union Air Lines and its subsidiary, West Coast Air Transport of Portland (operating between San Francisco and Seattle), WAE moved to expanded Los Angeles facilities in Alhambra near Montebello late in 1929.

*The Aero Corporation of California and Standard Airlines.* Across town at 102nd Street and South Western Avenue, Jack Frye, Paul Richter, and Walter Hamilton in 1925 formed the Aero Corporation of California as a dealership for the Alexander Aircraft Company and the Fokker Company of America, and in February 1926 they formed a subsidiary, Standard Airlines. In November Standard began service from Los Angeles to Phoenix and Tucson, later adding El Paso, Texas. Connections with the Texas Pacific Railroad allowed a 70-hour transcontinental service by February 1929, and an arrangement with Southwest Air Fast Express and the New York Central Railroad trimmed the time to just under 44 hours.

The first mail contracts, due to expire in November 1929, were extended six months to allow passage of the McNary-Watres Act. Hanshue, to strengthen his bidding position on new routes that would pass through Arizona, began buying Standard stock. By May 1930 Western controlled the company and promptly extended service through El Paso to Dallas.

*Maddux Air Lines.* Los Angeles Lincoln auto dealer John L. Maddux, after a demonstration flight in 1927, bought the Ford Motor Company's first production 4-AT Tri-motor transport and set about building his own airline. In July Maddux began service between Los Angeles and San Diego and added San Francisco in April 1928, carrying over 9,000 passengers by year's end with service to other cities including Riverside, Bakersfield, and Fresno. Phoenix was added the following February, and soon Maddux was operating the nation's largest fleet of Fords, 15 in all. Some 40,000 passengers were carried in 1929, and in November Maddux sold his thriving airline to the company that was about to join forces with a most reluctant Western Air Express.

*Transcontinental Air Transport (TAT).* May 16, 1928, marks the formation of Transcontinental Air Transport, with the backing of Curtiss Aeroplane and Motor, Wright Aero Corporation, National Air Transport, the Pennsylvania Railroad, and businessmen from St. Louis and capitalized at $5 million. Significantly, TAT was the first of the major air carriers whose stated objective was the transport of passengers, not mail.

Prodigious preparation and expenditure preceded the beginning of TAT's transcontinental service on July 7, 1929, guided by a technical committee headed by Charles Lindbergh. For the company's star New York-Los Angeles route, Lindbergh decreed handsome new terminals, spent $1.5 million for ground equipment and weather-reporting facilities over a 150-mile-wide strip all along the route with expert observers, and ordered a fleet of new Ford Tri-motors. Combined air-rail 48-hour transcontinental operations began on July 7, 1929, with spectacular, star-studded publicity. For all the merit of the new route, however, in its first 18 months TAT lost $2,750,000.

*The Model Airline.* Two major goals of the Guggenheim Fund focused on airline operations, particularly assistance in development of commercial aircraft and equipment. During 1926 and 1927 Daniel Guggenheim frequently visited the fund office on Madison Avenue and demanded that something be done for America's airline passengers. Finally, his son Harry invited the nation's leading contract airmail operators, including Harris Hanshue and Walter T. Varney, to meet in New York on May 27, 1927.

Harry Guggenheim proposed that the fund subsidize equipment loans of new trimotor planes to the airmail operators as a means of promoting inauguration of passenger airline service in the U.S. The fund, he suggested, would establish one or more "thoroughly organized" passenger routes with radio communications and meteorological services approved by the Department of Commerce's Aeronautics Branch. Reaction was mixed, but largely cool. "All of the big shots of the airmail in that stage of development threw water on the idea of flying passengers," said Harry. "In fact, only Hanshue and Varney had the vision to accept our proposition."

Western's acceptance revolutionized commercial aviation worldwide. On June 16, 1927, the fund board approved a grant to the airline of $400,000 for equipment loans "to promote the inauguration of passenger lines, on certain selected routes, in the U.S." Trimotor aircraft capable of continuing flight with one engine out were stipulated. Additional performance sought by Hanshue included 120 mph speed, 6-hour endurance, 1,000 lbs cargo capacity, accommodation for 10 passengers, and a 16,000-foot service ceiling. Of the possible airplanes, Western preferred the Fokker FVII, and fund advisors including Lindbergh concurred, asking Tony Fokker to modify the plane to the committee's specifications. The result was the F-X, which airlines and pilots in practice called the F-10 Super Trimotor. Built by Fokker's Atlantic Aircraft Corporation, it featured a 12-passenger cabin and three Pratt & Whitney 425 hp Wasp radial engines.

On October 4, 1927, Western and Guggenheim Fund officers announced implementation of the Model Airline between San Francisco and Los Angeles with three airplanes daily flying the route's 365 miles in three hours. The fund loaned Western $155,000 to be repaid over two years at five-percent interest, and three of the $50,000 airplanes went into service in May 1928, with two more added later. (Western later bought 21 more Fokkers based on the F-10, called F-10A, which served until March 1931 when apprehension about their wooden wings' durability forced their retirement.) The Guggenheim loan was fully repaid within 18 months.

As part of the Model Airline plan, the Guggenheim Fund undertook sweeping improvements in weather reporting, radio communications, and dispatch procedures along the 40-mile-wide airway; key contributions were made by pioneer meteorologist Carl Gustav Rossby and radio expert Herbert Hoover, Jr. Pacific Telephone provided free telephone service between stations and terminals. The fund managed these services from June 1928 to June 1929, when the airline users and the Weather Bureau took over. From May 21, 1928, users included WAE, Pacific Air Transport, Maddux, and private and airmail pilots. The initial 22 stations were increased to 40, and daily reports from three to six. Cooperation among participating agencies set a pattern unbroken to this day. At the end of the first year, 3,000 paying passengers had flown the line, which achieved a 99-percent on-time record in perfect safety.

*The Western-TAT Merger.* As the second round of bidding on postal contracts approached in 1930, Postmaster General Walter Brown may have set about his planning with serenity, but for Harris Hanshue the year was calamitous. Shortly after his bid conferences began in May, Brown informed the carriers that his master plan for the "central airway" into Los Angeles required a merger of the two competing bidders—Western Air Express and Trans-continental Air Transport. Over Hanshue's adamant objections, what airline historian Ron Davies calls the "most important airline merger during the first quarter-century of U.S. airline history" was ordered, and a new carrier emerged, Transcontinental and Western Air, Incorporated (TWA). To create a through trans-continental route, the participation of a third carrier, Pittsburgh Aviation Industries Corpo-ration (PAIC), was required, and the TWA assets were distributed with 47.5 percent each to WAE and TAT, and 5 percent to PAIC. One million shares were authorized, and the airmail contract was awarded on August 25. TWA operated its first coast-to-coast flight from New York to Los Angeles, stopping at Kansas City, with a Ford Tri-motor on October 30, 1930, the 36-hour single-plane operation permanently retiring the old air-rail service. Hanshue served as the carrier's first president until July 1931, when R.W. Robbins of PAIC took over. The Official Airline Guides of the 1930s show the combined schedules of the participating carriers, including Maddux. Western's Arizona routes were sold off to American Airways as part of Brown's comprehensive merger scheme.

The immediate result for WAE was bleak. Hanshue had resisted the merger, and WAE had acquired a major interest in a losing operation (about $200,000 per month), which actually challenged what was left of the independent WAE, particularly the Los Angeles-San Francisco route where Maddux was now a direct competitor. Hanshue sought financial assistance from General Motors' General Aviation Corporation, which acquired a majority of the company's stock for $900,000 early in 1933. Other financial consolidation included the sale of the Catalina Island route and equipment to the Wrigley family. The company retained the Los Angeles-Salt Lake City route, but gave up Seattle to Pacific Air Transport, a United Air Lines subsidiary, in March 1931 for $250,000. As a result of Farley's token rebuke of participants (however unwilling) in Brown's conferences, from May 1934 Western operated as General Air Lines before resuming its proper name on December 29.

Western's subsequent redevelopment was slow. Between 1934 and 1939 president Alvin Adams made the most of Western's route connections with United Air Lines, coordinating schedules and operating interchange flights to increase traffic. The arrangement nearly led to merger, but the plan was quashed by the CAB. Building a healthy route network was especially arduous and was achieved largely by absorbing small but strategically placed lines and applying frequently to the CAB for expanded authority. Among important acquisitions were National Parks Airways in 1937, Inland Airways in 1944, and Alaska's Pacific Northern in 1966. In 1941 the airline changed its name to the current Western Airlines, and in 1945 it won the coveted Los Angeles-Denver route. Service was begun in April 1946 with unpressurized DC-4s (passengers were issued oxygen masks), but Western's finances were so precarious that experts predicted the worst. In 1947, under the leadership of newly appointed president Terrell Drinkwater, the airline took the heroic step of selling the route to United Air Lines in order to raise desperately needed cash. Los Angeles-San Francisco rights had been regained in August

1943 and service begun on May 1, 1944. Few routes were won without protracted battles. Mexico City service was delayed nearly 11 years after CAB approval while negotiations with the Mexican government dragged on; the airline's 10-year struggle to get to Hawaii would make an exciting video game for the truly patient. Expansion of Western's network ultimately included Mexico City, Hawaii, Minneapolis-St. Paul, much of Alaska, and even London.

By 1982, as airlines groped among the trees of the deregulation forest, Western turned again to its origins and began to shape a dynamic hub-and-spoke network built principally around its founding communities—Los Angeles and Salt Lake City—from which it serves more Western U.S. cities than any other carrier.

*Trans World Airlines.* Although TWA's affiliations with Kansas City and New York are unshakable, the airline derives no small part of its substance and its image from California. From Los Angeles, TWA would acquire legendary men and airplanes. Fifteen months after the founding of its parent TAT in New York, Transcontinental and Western Air emerged from TAT's forced merger with Los Angeles' WAE, among whose ranks were men whose leadership would virtually define the young airline: Jack Frye became president of TWA in December 1934, Paul Richter his principal vice-president.

From the Maddux staff came Daniel W. "Tommy" Tomlinson, who began as a line copilot and became chief engineer in 1936. His high-altitude research in TWA's Northrop Gamma "flying laboratory" laid the groundwork for over-weather flying techniques and spurred development of pressurized airliners.

As vice-president of operations in 1932, Frye solicited the airplane that led to the DC-3, and when he and Richter became disenchanted with their board's management, they persuaded Howard Hughes to acquire control of TWA in April 1939, taking over from New York's Lehman Brothers and installing Frye as the new president. Hughes held control until December 31, 1960, when it was ceded to a voting trust. In 1965 Hughes sold his stock in the airline for nearly $550 million.

No sooner had Hughes bought into TWA than he and Frye went shopping for a new airplane to fly the transcontinental routes. Douglas, Boeing, and Consolidated each had sound reasons for passing up the project, but Lockheed's Bob Gross saw an ideal opportunity for his company. By June 1939 Hughes and Gross had a signed agreement, and Kelly Johnson was hard at work on yet another peerless design. Under a relentless barrage of suggestions from Hughes, Frye, Tomlinson, and others, Johnson's team worked in great secrecy on Model 049. When the sleek giant, whose elegant curves and triple tail would become synonymous with the postwar success of both Lockheed and TWA, rolled into the sunshine in December 1942, the legend of the Constellation was born.

For the first "Connie" flight on January 9, 1943, the left-hand seat was occupied by Boeing's Eddie Allen, at the time the world's most experienced four-engine airplane pilot, and in the right-hand seat was Lockheed's chief test pilot, Milo Burcham. The airplane flew in Army olive drab and with the military designation C-69. On April 16, 1944, Frye and Hughes delivered one airplane (for this flight painted in TWA colors) to the Army on a record-setting nonstop flight from Burbank to Washington's National Airport in six hours and 58 minutes. When TWA's last Connie was retired on April 6, 1967, the airline had flown 147 of them in eight different models.

By 1947 massive financing was needed for the airline's new fleet, and Hughes turned to his Hughes Tool Company and its financial leader Noah Dietrich to arrange $10 million in debentures. Dietrich's growing dissatisfaction with Frye's fiscal management ultimately led to the board's seeking Frye's resignation. LaMotte Cohu was named president, the first of several who would work in frequently strained conditions under Hughes until 1960. In 1950, in recognition of its new transatlantic authority, the company's name was changed to Trans World Airlines, a suggestion first made by Hughes himself in 1945. California has been a primary market for TWA from its very first flight, Los Angeles and San Francisco serving as principal originating cities for domestic and international routes.

*United Air Lines.* United's ties to California derive first from Pacific Air Transport, begun on September 15, 1926, by Vern C. Gorst, of North Bend, Oregon, whose initial transport enterprise was a profitable bus line. Gorst's successful operation over a route connecting Seattle and Los Angeles via San Francisco (CAM 14) began with meticulous survey and proving flights made by Claude Ryan himself and thrived with a fleet of Ryan M-1s. Gorst's line was acquired by Boeing Air Transport in 1928. Boeing, in turn, had its genesis in the partnership of William Boeing and Eddie Hubbard who had made survey flights between Vancouver and Seattle in March 1919, which led to a regular mail service between Victoria and Seattle the next year.

In 1929 Boeing joined with Pratt & Whitney to create United Aircraft and Transport Corporation, which in turn accumulated additional companies including Hamilton Propeller, Stearman Aircraft, and Sikorsky Aviation. Boeing won the Chicago-San Francisco mail route (CAM 18), the first commercial trans-continental route, flying the 1,900 miles on a 40-hour schedule using chief Boeing designer Claire Egtvedt's speedy and reliable B-40A. In June 1930, United acquired Walter Varney's Salt Lake City-Seattle operation for $2 million and in May 1930 culminating a long and complex battle, United Aircraft succeeded in buying out its principal competitor east of Chicago, National Air Transport. These transactions were all consolidated on July 1, 1931, in "the world's largest air transport system," United Air Lines.

In a footnote to the grander airline picture, both Gorst and Varney at one time had financial interests in Air Ferries, a briskly successful little operation that flourished from February 1930 until the Bay Bridge was completed in 1936. The diminutive airline used two Keystone-Loening Amphibians for the six-minute flight from San Francisco to Oakland, with a two-minute turnaround. Sixty thousand riders made the hops in 1930 alone.

United wielded enormous influence from the very first on trunk operations into California from all across the nation and became one of the two initially dominant airlines in the Pacifc Coast-Hawaii market (Pan Am was the first), partly as a result of its World War II contract work for the Air Transport Command. From September 1942, United operated C-54s over the 7,350-mile route across the Pacific from San Francisco to Brisbane, Australia, via Honolulu, Canton Island, and Fiji.

United's role in the intrastate California market dates from inauguration of its "Pacific Coast Airway" in 1926 when PAT began flights between San Diego and San Francisco via Los Angeles. On April 10, 1940, United made the industry's first serious attempt at low fares with its Sky Coach service between Los Angeles and San Francisco (with stops) using Boeing 247s and a fare of $13.90, a service discontinued in April 1942. United responded to California Central and PSA in May 1950 and resumed coach service with DC-4s and a fare of $9.95, and it remains the trunk airline most strongly identified with the busy corridor.

*Continental Air Lines.* Continental Airlines, which made its headquarters in Los Angeles from 1963 until 1983, enjoys a convoluted claim to California lineage through its own Varney origins. After selling his Salt Lake-Washington State operation to Boeing, Varney stayed active in both the Rockies and California. In 1932 Varney Air Service Limited was operating Lockheed Orions between San Francisco and Los Angeles, and soon became known as Varney Speed Lanes Air Service. Later that year, Varney negotiated with the Mexican government for a mail contract between Los Angeles and Mexico City. The coastal service was discontinued, and the Orions began flying to Mexico. Called Varney Speed Lanes System or Lineas Aereas Occidentales (presumably depending on which city was doing the calling), the operation lasted only nine months before the Mexicans abruptly terminated the mail contract.

Varney headed east to start up the Southwest Division of Varney Speed Lanes between Pueblo, Colorado, and El Paso, Texas. Adding Denver on

July 15, 1934, via Santa Fe and Albuquerque, the company was reorganized in December as Varney Transport Inc. In this form the outfit was acquired by Robert Six. Following the acquisition of Wyoming Air Service and the route from Denver to Pueblo in 1937, the tiny airline acquired a new home—Denver, and a new name—Continental Airlines. Under Six's energetic and unorthodox leadership, Continental earned a reputation as a scrappy and innovative competitor. Among the carrier's notable accomplishments were the introduction of progressive maintenance, which permitted efficient utilization of jet aircraft, pioneering air service in the central Pacific, and consistent profitability for many years.

In October 1982, following a bitter struggle for ownership of the airline, Frank Lorenzo's Texas Air Corporation bought Continental and moved its headquarters from Los Angeles to Houston (although 4,000 employees and such key departments as training and maintenance remained on the West Coast). Implementing a controversial plan to stem immense financial losses and regain a competitive position, Continental's owners filed for protection under the federal bankruptcy laws and repudiated costly union labor contracts.

*Hughes Airwest.* In April 1968 the CAB authorized the merger of three regional airlines into a single operation, which would affect air service throughout the Far West. The component companies were West Coast Airlines of Seattle, Pacific Airlines of San Francisco, and Bonanza Airlines of Las Vegas. The new entity was Air West, which would enjoy a brief and hectic moment in history before becoming Howard Hughes' last airline property.

Nick Bez, Air West's chairman of the board, began his airline career when he first applied to the CAB for an operating certificate in 1940, incorporating West Coast Airlines in Seattle on March 14, 1941. The board suspended applications in December, and Bez' three-year certificate waited until May 1946, with service between Seattle and Portland starting on December 4. In 1952 the CAB approved a merger of West Coast with Empire Airlines, of Boise,

Idaho, which had begun in September 1946. Empire, in turn, had merged with Zimmerly Air Transport, which had begun intrastate service between Lewiston and Boise in 1944. West Coast expanded to Oakland, and San Francisco, via Sacramento, in 1959. The world's first operator of the Fairchild F-27, West Coast was also the first permanently certificated Local Service Carrier.

Pacific Airlines (the name was adopted in March 1958), founded by John H. Connelly as Southwest Airways in 1941 with headquarters in Los Angeles, won its Local Service Airline certificate on May 22, 1946, and initiated service to San Francisco and Medford, Oregon, with DC-3s in December. The line earned some repute for its three-minute, one-engine-running station stops. Martin 2-0-2s joined the fleet in late 1952, pressurized 4-0-4s in 1959. Fairchild F-27s were added in 1958 and Boeing 727s in 1966. G. Robert Henry, who would serve as Air West's president, became president of Pacific in July 1967. In its prime, Pacific served more California cities than any other carrier.

Bonanza Air Lines has roots in Arizona and Nevada, having been founded as a flight school and charter service by Edmund Converse at Phoenix's Sky Haven Airport in December 1945, and moving to Las Vegas' Alamo Airport in April 1946, then to nearby Nellis Air Force Base where hangar space was rented from the Air Force. Bonanza's Local Service Certificate was awarded in June 1949, and flights began, first with DC-3s, between Reno, Las Vegas, and Phoenix. Ontario, California, and Los Angeles were subsequently added, and Fairchild F27s arrived in 1959.

Each carrier brought a strong tradition of independence to the merger, and Air West problems soon became the talk of the industry and the bane of passengers. Says Francis T. Fox, then Howard Hughes' director of aviation and responsible for assessing the airline for possible acquisition by Hughes, "It was not a merger, it was a collision." With three structures resisting consolidation, technology conspired to make matters worse when a computer installed to integrate reservations tasks failed for days at a

time. One vice-president was quoted as saying, "We actually had our people running out to meet a flight and asking . . . where are you from?"

In spite of the problems, Hughes' people found the company very much worth acquiring, with good routes and modern equipment. Discreet preliminary overtures on Hughes' behalf were made to Bez (both board chairman and principal stockholder) by Robert Maheu and Fox, leading to an offer of $22 per share for Air West stock. President G. Robert Henry expressed surprise at the offer and led stockholder opposition to the move. Efforts were made to secure alternative buyers, including Pacific Southwest Airlines' J. Floyd Andrews, who declined, saying, "It would take four years to bring [it] up to par." On December 27, 1968, at a special stockholders meeting, 73 percent of votes cast approved the Hughes bid.

Part of Hughes' purpose in acquiring Air West related to his grand plans for Las Vegas. Statements by Hughes himself and recollections of his staff describe plans for a world-class jetport to accommodate supersonic jets and act as a major hub for air travel throughout the Southwest region. The airline would play a major support role in such a scheme, and acquisition of additional carriers such as Los Angeles and San Francisco helicopter airlines was contemplated.

As with so many Hughes projects, the Air West deal was not without drama. On the day the tender offer was to expire, Fox was called in Los Angeles and asked to fly to Seattle immediately because an approaching storm threatened to prevent Hughes lawyer Chester Davis and Maheu from landing in Seattle. Fox's United plane was the last to land before driving snow closed the field. When the record-breaking snowfall abated in the early evening, Fox volunteered to supervise the plowing (he'd cleared plenty of snow while working as airport manager in Worcester, Massachusetts) for Airport Manager Don Shay, who'd had no experience with deeply drifted runways. Directing a gang of plows hastily commandeered from the city, California-clad Fox shivered through the exercise to complete the job in time to permit the Hughes corporate jet to land and the trio to rush to Bez' home in time for the signing at only 20 minutes before midnight. Bez, then 73 and terminally ill, was a confirmed admirer of the Hughes legend and asked Maheu if Hughes might be reached by phone. Maheu did get through to Hughes, who talked with a pleased Bez for nearly an hour.

After the CAB approved the purchase in mid-1969, management set about putting things right with fierce determination, and real improvement was swiftly apparent, especially on the balance sheet. From a 1969 loss of almost $21 million, by 1972 Hughes Airwest (the name was formally adopted in April 1970) showed a net profit of almost $2 million, a trend that continued for six years. Headquarters were located in San Mateo, midway between San Jose and San Francisco, and in 1980 the fleet included 41 DC-9s and six Boeing 727-200s. In October 1980 Republic Airlines of Minneapolis acquired the assets of Hughes Airwest for $38.5 million in cash and convertible debentures.

*American Airlines.* The final trunk airline of early significance on the Pacific Coast is American Airways, formed in January 1930 from an imposing array of 85 smaller companies, many of which had become subsidiaries of American's parent Aviation Corporation (AVCO). Of special note is Century Pacific Lines, which dated from July 3, 1931, and was the creation of Auburn Motor Company owner Errett Lobban Cord. Cord offered frequent service between San Francisco and Los Angeles via Oakland, Fresno, and Bakersfield, with a San Diego-Phoenix spur. Fares were below those charged by the railroads, and Cord carried 55,000 passengers during the few months he operated. Unable to secure a mail contract (Walter Brown was at least impartial in his exclusion of small operators), Cord offered his lines to AVCO for 140,000 shares of American Airways stock and enjoyed control of the big company for some time after April 1932. American Airlines, as one of the nation's largest carriers, continues extensive services to and from California, and its recent massive order for

McDonnell Douglas MD-80s verified the powerful connections between airlines and California airframe builders.

## THE ROUTES BEYOND
*Pan American.* A strong pretender to first place in sustained and compelling drama among all the world's airlines, the story of Juan Trippe's Pan American World Airways briefly but brilliantly illuminated California shores beginning in 1933. Pan Am had built its formidable foundations as America's "chosen instrument" in the Caribbean and Latin America from 1927 and only six years later was contemplating conquest of both the Atlantic and Pacific oceans. That such audacity was suddenly attainable was due in large part to the mushrooming technologies of aircraft manufacture, navigation, communications, and meteorology—all of which had been significantly advanced by an unprecedentedly able team of scientists and engineers assembled and inspired under Juan Terry Trippe's ambitious leadership.

Pan Am's first visible Pacific effort was the survey flight of a great circle route from New York to China undertaken by Charles and Anne Morrow Lindbergh with a modified Lockheed Sirius in July 1931. The route proved impractical, in part because the Russians refused to allow the needed overflights. Next came action to secure an Eastern terminus for the route across the Pacific, and shrewd planning managed this objective while simultaneously blocking German incursions in the Far East and delaying Japanese advances.

China's extant treaties required equal treatment of all nations, meaning that any concessions Pan Am might win directly would be available to foreign airlines; so Trippe sought access at a port already controlled by a foreign nation, the British crown colony of Hong Kong. On March 3, 1933, Trippe contracted with the Chinese Nationalist government for a 45-percent interest in China National Aviation Corporation (CNAC), which had been founded in 1929 by the Curtiss-Wright Corporation but had remained unprofitable. CNAC began operations along the China Coast on October 23, 1933. The next requirement was a suitable airplane: by late 1934 a plan emerged, and on March 23, 1935, a Sikorsky S-42 flying boat outfitted for extreme long range and tested in the Caribbean was ferried to the newly formed Pacific Division's Headquarters at Alameda in San Francisco Bay.

Establishing a string of stepping-stone bases was greatly facilitated by the United States Navy which, already concerned about Japanese intentions for the Pacific Basin, welcomed the opportunity to acquire both ready-made bases and operational knowledge about the Pacific region. Permits were swiftly arranged for Midway, Wake, and Guam, and on March 27, 1935, the steamer *North Haven* sailed from San Francisco with men and material to establish preliminary facilities where there were, literally, only desert islands, in an amazing 55 days. The Japanese press wasted no time in loudly protesting the preparations as a clear military threat to Japan.

During October and November 1935, Pan Am took delivery of the Martin Company's new M-130 flying boats, the first of three being the famed *China Clipper*. Following several proving flights, on November 22, 1935, at 3:45 p.m., *China Clipper* set out on her six-day, island-hopping voyage to Manila. Every detail of its inauguration emphasized the historical significance. The pre-departure ceremonies included elaborate radio links to the Pacific stations and nationwide network broadcast. Across the nation and the ocean listeners heard Trippe's voice intone: "Captain Musick you have your sailing orders. Cast off and depart for Manila in accordance therewith." The Martin was weightier even than the prose, and most observers thought it part of the schedule when the Clipper lifted slowly into the air after a long takeoff run and flew beneath the Oakland Bay Bridge, then under construction. Actually, Musick was unable to gain sufficient altitude in time to fly over the obstacle. Soon the schedule had become almost routine, although the 130s could carry only relatively small payloads, but setbacks were encountered with two fatal accidents in 1938. First the Sikorsky S-42, *Hong Kong Clipper*, exploded during fuel dumping on

approach to Pago Pago; and then *Hawaii Clipper* disappeared westbound between Guam and Manila. The Pago Pago crash was an especially cruel blow, claiming the life of Captain Edwin Musick, the airline's world-famous pioneer pilot much beloved by his colleagues.

In 1937 Auckland, New Zealand, had been added to the network, and in January 1939 the first of Boeing's wondrous B-314 flying boats—the ultimate refinement of the seaplane—came on line at a unit cost of $550,000 to $696,000. On August 10, 1941, the first regular local service between the mainland and Hawaii was inaugurated by the 314s, but destiny abruptly shattered Pan Am's transpacific odyssey on a December dawn. During the Japanese attack at Wake, nine airline employees were killed outright and 81 captured. Staff and crew at the other stations all endured dramatic encounters or escapes, none more impressive than that of the crew of the *Pacific Clipper* caught between New Caledonia and New Zealand when notified of the Japanese onslaught. Proceeding to Auckland in radio silence, Captain Robert Ford and his crew of 10 decided to bring their urgently needed Boeing home the long way 'round. When the weary pilot set his ice-laden Clipper gently onto the gray waters of New York's Flushing Bay just after dawn on January 6, 1942, it became the the first commercial aircraft to circumnavigate the globe, after a journey of 31,500 miles.

Pan American's presence in California remains commanding, the airline's globe-spanning flights regularly departing from Los Angeles and San Francisco with only a little less drama than the halcyon days of the 1930s.

UNIQUELY CALIFORNIA
*The Intrastate Phenomenon.* Frequently an idea whose time has come appears deceptively simple. Success often masks the complex ordering of events upon which it is built, and the frequent and speedy flights among California's major cities that millions of passengers take for granted is a telling case in point.

Before 1938 airlines in California effected market entry and exit (small and unsophisticated though the market was) with practical freedom from government regulation of procedure, equipment, routes, and fares. Each operation contributed to the industry's experience pool. New airliners, particularly the DC-3, brought economic viability within reach of competent airline management and attracted a growing public.

For the duration of World War II the process was arrested, and in 1946 radically changed circumstances prevailed. Surplus transport planes were easy to acquire, public awareness of air travel had increased by an order of magnitude, and uncounted flyers returned to civilian life eager to make their fortunes in aviation. Richard Thruelson, chronicler of Transocean Airlines, estimated that some "2,000 groups of ex-war pilots tried to form their own aerial transport enterprises of one kind or another during the immediate postwar period." New airline ventures sprang up nationwide, with a high proportion clustered around Oakland, Burbank, Long Beach, Ontario, and San Diego. Many took off, most landed abruptly, some rode high for a short time, but a very few lasted long enough to enjoy measurable success.

Brevity was the general rule, and California's first postwar intrastate airline set the too-frequent course. Pacific Air Lines began bravely in April 1946 with DC-3 flights from Burbank to Sacramento, adding San Francisco, Fresno, Modesto, and Stockton before the year was out: by June 3, 1947, the flying was over and the bankruptcy files closed in December.

*Pacific Southwest Airlines.* John Newhouse understated the perils confronting airline managers when he wrote: "Running an airline . . . is formidably difficult." In the fierce postwar competition, the road to success was an almost oblique easing into the airline business from some related aero endeavor not quite so unforgiving. At least that is how California's one unequivocal intrastate airline success story began when Kenneth G. (Ken) Friedkin and Joe Plosser, Jr., set up their modest flying school and fixed base operation at San Diego's Lindbergh Field in 1945. Offering flight instruction and instrument training leading to objectives from

the basic licenses to Flight Instructor and Air Transport Pilot ratings, the school thrived on a student body largely financed by GI Bill education benefits. The student roster sometimes included as many as 200 students, and the actual flight equipment consisted of one PT-19 which Friedkin rebuilt himself.

Progress was steady if unspectacular, and the partners incorporated in 1948 as Friedkin Aeronautics even as the training boom began to wane and they "searched for alternatives" to keep the operation going. The idea of an airline began to take shape in occasional flight operations into the Imperial Valley somewhat grandly called "Friedkin Airlines," and flight instructor J. Floyd Andrews soon became a frequent advocate of starting a scheduled operation in earnest.

On May 6, 1949, the airline idea became a reality when the company leased a 31-seat DC-3 and inaugurated weekend service between San Diego and Oakland via Burbank for fares ranging up to $15.60 for the longest stage. By year's end Friedkin Aeronautics, doing business as Pacific Southwest Airlines, with 50 employees on the payroll, had leased a second DC-3, carried 15,011 paying passengers, and banked a small but encouraging net profit of almost $12,000.

With fares well below those offered by competing certificated airlines and strong community support, particularly among San Diego's military population (PSA locally was frequently taken to mean "Poor Sailors' Airline"), the company behaved like a family concern, its employees genuinely believing they were running an "airline for the people." PSA not only pleased its customers, but moved the competition, certificated and otherwise. William Jordan, a prominent commentator on air carrier regulation, says, "Without question, the certificated carriers' inauguration of coach service was in response to the services and fares introduced by the California intrastate carriers in 1949."

By 1952 the fleet included four DC-3s, and in November 1955 Friedkin turned to Capital Airlines to purchase two 70-seat DC-4s. Two more DC-4s were added, one each in 1956 and

1957. Passenger boardings continued to climb, reaching 295,818 in 1958, justifying a giant step with the lease of three Lockheed propjet Electras in November 1959. Passing through San Diego one afternoon shortly after PSA introduced its Lockheeds, Eastern Airlines president Eddie Rickenbacker spied Ken Friedkin about to board one of the new Electras and shouted across the ramp, "It's a money-making S.O.B.!"

Success followed success, from popular "grocery receipt style" tickets to flight hostesses famed throughout the industry for brisk competence and remarkably good looks enhanced by trendy uniforms. Inevitably the airline acquired more of the trappings of corporate success, "going public" in 1963 and beginning a program of diversification in 1967 that included car rentals, hotels, fuel exploration, and radio broadcasting. PSA has long provided crew training for other airlines, and its training facility is a substantial revenue producer. Some indication of the carrier's stature lay in its consideration of several merger possibilities, with PSA in every instance viewing itself as the surviving carrier. In 1968 the company bid on then-ailing Western Airlines with an offer of $261 million; the brief flirtation with Air West took place in the same year. In 1970 and again in 1973, PSA and Air California explored merger, with PSA withdrawing only in the face of antitrust action by the Justice Department; and in 1982 PSA came very close to adding a 16-city division based upon acquiring assets of the defunct Braniff Airways.

The airline's routes suggest the strength of the intrastate market. From 1949 to 1965, its period of establishment and greatest growth, PSA's operations averaged four airports and a route system of 1,086 miles. PSA in 1972 served 11 airports and 25 city pairs, and in 1973 system route mileage grew to 9,760 miles. After Friedkin's death in 1962, Andrews assumed the presidency and earned high marks throughout the industry for his astute leadership. PSA's fleet selection has taken full advantage of available technology for its homogeneous routes, moving from Electras to Boeing 727s in 1965 (two Lockheed TriStars joined the fleet for a few

months in 1974-1975, but recession and fuel quotas soon proved the wide-body unsuitable even for the Los Angeles-San Francisco corridor), and from the Boeings to the ultra-quiet and fuel-efficient MD-80s in 1980 (PSA was the nation's first operator of the type). Late in 1983 the carrier announced an order for 20 100-passenger British Aerospace BAe 146 four-engine jet transports to improve service on lower-density route segments. Under the leadership of William Shimp (who became chief executive officer when Andrews retired in 1976) and president Paul C. Barkley, PSA has adroitly entered the 1980s and explored diverse options for expansion while maintaining its basic strengths.

Deregulation has posed monumental problems for the airline industry, but Pacific Southwest Airlines seems mightily unruffled, perhaps because the scrappy outfit has been the model of how to succeed under deregulation for 35 years already.

*Colonel Charles and Edna Sherman.* PSA's story continues in a handsome headquarters building at Lindbergh Field, in glossy annual reports, aboard a gleaming jet winging up the coast. But the tale of its primary competitor during those zesty years from 1949 to 1955 is found in two dusty cartons in the Federal Archives Building marked simply 59560 & 61-PH—the 1954-1955 bankruptcy proceeding records for California Central Airlines and Airline Transport Carriers. But there amongst the lawyers' lists and creditors' demands is irrefutable evidence of the spirited determination of a husband and wife whose airlines must be judged by history, not by a bankruptcy referee.

Colonel Charles Sherman came home to Southern California in 1945 after an action-filled wartime career with the Air Transport Command in the Pacific, in Alaska, in Latin America, and on the famed Fireball Run, which supplied Allied troops in North Africa. His peacetime career was hardly less dramatic, and Sherman and his wife, Edna, orchestrated at least two historic airline ventures. One began with their incorporation of two companies: Air Transport Carriers in 1946 as a Large Irregular

Carrier, which began flying between Oakland and Burbank on schedules sufficiently regular to be curbed by the CAB; and California Central Airlines, organized in 1947 as an intrastate carrier to take over ATC's board-offending services. CCA duly petitioned the PUC and on January 2, 1949, resumed DC-3 flights for $9.99. Traditionalists could still make the trip with Western or United for $21.05, and long months would pass before the certificated carriers took the CCA and PSA gauntlet for the timely challenge that it was.

The Shermans found the DC-3s unable to cope with the flood of reservations. In 1949 eighty-three thousand passengers were boarded; in 1950, ninety-three thousand (compare PSA's first full year figures of 45,390); 1951, one hundred forty-five thousand (PSA, 75,995); 1952, one hundred ninety thousand (PSA, 92,484); 1953, one hundred forty-eight thousand (PSA, 115,028); 1954 (through November 18) one hundred forty-three thousand. In August 1951 the Shermans acquired five speedy Martin 2-0-2s (from Northwest Airlines) to serve Los Angeles, San Francisco, Oakland, and San Diego from their Burbank headquarters. Over the next seven months traffic grew by 43 percent. But a harsh truth was accumulating almost as fast as the passenger figures: CCA's fares were simply not high enough to cover expenses. By the summer of 1953, late tax payments and mounting debts clouded the future, and the Shermans reorganized CCA as a Nevada corporation and tried to postpone the inevitable. But that was not to be: on December 3, 1954, they sought the protection of a Chapter 11 bankruptcy filing.

Allowed to continue operating under the court's supervision as "debtor in possession" while they reorganized, the Shermans and their team struggled to put the company in the black. They applied for a route to Tijuana; they set up the state's first "fly now, pay later" ticketing scheme; they sought fresh capital; they pledged their stocks and personal assets, all to no avail. In January 1955 the Martins were sold to Southwest (soon to become Pacific) and Allegheny Airlines, and the Shermans

themselves bought the meager remaining assets to organize yet another carrier, California Coastal Airlines, which limped along from March 1955 until August 1957 (with DC-3s over a reduced route system) when it too folded its wings.

Sherman had also entered the national low-fare stakes with fellow entrepreneurs at North American Airlines. That race would end not in red ink but red tape when the certificated carriers effectively strangled NAA in the hearing room and the courtroom.

In California, Western Airlines rose to the CCA and PSA challenge on August 19, 1949, when the CAB refused to let the trunks match the upstarts' low prices. Western formed an intrastate subsidiary, Western Airlines of California, to which it then leased equipment for the operation of California flights at reduced rates. As soon as the CAB moved to allow comparable fares, Western dissolved the subsidiary on May 31, 1950.

*Air California.* The other intrastate carrier to stay the course, Air California, arrived in December 1965, the brainchild of Orange County businessmen who believed the mushrooming business communities in their area ought to have improved air service from their own airport. J. Kenneth Hull, former Lockheed Aircraft International president, was chosen as the first president. The PUC granted an operating certificate in September 1966, and service from Orange County Airport to San Francisco began in January 1967 with two used Electras. The PUC refused PSA's application for parallel service, setting a policy of balancing available markets among rival carriers, which it long pursued, much in the pattern of the pre-1977 CAB. The old investor's saw that "timing is everything" took on special meaning for Air California: in its first year 300,000 passengers were boarded; in 1968 the figures more than doubled to 650,000—traffic that sorely pressed the fleet now grown to four Electras and two DC-9s.

Equipment leasing provided at least a temporary solution, and six Boeing 737s replaced the first fleet before 1968 was out. The

Westgate Corporation purchased controlling interest in the airline in 1970, and full ownership in 1977. Following deregulation, which freed the airline to expand outside the state, early in 1981 two partners formed AirCal Investments and outbid Air Florida System to buy the carrier; and on April 6, 1981, the name AirCal was adopted. Headquartered in Newport Beach, AirCal by 1983 operated seven MD-80s and 15 Boeing 737s: 1981 passenger boardings were 3.5 million over a route system embracing 15 cities in California, Nevada, Arizona, Oregon, and Washington.

*Holiday Airlines Corporation.* Occasionally a small operator entered the marketplace, usually with predictable results. One example is Holiday Airlines, which began in Oakland in June 1956 and later moved its headquarters to Los Angeles. Starting out with DeHavilland Doves, Holiday eventually acquired two secondhand Lockheed L-188 Electras and operated services between Oakland, San Jose, San Diego, Burbank, Lake Tahoe, and later Los Angeles. A third Electra was added in mid-1974, but by November the under-capitalized little line collapsed, and by the following May the airplanes had gone to the creditors.

THE SUPPLEMENTALS

*North American Airlines.* The CAB's long struggle with the issue of the Supplemental Carriers was vividly illustrated by California-born North American Airlines, which began in November 1945 as Fireball Air Express (Charles Sherman's African experience must have been fresh in his mind as he met with his cohorts, including Stan Weiss). The company first operated DC-3s from Long Beach to New York, via Kansas City and Chicago. In 1946 a more decorous "Standard Air Lines" was affixed to the newly awarded CAB Large Irregular Carrier certificate.

Across town at Burbank, Ross Hart and Jack Lewin had started Viking Air Lines, and in January 1950 the promoters of the two carriers formed North American Airlines Agency with several other Large Irregulars—Twentieth Century, Trans-National, Trans-American, and Hemisphere Air Transport. With their combined

fleet of 14 DC-3s, they began a coordinated schedule of transcontinental flights via Albuquerque, one way for $99, $160 round trip.

A 1948 CAB decision set a limit of eight to twelve flights per month for any single Large Irregular Carrier. By combining their point-to-point authorities, the North American Airlines group established regular, frequent service within the letter of law, much to the obvious consternation of their certificated brethren and the CAB. Flights routinely operated 85-percent filled, and big DC-4s were added in 1951. By 1954 they had acquired a brand-new DC-6B and had carried 194,000 passengers over 329 million passenger miles. By May 1955 the group's nonstop transcontinental fare was $88, but by now the opposition was on the march in Washington, D.C.; in July a CAB order revoked the airlines' certificates.

During 1955 two hundred seventy-two thousand passengers were carried, and the group made $1 million profit on revenues of $15 million. But continued legal challenges, culminating in an adverse U.S. Supreme Court ruling, finally sank the upstart, and in 1957 the seven DC-6Bs were leased to Eastern. But Weiss, Sherman, and their colleagues had forced the certificated operators to recognize the merit of low fares 30 years before pricing would become the airline manager's primary marketing weapon.

*Flying Tiger Line.* Of the uncounted attempts to establish all-cargo airlines in California during 1945 and 1946, only one would survive to see 1984. That hardy carrier is the Flying Tiger Line headquartered at Los Angeles International Airport, which began as National Skyway Freight Corporation on June 25, 1945. The work of Robert Prescott and 11 pilots and fellow members of General Claire Chennault's famed volunteer Flying Tigers aviators, and Sam Mosher of Signal Oil Company, the carrier was in the vanguard of every battle to be fought by an often-beleaguered air cargo industry. The line's first airplanes were 14 all-steel Budd Conestogas picked up for a bargain, but they were soon replaced by more practical C-47s, C-54s, and C-46s, some 22 of which were on the line by 1950.

Concerned about losing an entire class of revenue generation, the trunk lines resisted every move of the would-be cargo outfits, and the freight carriers soon found themselves shut out of the vital mail and air express markets. Unrestrained rate-cutting among themselves made even full airplanes losing propositions. Most operators simply threw in the towel by the end of a particularly vicious rate war in April 1948.

For Prescott and his crew, the first glint of success came in 1946 as an Air Transport Command Pacific contract to be flown with surplus C-54s. The award of the contract allowed the company to move from Long Beach to facilities at Burbank, and in February 1947 the Flying Tiger name was adopted. With 28 contract flights per week over the Pacific, the Tigers soon had sufficient funds in the bank to feel some stability.

The company was awarded the nation's first all-cargo route certification on April 25, 1949, and by 1950 the Tigers had expanded the route network to 22 stations. Continued route expansion, growing marketing sophistication, and continued military charter contracts all contributed to the company's growth. In 1957 Prescott bought 15 Lockheed Super H Constellation freighters for $20 million; Canadair Swingtail CL-44s in the early 1960s; Boeing 707s by 1965; and the industry's first stretched DC-8-63Fs in 1968. In 1973 Boeing 747-100 converted freighters joined the fleet. Flying Tiger assumed dominance in the cargo markets across both the Atlantic and the Pacific oceans with its merger acquisition of New York-based Seaboard World Airlines in 1980.

*World Airways.* Among successful postwar operators was Edward J. Daly, who bought a struggling non-sked in 1950 for $50,000 and turned two leased C-46s into an aggressive supplemental airline more often than not leading its branch of the industry into battle with the certificated establishment. The outfit the 27-year-old Daly acquired had been incorporated in March 1948 and was ambitiously called World Airways. Before Daly finally managed to stabilize its fortunes, he once

had to sell all his airplanes to keep World ahead of the creditors. Military charter work kept the airline in business, and the turn came in 1956 when he picked up a bargain C-54—a burned-out hulk in an RAF hangar at London. After 90 days of restoration, the airplane became the nucleus of a fleet providing global service.

The airline's move from New Jersey to its present Oakland headquarters was made in 1957 as part of a massive Pacific contract with the military. Douglas DC-6s and Lockheed Connies joined the fleet, and Daly continued to press the CAB for expanded authority to conduct passenger charters. The board's eventual liberalization of its charter rules to allow the Supplementals into the market was doubtless accelerated by World's endless briefs to Washington. In 1962 World became the first buyer for Boeing's long-range 707-320Cs and the first Supplemental airline to order jet transports. The company became a public corporation in April 1966 and in 1973 opened a seven-acre hangar and office facility in Oakland; World took delivery of its first 747 on the same day. When Daly relinquished day-to-day control of World in 1982 because of declining health, World faced serious financial problems, partly because of the very deregulation for which he had fought so hard. Daly died at his home near San Francisco in January 1984.

*Transamerica Airlines.* Just another in a long list of hopeful shoestrings when he began it in 1947 as Los Angeles Air Service with a lone DC-3, Kirk Kerkorian's first airline venture continues today as a highly profitable division of a multi-billion-dollar global conglomerate, the Transamerica Corporation. The airline incorporated late in 1948, earned its CAB certificate on July 8, 1949, and settled down to worldwide military and civil contract and charter work. The name was changed in July 1960 to Trans-International to avoid confusion with L.A. Airways. As TIA, the airline became the first Supplemental jet operator with the DC-8-51 on June 22, 1962. In October Kerkorian sold the operation to the Studebaker Corporation, only to buy it back two years later at a substantial profit as the fiscally ailing auto builder sought to raise cash. The company was made a public corporation in June 1967 and acquired by Transamerica on February 23, 1968.

The next major step was expansion into the cargo realm with the acquisition in 1976 of Saturn Airways Incorporated of Oakland, which had in turn been founded in Miami as All American Airways Incorporated and had absorbed AAXICO (American Air Export & Import Company) in 1965. The Saturn addition overnight made the carrier one of the world's largest specialty cargo operators. The current name, Transamerica Airlines, was adopted in 1979.

*Transocean.* United Air Lines' World War II work for the ATC in the Pacific provided a taste of foreign romance and a great deal of long-haul experience to the carrier's pilots, as well as time to dream. One pilot who turned his cockpit musings into an airline of his own, Transocean, was Orvis M. Nelson. With a big loan and a modest subcontract from United to fly military cargo between San Francisco and Honolulu with DC-4s in 1946, Nelson was in business. For the next 14 years, his outfit roamed the globe with extensive charters of every kind, from race horses to Mecca-bound pilgrims. Transocean's Stratocruisers even saw duty in the non-sked wars of the late 1950s, but as with many other doughty Supplementals, the competition proved too severe. In 1960 Transocean was merged with United States Overseas, which itself expired in November 1964.

*Helicopter Carriers.* Los Angeles Airways, incorporated on May 11, 1944, contributed to U.S. aviation out of all proportion to its small size. Innovative and persistent under the courageous leadership of Clarence Belinn, the little helicopter airline defied convention from the first and began with more complex problems than many airlines face during their entire lifetimes.

To begin with, the machines themselves posed inherent problems. They were expensive to maintain, and they were slow, small, and noisy. There were few pilots and virtually no available data on such critical matters as suitable weather minima and operating altitude for the aircraft,

and commercial data was nonexistent. But Belinn filed his application with the CAB in 1944 and set about gathering all the information and support he could. Experimental flights with Sikorsky S-51s were conducted over the basin from April 1947, and on May 22 the board awarded a three-year certificate for local mail service. LAA began the world's first regularly scheduled helicopter mail service on October 1, 1947, over a network branching out from Los Angeles International Airport to the Post Office Terminal Annex Building downtown and to the San Fernando Valley, San Bernardino, and Newport Beach.

In July 1951 the CAB extended the certificate and added authorization for passenger service. Large S-55s were added in October 1950, and the route now covered 356 miles. In LAA's first year 209,325 lbs of mail were flown; in 1954 the total was 6,126,440 lbs. Encouraged by Belinn's results in Los Angeles, similar services were inaugurated in Chicago and New York. LAA put the big gas turbine-powered S-62 into service in December 1960. The amphibious S-62 was so well-suited to overwater service that it was the first aircraft chosen by San Francisco & Oakland Helicopter Airlines, which was founded in January 1961. In another milestone, LAA began the world's first multi-engined, turbine-powered helicopter service on March 2, 1962, with the Sikorsky S-61L. This machine, called by Peter Brooks the "first practical transport helicopter," could carry up to 28 passengers at 135 mph.

The economics of helicopter transports, however, are brutal, particularly because of their comparatively low utilization and high maintenance costs, which balance poorly against relatively low revenue yields. LAA's survival was possible in large part through substantial federal subsidy. An alternate proposal came from the CAB in 1965 when it terminated helicopter subsidies: allow United and American, which benefited from the feeder functions the helicopter line provided, to acquire control of Los Angeles Airways through a $3.2-million loan agreement. Late in the 1960s Howard Hughes considered buying LAA as part of his comprehensive plans for aviation throughout the Western states, but the plan was shelved amidst complex litigation. In 1971 the pioneer operation was purchased by Golden West, a commuter operator that would enjoy some success itself, but not with helicopters. Not until Jack Gallagher organized Airspur early in 1981 and began service with Westland helicopters in May 1983 did scheduled rotary-wing passenger service return to Los Angeles.

San Francisco & Oakland Helicopter Airlines was founded on January 6, 1961, and had two S-62s leased from Sikorsky in service over the Bay by June. By December 1962 the line had almost 100 flights daily and in February 1963 bought three S-62s for one million dollars. Sufficiently healthy to be able to forego subsidy, the carrier was awarded the first permanent CAB certificate for any helicopter airline, and it did take up the board's recommendation for a trunk affiliation, moving its San Francisco terminal to American Airlines' concourse. By 1975 changing economics induced the owner to liquidate the airline's assets.

*Commuters.* The commuter phenomenon emerges from the air taxi operators and is first visible in the early 1960s, even though countless small operators had been in business wherever suitable markets existed for years. Their first categorization was as "Third Level Carriers," and their records were compiled by the Federal Aviation Administration, not the CAB. In the absence of restrictive economic regulations, these customarily small outfits have steadily expanded their utility, particularly in California. Their entry and exit from the market has been considerably more facile than other kinds of carriers, and survival has frequently depended upon serial merger tactics.

A not atypical example was Aero Commuter, founded in 1967 to provide service between Long Beach and Catalina Island with DeHavilland Twin Otters. Catalina Airlines and Cable Commuter were merger partners less than two years later, followed by acquisition of Golden West and Skymark to form Golden West Airlines, at one time the country's largest third level carrier. Cable Commuter Airlines had

gotten underway in November 1966, providing service between Ontario, Los Angeles, Ventura, and Santa Ana—also using the Otters. Golden West, critically overextended by the acquisition of a fleet of DeHavilland of Canada Dash Sevens, filed for bankruptcy in 1983. Golden Gate Airlines, based in Monterey until its demise in August 1981, had also achieved a significant scope of operations if not solvency. The line, operating nine Dash 7s and 11 Swearingen Metroliners, was formed in March 1980 by the merger of Air Pacific and Gem State Airlines, and served 20 cities with 1,400 weekly flights in California and five other Western states.

Imperial Airlines of Carlsbad has provided a more optimistic example since its formation in 1967. With 150 daily flights between nine Southern California cities by the end of 1983, and an efficient fleet of a dozen Embraer and Shorts turboprop aircraft, Imperial appeared to have identified a suitable market niche and validated the idea that small, well-run carriers may yet provide needed services and remain viable.

*Santa Catalina Island.* When Glenn Martin made the very first flight from the mainland to Santa Catalina Island on May 10, 1912, he could scarcely have anticipated the tide of little airplanes that would flow across the channel in his wake. When he launched his cheery summer project in 1919, Syd Chaplin's foresight probably wasn't much better. But the lovely island resort has inspired something of an aeronautical legend for seven decades.

After Chaplin quit St. Catherine's Bay, Foster Curry put together Pacific Marine Airways in 1920 and began a San Pedro-Avalon Bay operation in 1922 with two HS-2L flying boats, replaced in 1928 with more luxurious C2-H Loening amphibians that permitted the mainland terminal to be located ashore. By 1927 fifteen thousand passengers had been carried, enough to attract the attention of Harris Hanshue. Western Air Express negotiated with PMA's president E.A. Bacon and the Wrigleys, and on June 29, 1928, WAE became the first of two trunk airlines to find the lilliputian route rewarding.

When the WAE contract ended in 1931, Philip K. Wrigley bought the route, believing that continued development of his island resort would benefit from carefully coordinated transportation from the mainland. To complement his Santa Catalina Island Company's steamship service (the SCI Company in 1924 had built the handsome 300-foot SS *Catalina*, which made the 2-1/2 hour crossing from Wilmington with some 1,500 passengers daily in the summer season), Wrigley organized Wilmington-Catalina Airline, which began flying Douglas Dolphin amphibians across the channel on June 6, 1931.

In 1939 the new CAB (perhaps overlooking the length of the route) granted the airline, possibly the world's smallest at the time, its certificate as a "Grandfather Carrier." The next step was to make the rugged island accessible to land airplanes, and in August 1940 work began on a lofty site nine miles from Avalon called Buffalo Springs. In the interim, the company was renamed Catalina Air Transport, the name by which it had been familiarly known since 1932. On July 22, 1941, the route certificate was amended to add Los Angeles as the terminal and Wilmington and Long Beach as intermediate stops. On September 3, 1942, service was suspended under wartime regulations. Two Lockheed Lodestars that had been ordered were preempted for Lend-Lease delivery to Britain, and the Dolphins were turned over to the Army Air Corps. During its 11 years the line made 44,000 trips with 300,000 passengers.

The next chapter began in June 1946 when United Air Lines decided to operate the route to the newly finished "Airport in the Sky," whose construction had required the filling of two large arroyos with the tops of two mountains to obtain 3,400 feet of relatively level ground. Agreement from the SCI Company was secured, and the CAB certificate transferred in time for the inauguration of DC-3 service from Los Angeles, Burbank, and Long Beach to Catalina Airport on July 1. During the eight years United operated the route, the DC-3s carried 400,000 passengers.

After United's final flight on September 30, 1954, the Wrigleys engaged Avalon Air Transport, which had actually begun service with the Grumman Goose between Long Beach and Avalon harbor in August 1953. On July 1, 1955, airmail service was approved under a CAB Star Route contract, and in 1957 the airline acquired a 47-passenger Sikorsky VS-44 four-engine flying boat to supplement the eight Grummans then in service. By 1963, when the company changed its name to Catalina Airlines, Inc., 80,000 passengers were being carried yearly. Service to the island has been flown by several commuter lines in recent years, including Aero Commuter, Cable, and Golden West Airlines.

Perhaps not so grand as the mainland airline saga, the tale of Syd Chaplin's breezy 30 miles still provides a fitting colophon to California's continuing airline history.

*Western Air Express came into being largely through the tireless efforts of Harris M. "Pop" Hanshue, a blunt and irrepressible 40-year-old auto salesman who became WAE's first president and a major force in the development of U.S. airlines. Hanshue is shown here at Vail Field in Montebello during WAE's first year, 1926. Courtesy, SPNBPC/LAPL*

*Above: Anthony Fokker's F-10 was the ideal ship for WAE's Model Air Line. Three of them entered service in May 1928, and two more were added later in the year. Assembled in Fokker's New Jersey plant, the $80,000, 12-passenger, 2,000-pound F-10 was 50 feet long with a span of 79 feet, and was powered by three P&W 420 hp Wasp engines. Courtesy, Gordon Williams*

*Opposite, top: A United Airlines Boeing 40B-4 (one of 38 built) was photographed at Oakland's Boeing Field in 1934. It was the final growth version of the original 40A, which had brought dependability to the transcontinental mail service from 1927. Courtesy, Gordon Williams*

*Above: Hired early in 1929 to help develop communications systems for WAE, Herbert Hoover, Jr., made lasting contributions to communications technology and procedure. Here he seems somewhat bemused by whatever humor is passing between the first two pilots WAE hired—Charles "Jimmy" James (left) and Olympic gold medal hurdler Fred Kelly (right). Courtesy, Western Airlines*

*Right: Igor Sikorsky's first amphibian, the nine-passenger S-38, was manufactured from May 1928 until 1930, some 100 examples in all. WAE bought this one in 1928 for the Catalina route, where it served until 1931. Courtesy, Western Airlines*

Below: TWA's Navy-trained Daniel W. "Tommy" Tomlinson IV, "as much scientist as airman," conducted high-altitude research, which was sponsored by Northrop, GE, the Army, and TWA, with the Northrop Gamma "flying laboratory" from 1936 to 1940. He was able to provide data for airliner design and operation. Courtesy, R.E. Falk

Bottom: TWA president Jack Frye (left) and principal stockholder Howard Hughes (far right) seem pleased during a 1943 flight in Kelly Johnson's prototype Lockheed 049 Constellation—the second great airliner precipitated at Frye's urging, and a consuming Hughes interest. Courtesy, CALAC

In 1927 Los Angeles Lincoln dealer John L. Maddux bought a Ford Tri-motor transport with which to start his own airline. His line flourished with service between Los Angeles (whose elegant downtown ticket office is shown here), San Diego, San Francisco, and other California cities before it was sold to Western Air Express in 1929. Courtesy, SPNBPC/LAPL

*Left: This 1949 San Diego Airport scene of passengers boarding a Pacific Southwest Airlines DC-3 during the airline's first year suggests that the "Poor Sailors Airline" appellation for PSA was well founded. Courtesy, PSA*

*Top: California Central Airlines (1949) acquired five Martin 2-0-2s to serve a Los Angeles-Bay Area low-fare network from their Burbank headquarters. With good block times, handsomely furnished cabins, and ventral stairs, the Martins offered a high standard of service. The* City of Burbank *is shown here. Courtesy, Gordon Williams and R.E.G. Davies*

*Right: PSA president Ken Friedkin (left) and Lockheed-California chief operating officer Burt C. Monesmith execute documents in Burbank in July 1959 for November delivery of the airline's second order of L-188 Electra turboprops. Courtesy, CALAC*

Lifting off the runway at Long Beach Airport on a delivery flight to Continental Airlines in the mid-1970s is a Douglas DC-10. At the end of 1983 the airline operated 13 of the wide-bodied airliners. Courtesy, MD

The Flying Tiger Line's first planes, 150-mph, stainless steel Budd Conestogas acquired in 1945, were replaced by 1947 with more conventional planes, Curtiss C-46s and Douglas C-47s. Courtesy, Flying Tigers

Clarence Belinn, founder and president of Los Angeles Airways, pauses during the 1962 celebration of Burbank Airport. This was the day his airline inaugurated turbine-powered helicopter service there with the 25-passenger, 135-mph Sikorsky S-61L (background). Courtesy, CALAC

# CHAPTER EIGHT

# THE AVIATION COMMUNITY

The major aero manufacturing firms, research institutions, military services, and airlines in California provide a most hospitable and symbiotic environment for related activities and industries. Across air controllers' glowing radar screens at the Palmdale Regional Air Route Traffic Control Center flows an endless stream of targets representing aircraft headed toward Los Angeles International, suggesting the vital role of airports in the state. In theaters around the world, larger screens frequently reflect Hollywood's vision of the world of flight. And from air races to vintage aircraft collections, the activities of the diverse community of aviation are nowhere more colorfully represented than in California.

## AIRPORTS
Spirited technology in a few decades has transformed frail kites into elegant marvels. Each day thousands of passengers fly over continents and oceans in carefree comfort close to the speed of sound—or twice that pace for a premium fare on a few routes—in a global transportation system like nothing so much as a Jules Verne or H.G. Wells dream. Marvelous indeed, but one man's dream may be another's regularly interrupted nightmare. And for communities buffeted beneath numberless thundering takeoffs and shrieking approaches, jet airplanes make problematic neighbors. Airframe and engine manufacturers, air carriers, the military services, federal, state, and local governments, courts, business people, and homeowners continue to confront conflicting challenges raised by modern air operations. Few people dispute the advantages of rapid air

transport; fewer still welcome an airport next door.

In Southern California, not long ago dotted with airfields that fostered the growth of one of the state's principal industries, a 20-year battle continues to rage to establish additional airports to handle the relentless traffic growth of three of the world's ten largest air commerce centers.

When the airplane was new and exciting, families packed picnic baskets for special afternoons in delighted awe of daring airmen and their unlikely machines. The local airfield—often an unassuming grass strip contrived from idle farmland—was a friendly place, a happy curiosity. Today, a modern big-city airport often enjoys much the same welcome as a dump, a prison, or a chemical plant.

To some visionaries, the problem was evident early. In 1926 Orville Wright told a Congressional committee: "The greatest present drawback to the use of aircraft for civil purposes such as commerce, mail, travel and sport is the lack of suitable airports."

In 1983 an aviation industry task force reached essentially the same conclusion when it found that: "The growing lack of needed airport capacity is one of the most serious problems facing the U.S. aviation industry."

Industry sources have pinpointed the phenomenon even more specifically to California. The state's economy relies heavily on aviation to move passengers and an ever-increasing variety of goods, from agricultural commodities to high-tech products. Clifton A. Moore, general manager of the Los Angeles Department of Airports, whose Los Angeles International Airport is currently one of

America's three largest air centers, says: "If Southern California is going to stay vital, it has to provide adequate air commerce. We don't have a backup transportation system. If our lack of capacity stifles commerce, that backs up down the chain and then you have an economy that stagnates."

With five major airports providing scheduled passenger services, and a galaxy of general aviation airports, Southern California today reflects a unique heritage of aviation pioneering in the airfields from which the great inventors and builders first flew their historic creations.

Throughout the California southland in the 1920s, the motion-picture industry was significant in airport and flying development. Among early fields was Venice Airport, sometimes known as Ince Airport because of its close connection with early motion-picture mogul Thomas H. Ince, who built a major studio in Culver City. Close by the town that hoped to become the "Venice of America," with canals and Italianate architecture, Venice Airport saw much wing-walking and aerial acrobatics used in feature films and newsreels.

From 1919, the Los Angeles intersection of Wilshire Boulevard and Crescent Avenue (now Fairfax) was an aerial crossroads as well. Cecil B. De Mille owned Mercury Aviation Company, which operated from the area northwest of the intersection. Turned down for wartime pilot training, De Mille learned to fly in a war-surplus Jenny and was active in aviation throughout his career, at one time operating three airports in the Los Angeles area.

The field across Wilshire from Mercury was operated by Syd Chaplin, who came to Los Angeles in 1919. Although his background was in the manufacture of ladies' garments and managing his soon-to-become famous brother, Charles, Syd Chaplin earned distinction in airline history with his 1919 San Pedro-to-Catalina Island airline. Chaplin's company also promoted its 1919 record-breaking round-trip, one-day flight between Los Angeles and San Francisco; his Curtiss Oriole delivered a package of securities destined for a ship departing for Tokyo after a flight of four hours, 34 minutes;

the return trip took just four hours, two minutes.

When both De Mille and Chaplin began to concentrate full time on movie interests, their separate airport operations were sold to Chaplin's former partner, Emory Rogers, who combined them into Rogers Wilshire Boulevard Airport. The airport included a flying service that advertised "theoretical and practical flying . . . expert instructors in charge." Following Rogers' death during an air race in November 1921, his wife operated the company until 1923, when the property was subdivided for commercial and residential development.

Burdett D. Fuller learned to fly in Michigan in 1916, served as a Naval Reserve pilot in World War I, and in 1919 began his California flying career. His first ventures in Long Beach and then Alhambra were general fixed-base operations, but what Fuller did consummately well was teach others to fly. At the Burdett School of Aviation at Manchester and Cypress and his second airport facility, Burdett Airlines at 94th and Western Avenue, opened in 1922, Fuller's many students mastered flying. It was quite a group of graduates, including among hundreds, Bobbie Trout, Jack Frye, Paul Richter, and Jake Moxness. The 94th Street and 104th Street operations were sold to Frye and his colleagues in 1927 and 1928, and as the Aero Corporation and Standard Airlines became part of Western Airlines' and TWA's foundations. Fuller later worked for Donald Douglas as a test pilot and administrator. At his death in 1949 the *Los Angeles Examiner* called Fuller "the area's outstanding flying instructor of the 1920s."

Ross Field in Arcadia, now the site of Santa Anita racetrack, was operated by the federal government as a balloon station and school for operators and balloon observers. Life for the balloon pilots and observers often became exciting when one of the unpowered "sausages" broke loose, flying freely over the countryside.

Earl Daugherty's "Chateau Thierry" airport in Long Beach launched one of the era's more inventive publicity stunts when Daugherty and Miss Catherine Hall were married in September 1923 while flying over Long Beach in his four-passenger Orenco biplane. This was one of a fleet more mundanely utilized for wing walking and flying under Long Beach bridges.

Waldo Waterman, an early airplane builder and Venice Airport tenant, was first general manager and helped establish Los Angeles Metropolitan Airport at Van Nuys, site of the present Van Nuys Airport. Van Nuys has become one of the nation's busiest general aviation airports, home for hundreds of flying clubs, private pilots, and major companies providing aviation and aerospace services and support.

Farther out from Los Angeles' business activities was Sierra Airport (sometimes called Hastings Airport) built by Walter Wright Alley, an engineer under Donald Douglas at the Martin Aircraft Company in Los Angeles. Bell Airport was advertised as being "six miles from Los Angeles' main post office, fully equipped with wind pennant," and "in the heart of Bell." Part of Southern California's sprinkling of fields was Las Turas Lake Airport on the Los Angeles/ Ventura County line in Thousand Oaks. In Montebello, Vail Field in 1926 became head-quarters for Western Air Express.

Santa Monica's Clover Field, dedicated in 1923 with a program that included a formation flight of "all available airplanes in Southern California (flying) over Los Angeles and returning to Clover Field," is one example of a California airport that fostered major aviation growth and then fell under the hue and cry of disgruntled neighbors complaining about noise. As Douglas Aircraft expanded in Santa Monica in 1928, it moved operations to Clover Field, continuing major production there until the 1960s. A second plant adjacent to the larger Long Beach Airport was opened in 1940 to meet wartime production demands. Operations at Clover Field were gradually reduced to general aviation, and some residents and city officials now seek to shut down the field altogether.

Across the great basin, Glendale Airport, later Grand Central, was to earn national distinction as the western focus of transcontinental air services. Dedicated in 1923 with an air rodeo, Grand Central was not officially opened until

February 1929. First operators to fly from Grand Central Terminal were Maddux Airlines and Transcontinental Air Transport. Cross-country air service was inaugurated from Grand Central's handsome terminal building in July 1929, with Charles Lindbergh as pilot and Eddie Bellande in the right-hand seat of a resplendent TAT Ford Tri-motor, duly splashed with Prohibition grape juice by Gloria Swanson and Mary Pickford.

Long Beach Municipal Airport, now providing scheduled commercial service for several carriers as well as Douglas Aircraft Company production together with other aviation-associated businesses, was Southern California's first municipal airport.

## AN AIR SHOW INSPIRES WORLD'S THIRD-BUSIEST AIRPORT
Just as Dominguez Hills in 1910 provided the original catalyst for Southern California aviation, an air show in 1928 resulted in the creation of what would become Los Angeles International Airport, for many years known as Mines Field (honoring the real-estate agent who handled the property sale to the city). An open field planted in wheat, barley, and beans, the site was one of 27 proposed in 1926 by the Los Angeles Chamber of Commerce, vigorous promoters of a municipally owned and operated airport. The needed push for a municipal airport for Los Angeles came with the selection of Mines Field for the 1928 National Air Races. Veteran aviation enthusiast and later airport general manager Cliff Henderson personally took charge of work on the unprepared site. The air show would attract 200,000 people and feature the nation's air hero, Charles Lindbergh. When Mines Field was selected for the 1928 National Air Races, Los Angeles County had a total of 52 landing fields, 37 of which were privately owned or leased. Lindbergh, in advance of his National Air Races appearance, played a role in focusing attention on the Inglewood field when he landed a Maddux Airlines Ford Tri-motor there prior to the decision. Lindbergh had not originally been billed as part of the races entourage, but he replaced Lt. J.J. Williams as the

third man in the Army Air Corps exhibition team, the "Three Musketeers," when Williams was killed in a crash on the meet's third day.

Following the Air Races, the City of Los Angeles took over operations at Mines Field. In 1928 Henderson was named first Director of Airports at $400 a month. One of the first Mines Field airport employees was Henry G. Bakes, hired in 1928, who retired in 1970 as Director of Operations. During the first month of Los Angeles Municipal Airport operation, Bakes did his work out of a phone booth, no other facilities being available. The airport was officially dedicated in June 1930. Because of L.A. Municipal's modest facilities (though they had grown some since Bakes' phone booth), most airlines continued to operate out of either Grand Central Airport in Glendale or United Air Terminal (now Glendale-Burbank-Pasadena). The major criticism of Mines Field (although officially Los Angeles Municipal Airport, it continued to be called Mines Field until well after World War II) was that it was "located too far from the center of the city . . . and no one would use so isolated a field." Nonetheless, Mines Field continued to receive publicity with such events as the 1929 landing of the German dirigible, *Graf Zeppelin*, during its record-setting around-the-world flight. The National Air Races were held at Mines Field in 1933 and 1936, enhancing the image of Southern California as an aviation center.

By the early 1930s Mines Field began to attract a modest number of manufacturers. Moreland Aircraft located a production site adjacent to the airport. When Moreland failed, Northrop Aircraft, then a division of Douglas, took over the plant operation, which later became the Douglas El Segundo Division. In 1936 North American Aviation moved to Mines Field. Rockwell continues to operate major facilities at Los Angeles International (LAX), as does Northrop Corporation. Hughes Aircraft began moving some of its facilities closer to LAX and is now headquartered in the airport area, along with hundreds of other companies that have made the area a center for business, commerce, and transportation for all of Southern California.

During World War II Los Angeles Airport was operated by the U.S. government. Taken over by Army and Navy air transport services, it became a major military air transport center and delivery base and takeoff point for thousands of military aircraft produced by local manufacturers. The facility was camouflaged to look from the air like a farm complex.

By the end of 1946, as part of the postwar business boom, TWA, American, United, Pan American, and Western Airlines moved into the airport. For all its growing importance, LAX in the immediate postwar era sported an almost provincial look, its jury-rigged wood-frame terminal buildings presided over by Mike Lyman's Grill and plank balconies where visitors watched the ceaseless tides of DC-4s and Connies in grit-laden, prop-washed wonder. The architectural theme was chain-link temporary, but the mood was bustling vibrant.

In 1949 the Los Angeles Department of Airports took a first step towards regional operation when it acquired Van Nuys Airport from the War Assets Administration for one dollar. In 1950 the airport was officially designated Los Angeles International (LAX). Los Angeles Airport showed its first profit in 1952; it has never since lost money. Ontario Airport in 1967 became part of the Los Angeles Department of Airports Regional Airport System.

Over the years LAX has been a pacesetter in airport development. When the runways required lengthening and strengthening to serve the larger aircraft of the 1950s and 1960s, Sepulveda Boulevard underpass, the first tunnel of its kind, was constructed. It permitted the extension of two main runways over the highway. The jet age was anticipated in earnest in 1957 with ground breaking for an entirely new complex, and jet service was inaugurated in January 1959 with American Airlines' Los Angeles-New York flights.

The year 1961 saw most of the new terminal construction completed. President John F. Kennedy was scheduled to formally open the major terminal area in June but injured his back just before the event and pressed the Vice-President to do the honors. Lyndon Johnson arranged to do so during a stopover en route to Washington after an exhausting visit to the Far East. The new Los Angeles mayor, Sam Yorty, was late for the dedication but showed up at the Vice-President's plane shortly afterward and asked to meet with Johnson. Johnson had retired for some much-needed rest and somewhat grudgingly dressed for his second ceremony— greeting the mayor before the cameras at the 707's doorway.

During the decade, both LAX itself and the Los Angeles airport system expanded, and the L.A. Department of Airports General Manager Francis Fox played significant roles in national and international airport planning, including participation in Project Horizon (Kennedy's advisory group on federal aviation policy). Immersed every day in almost every imaginable issue of modern airport operation, it is not surprising that LAX was a major research focus for novelist Arthur Hailey when he set about writing *Airport*. Hailey spent long hours at Airport Commission meetings, and he and Fox became good friends. Invited to read the manuscript before publication, Fox felt that Hailey's airport manager character might be a little too recognizable. And so the novel's airport was moved to more northerly climes.

Anticipating passenger growth and the 1984 Olympics, LAX undertook a $700 million airport modernization and expansion program completed in mid-1984, just before the games. Despite massive congestion caused by the almost total rebuilding, LAX managed to annually handle approximately 33 million passengers during the construction. In contrast to other airports, notably Atlanta, Chicago's O'Hare, and Dallas/Fort Worth where new airport facilities were constructed and then operations moved from the old site, LAX operated continually while being rebuilt.

SAN DIEGO HAS NO MUNICIPAL AIRPORT UNTIL 1928

Although San Diego's North Island was the scene of America's first military flying school, and its harbor was used as a "landing strip" for the earliest floatplanes, the city did not have a municipal airport until nearly two decades after these embryonic aviation feats. The catalyst was Charles A. Lindbergh and an airplane named for another city.

Although city leaders interested in San Diego's aviation future began to study airport needs in 1925, Claude Ryan said it was the Lindbergh airplane and San Diegans themselves that provided the impetus to "do something."

"The people were pretty enthusiastic. They were really for it. Lindbergh's flight, that's what set it off. The people realized that the plane was built here and were proud of that," Ryan recalled 50 years later.

The chamber of commerce wanted a municipal airport constructed that would help retain aircraft manufacturers located in San Diego; would provide direct airmail service to San Diego; would improve transportation in and out of the city; and, in view of the city's relationship with the Navy, would convince that service to base one of its two gigantic aircraft carriers (*Enterprise* and *Saratoga*) at North Island.

The location chosen was a marshland on the harbor, close to the old cannery in which Ryan was building airplanes. The site could be made into an excellent airport and transportation center close to downtown; dredging of the harbor to provide landfill for the field would deepen the harbor, making it more attractive for a Navy carrier. In addition, seaplanes could use the facility and the filled land would provide a runway of more than 7,000 feet.

San Diego in the 1920s was in the midst of a boom not unlike its growth of the late 1970s and early 1980s. From the turn of the century to 1920, San Diego's population doubled every ten years; in 1920 it began to double every five years. Land values were climbing at 20 percent per year.

In the midst of this boom along came Lindy and his dreams of conquering the Atlantic. His selection of Ryan to build what became the most famous airplane in American aviation history came only after he had been turned down by other major manufacturers. And, time to build it was only 60 days. His enthusiasm, and ultimate triumph, were contagious, and San Diegans caught the fever.

Following his 1927 conquest of the Atlantic, Lindy made a triumphal return to San Diego, where 60,000 people packed Municipal Stadium (another 90,000 tried to get in) to salute the city's hero. By then Lindbergh, Ryan, and San Diego were definitely "on the map" and assured a place in history. In August 1928, the day before the official dedication, the first plane—a Consolidated PT-1—landed at Lindbergh Field. The airplane was piloted by San Diego city councilman Frank W. Scifert, the strongest supporter of the airport; in the rear cockpit was Mayor Harry C. Clarke. The next day thousands of San Diegans on foot and in automobiles turned out for the flying show and official dedication of their new municipal airport.

One of the city's early, businesslike moves was to assure that the Harbor Commission with its vast experience included operation of the city's newest "port." Today the San Diego Unified Port District, in charge of Chula Vista, Coronado, Imperial Beach, and National City as well as San Diego, directs the city's sea and air commerce.

Even though a field existed in 1928, there was no structure. The first building was begun in 1929, but the Depression intervened; the city ran out of money. Once again, Claude Ryan stepped to the fore. Ryan said, "The city didn't have money to spend on the air terminal . . . so we worked out a deal. We (Ryan Air Lines) would design a building, subject to the city's approval, and lease it out." Construction began in 1932 on the Spanish-style air terminal to house the terminal, Ryan's offices, and a number of concessions. That classic California building served as Lindbergh Field Air Terminal until 1967 when the present site across the field was first occupied.

Lindbergh Field today has a modern, efficient terminal complex with an annual passenger capacity of eight million to meet the increasing requirements of a wide diversity of industry, local business, and the military, which continues to play a major role in San Diego's economic base.

San Diego and Lindbergh Field were benefactors of a major boost when Consolidated Aircraft (later Convair and ultimately General Dynamics) located aircraft manufacturing facilities adjacent to Lindbergh Field. Partially because of Lindbergh Field's capabilities, Reuben Fleet first selected San Diego for his Consolidated Aircraft Company when it moved from upstate New York. An evolution of PBYs, B-24s, Convair Liners, and Convair 880 and 990 jetliners were first delivered at Lindbergh Field.

Because of the field's close proximity to the city center, San Diego's airport has been a particular target of environmentalists and community neighbors who want to move this center of air commerce to another location. Just as with other California, and American, cities, an argument over site selection continues.

## THE BAY CITY OPENS AN AIRPORT IN 1921

Like San Diego, it took San Francisco nearly two decades after the first pioneering aviation efforts to create a municipal airport. City fathers and shakers and movers made extensive studies of six possible locations, spotted up, down, and across San Francisco Bay. Selection was finally made of property that had originally been the Mills estate. The man who headed the study effort said in 1926 that "Mills Field will serve the aviation needs of San Francisco adequately for the next five years." It was dedicated in 1927.

In a pattern quite similar to San Diego, Charles Lindbergh played a significant role in the initial development and, unfortunately, political fortunes of the airport in the late 1920s and early 1930s.

In what became known as the "Lindbergh Incident," the new American hero had agreed to make a stop in San Francisco on a triumphal American tour. Thousands were on hand at Mills Field to greet the conquering hero. Following his landing Lindy turned the aircraft around, hit a soft spot on the field, and became stuck in the mud to make front-page reading for the entire nation. Lindy unwittingly dampened the air-minded spirit in San Francisco. Political problems had caused great questions to be raised about Mills Field, and the incident embarrassed the city and boosted anti-airport forces.

Adding to that embarrassment was the fact that officials of the Dole Race had selected Oakland Airport across the Bay as departure point for their transpacific, nonstop flights to Hawaii. And then there was the weather. The then-superintendent of Mills Field, commenting on the first attempt to establish San Francisco as a terminal city for commercial airline operations, said:

*Unfortunately, the first day that the field ever had been covered with fog since it opened was the day set for the official takeoff of the first airmail plane. Boeing officials were chagrined and their first impressions were lasting. Certain of their pilots apparently had preconceived opinions that Mills Field was unsafe and a month later, in November 1927, Boeing left the airport.*

But there were bright sides. In May 1928 Western Air Express and Maddux Air Lines chose Mills Field as their Bay region base of operations. In June 1931 San Francisco supervisors changed the name from Mills Field to San Francisco Airport. In 1932 additional tenants were signed, including several airlines, among them Cardiff and Peacock Airlines, flying from San Francisco through the San Joaquin Valley, and Valley Airlines, operating between San Francisco, Stockton, and Sacramento. They were followed by Pacific Air Transport, TWA, and Varney Speed Lines.

Airport management conceived varied events to promote the new field. In November 1932 an air show was held that included Army and Navy planes, including one Army pursuit plane on a cross-country training flight from March Field piloted by Lieutenant Colonel "Hap" Arnold. By 1936 the Public Utilities Commission, which controlled the airport, reported: "The status of San Francisco is passing that of national to international renown."

United Air Lines provided a major boost for the airport and its surrounding area in 1940 when it established major maintenance facilities at the airport. The United/San Francisco airport lease was for a 20-year period. In that same year

the U.S. Coast Guard Air Station was commissioned, providing San Francisco additional protective service for its vital shipping industry.

The station was a precursor of more extensive military operations that were to come after December 7, 1941, when military authorities took over San Francisco Airport, permitting airlines to continue operations under wartime conditions. Civil and military aviation agencies combined to share the burden of wartime assignments. In 1943 the Army and Navy departments spent $10 million improving the airport, including reclamation of 93 acres of land, in exchange for a deed to Treasure Island, which the City of San Francisco owned and operated. "The Army's interest in Mills Field (San Francisco Airport) is in the necessity for providing a suitable airport for transpacific operations as a reserve station if existing Army installations become overloaded," stated the assistant to the director for Army Air Forces. On the Navy side, the Assistant Navy Secretary for Air said, "That the Navy Department considers these seaplane facilities to be of great value in the prosecution of the war effort is indicated by the expenditure of over $3 million in their development."

Pan American World Airways, serving as contractor to the Naval Air Transport Service in 1944, moved its Pacific-Alaska division headquarters from Treasure Island to San Francisco Airport.

Following the war the area surrounding the airport was the scene of a major land boom and an economic infusion as a result of aviation business and workers on the payrolls of Pan American, Southwest Airways, TWA, United, Western, and Slick Airways. Only 20 years before there had not been a single airport tenant or payroll producer.

As the Bay Area expanded in the postwar years to become a West Coast business and financial center, San Francisco Airport grew with it. By 1954 new facilities and a $14 million administration and terminal building were added as part of the dedication of what was now San Francisco International Airport. Annual passenger traffic was projected at 10 million people. On the eastern edge of the field, a $100,000 structure was built exclusively for general aviation use. Today about 20 percent of flight operations at SFO are third-level carriers, military aircraft, and general aviation. A new international terminal was completed in 1983 that can simultaneously accommodate 10 wide-bodied aircraft and has the capability to handle up to 1,500 international passengers per hour.

Despite the fact that, like other major California air centers, SFO has little space (its maximum available land is about one-third that of Dallas/Ft. Worth and one-fifth that of Montreal), SFO is currently the seventh-largest U.S. and eighth-largest world airport as measured by passengers handled. But, like its California sisters, SFO—and the entire Bay Area—faces the necessity of expansion or relocation in order to continue to meet the ever-growing transportation requirements of Californians.

## ACROSS THE BAY A SECOND MAJOR AIRPORT IS BORN

On the eastern shore of San Francisco Bay, Oakland city fathers, also inspired by a history-making flight prospect, began development of a municipal airport for Oakland. This development began in 1927; estimated cost was $1 million.

The Oakland site had been selected by the U.S. Army for the first transpacific flight. That selection served as a catalyst to advance site development and construction in order to complete it by June 25, 1927. Came the magic date, the airport developers anxiously awaited the Army's approval. Pilots inspected the site and put their stamp of acceptance on the construction work. On June 28, 1927, an Army Fokker monoplane with a crew of three took off from Oakland, reaching Hawaii the next day. It was the first successful flight across the Pacific to the island territory. A second flight was made a few weeks later. Oakland Airport subsequently was the launching point for the famed Dole Races to Hawaii, the aviation event that did much to demonstrate aviation's overwater and

long-distance capabilities. Oakland was selected by pilots because it had a large expanse of flat land, good runways, and no surrounding obstructions.

Although Oakland still remains in the shadow of San Francisco and its massive international airport, the airport today serves major areas of Northern California with flights to the East and intrastate operations. It is the headquarters for charter airline operations, including World Airways as well as several major freight carriers.

## A POCKET OF CALIFORNIA'S AVIATION HERITAGE

Far from the madding crowds of LAX, SFO, SAN, and OAK and the general aviation hustle and bustle of two of America's busiest general aviation ports, Van Nuys and John Wayne, is a West Coast capital for historic aviation buffs.

Santa Paula Airport retains the flavor of 1920s aviation. A little run down around the edges, Santa Paula has a well lived-in look; old, corrugated metal hangars and an absence of carefully surfaced runways and taxiways combine to make it a step back into history. Unlike other California airports, Santa Paula was created in 1929 by a group of local ranchers who owned airplanes and simply wanted a place to operate them. No economic pressures were involved. Residents and ranches along the Santa Paula River in 1929 were victimized when a dam broke, sweeping away houses, killing hundreds of people, and doing millions of dollars in damage. One fortunate outgrowth, however, was that the river banks were swept clean, leaving land that could be developed for an airport. The Santa Paula Airport Association sold stock; an airport was opened in August 1930. For more than 50 years Santa Paula has been supported by local interests; no public money has ever been expended for the airport. Far enough away from the Los Angeles and San Francisco centers, Santa Paula provides an aviation enthusiast's haven, from ranchers and farmers to Hollywood stars. Movie actor Cliff Robertson keeps a fleet of antique aircraft at Santa Paula; Clete Roberts, Los Angeles television personality, is a regular flyer at Santa

Paula; the late Steve McQueen kept his Stearman and Pitcairn Mailwing airplanes at the airport and once observed, "Santa Paula is my kind of country club." Aviators from all over the United States, and even the world, gravitate to Santa Paula, piloting antique and experimental aircraft.

Harking back to a time in the '20s and '30s when wide-eyed citizens flocked to local airports to see wondrous denizens of the air, Santa Paula on weekends still draws the curious and worshippers. They're not disappointed. They often see Ryans, Moths, Stinsons, Stearmans, Staggerwings, and even Messerschmitts taking off, performing flying displays, and landing. Several of aviation's jewels in Washington's National Air and Space Museum (and other air museums around the country) were built or restored at Santa Paula. There is a Messerschmitt Me 108 at Santa Paula; a Boeing F4B3 was hand-built. In many respects, Santa Paula has become a private sector, West Coast version of the Smithsonian's Silver Hill, Maryland, restoration facility. It's living testimony to aviation's heritage.

## CALIFORNIA AVIATION MADE AIRPORTS— AND VICE VERSA
California airports range from tiny strips serving such exotic spots as Catalina Island . . . to Alameda Airport (originally Curtiss-Wright Airport) on San Francisco Bay (once billed as "serving yachtsmen and air pilots") . . . to Los Angeles, San Francisco, and San Diego that are served by feeder/commuter/regional airlines in the "hub and spoke system" of air routes.

The Federal Aviation Administration projects that the number of airline passengers will double within the next 20 years. Unfortunately, rising land costs, depletion of major land areas suitable for airport development and close to big cities, and, most important, community resistance to having a noisy airport as a neighbor, combine to impede aviation progress. Public laws severely limiting aircraft noise at three measuring points—takeoff, sideline, and landing—will go into effect across the U.S. on January 1, 1985. Known as Federal Aviation

Regulation (FAR) 36, these rules are an answer to the citizen protest created by the advent of larger, noisier jets that increasingly populate the world's skies.

To its great credit, the aviation industry— aircraft and engine manufacturers, airlines, and the airports—has faced up to the problems of airplane noise. Although doomsayers little more than 10 years ago predicted that jet-engine/airplane noise could not be reduced, technology has succeeded in doing just that. New-generation aircraft and advanced technology turbofan engines have resulted in noise reductions up to 75 percent from first generation jetliners. Power plants for two-, three-, and even four-engine transports, with turbofans and nacelles that surround and dampen engine noise, are being produced by the world's leading jet-engine manufacturers.

## WOMEN ALOFT: A FEMINIST AIR FORCE
If aviation wasn't the prime force in feminism, it surely provided a great lift to women's rights around the world and in California. The feats of aviation achieved by the state's women aviation pioneers together with record-breaking flights originating in California are hallmarks in the annals of aviation and women's rights.

In 1918 Ruth Law, one of the most publicized fliers of her day (sister of Rodman Law, whose publicity stunt parachute leap from the Statue of Liberty helped launch America's newsreel industry), wrote an article entitled "Let Women Fly!" for *Air Travel* magazine. Summarizing women's independence, circa 1918, the adventuresome Law wrote: "It would seem that a woman's success in any particular line would prove her fitness for that work." Miss Law had been rejected by the Army in her bid to serve as a WW I combat pilot. She said: "There is the world-old controversy that crops up again whenever women attempt to enter a new field, are women fitted for this or that work?"

Earhart, Cochran, Troop, Smith, Foy, Knapp, and even "Rosie the Riveter" would help demonstrate women's "fitness" for aviation. Nonetheless, even with more and more women today in the "front offices" of military and civil aircraft, the controversy over women pilots continues.

As early as 1912 Julia Clarke was the first woman student at the Curtiss Flying School at San Diego's North Island; she was the third American woman licensed pilot.

One Ruth Law record was broken by Katherine Stinson, a female stunt flier, who in 1917 set a nonstop distance mark, flying 610 air miles between San Diego and San Francisco. "Passing over Los Angeles, I began to rise gradually over Tehachapi Pass," she recalled. "I knew that aviators had tried to cross it and failed and I knew too, that once over the top I would have no trouble." She didn't, ultimately landing at Presidio Army Base in San Francisco.

Hollywood's glamour combined with the drama of flying to lure women aviators. Andre Peyre, who had learned to fly in France, arrived in Los Angeles in 1919 under contract as an actress to United Studios. Flying her Farman Sport plane, she was a familiar sight at local airports. One of Cecil B. De Mille's writers, Jeannie Macpherson, was an accomplished pilot. Early film stars Ruth Roland and Mary Miles Minter were often photographed at Los Angeles airports when movie people gathered. Actress Blanche Noyes demonstrated her flight skills as an entrant in the 1929 Women's Air Derby.

Ruth Elder was already a proven pilot (she and George Haldeman in 1927 attempted a transatlantic flight but were forced down at sea; Miss Elder placed fifth in the 1929 Women's Air Derby) and was soon wooed by the glamour of Hollywood to become one of the era's leading film actresses.

The most famous working woman pilot in Hollywood annals was Florence Lowe "Pancho" Barnes. Granddaughter of pioneer balloonist Thaddeus S.C. Lowe, who commanded the Union Army's observation balloons in the Civil War, Pancho was a socialite, actress, stuntwoman, animal trainer, and script girl. Fiercely independent, Pancho Barnes in 1928 won the first 100-mile, closed course women's air race, was an entrant in the 1928 Air Derby, in 1930 set a new world's speed record for women (breaking Earhart's record), and was the only

woman founding member of the Associated Motion Picture Pilots, the movie stunt fliers' union chartered in 1929 by a forerunner of the AFL/CIO.

Pancho Barnes' feats have become legend. In the film based on Tom Wolfe's *The Right Stuff*, her famed "Happy Bottom Riding Club," a ranch near Edwards Air Force Base used by test pilots for off-duty relaxation, is part of the story. Moreover, in 1980 the "Pancho Barnes Room" was officially dedicated by the Secretary of the Air Force at Edwards AFB's officers' club. For more than 30 years Pancho Barnes was a symbol of independence and pioneering spirit in California's aviation heritage.

Nineteen twenty-nine marked a significant turning point in women's aviation in the United States. In August the Women's Air Derby, the first cross-country competition for women, was an official event of the National Air Races. Taking off from Santa Monica's Clover Field on August 18, twenty of the world's top women pilots faced a 2,800 mile challenge to Cleveland's Municipal Airport, finishing August 26. Amelia Earhart called it "the event that started concerted activity among women fliers."

After nine days of grueling daylight cross-country flights, 15 women aviators landed in Cleveland. Louise Thadden was the winner, Gladys O'Donnell second, Amelia Earhart third. Thadden was hailed as America's top aviatrix. Such illustrious entrants as Blanche Noyes, Bobbi Trout, Pancho Barnes, and Ruth Nichols were plagued by problems and failed to finish. Even with the triumphant finish of 15 of the 20 starters, one fatality marred the Air Derby's reputation when Marvel Crosson was killed bailing out of her stricken airplane over southwestern Arizona, too low for her parachute to function.

Despite a barrage of negative publicity, the women pilots banded together in 1929 to form the Ninety-Nines, an association of women flyers whose name derived from its original 99 charter members.

That same year two stalwart and competitive women pilots, Bobbi Trout of California and New York's Elinor Smith, established a new in-flight endurance record. The 23-year-old Trout and 17-year-old Smith had taken turns breaking each other's flight records. In late 1929, accepting the challenge of a California businessman, the two women fliers joined ranks, vowing to stay in the air at least one month. Midst much publicity, Trout and Smith made two abortive efforts at a new record. On November 27, 1929, despite aircraft problems in the "flying gas station" from which they were refueled, the pair set a new women's endurance in-flight record of 42 hours and were the first women to refuel an aircraft in flight.

Although neither were native Californians, the two women who most affected American aviation achieved or began their most famous records in California. Amelia Earhart and Jacqueline Cochran (who became close friends) made giant strides in world aviation and for the stature of women pilots.

When her parents moved to Los Angeles soon after WW I, Amelia Earhart—later known the world over to flyers and nonpilots alike as "AE"—came West to join them. Learning to fly under the tutelage of Neta Snook, AE had by 1922 set a women's altitude record of 14,000 feet, and in 1928 became the first woman to cross the Atlantic by air.

As evidence of Amelia's fierce independence, her 1931 marriage at age 34 to publisher George Putnam made headlines when she presented Putnam a "declaration of independence" immediately prior to the ceremony. Putnam was devoted to his wife and dedicated to promoting her flying career.

In 1932 Earhart and Bernt Balchen successfully flew the Atlantic in a Northrop-designed Lockheed Vega in 15 hours, 18 minutes, establishing a transatlantic record. By this time AE was becoming a sort of female counterpart of America's hero, Charles Lindbergh. Only three months after her transatlantic achievement, she flew her Vega nonstop from Los Angeles to Newark, New Jersey, in 18 hours, 5 minutes, establishing a new women's long-distance record. In 1933 she shortened her own solo transcontinental mark by two hours. By this time AE was very much a world leader in the

drive to get women into the air and to be recognized for their triumphs. Her natural, longtime independence and prodigiously skilled airmanship were a compelling combination; it may have been inevitable that AE would emerge a powerful feminist symbol.

With a new and improved Vega and strong support from movie stunt pilot Paul Mantz, AE in 1935 became the first person to make a nonstop solo flight across the Pacific from Hawaii to California. Touching down at Oakland 18 hours and 15 minutes after takeoff, AE and her team collected the $10,000 prize offered by a group of Hawaiian businessmen to the first pilot to successfully achieve the flight. Only three months later Earhart set a new Los Angeles-to-Mexico City nonstop mark, the first step in a grander scheme. She planned to fly from Mexico City to New York across the Gulf of Mexico and in April 1935 landed at Newark Airport after a record flight of 14 hours, 19 minutes. With transatlantic, transpacific, and transcaribbean records in her logbook, Earhart determined to make the first woman's around-the-world flight.

To realize her dream, Amelia Earhart acquired a new, advanced, twin-engine Lockheed Electra, an aircraft with a top speed of 200 miles per hour and more than adequate room for extra fuel and equipment. For a trial run AE flew the Electra in the 1936 New York-Los Angeles Bendix Race. Although she had aircraft problems, Earhart finished fifth. To AE's great delight, however, Louise Thadden and Blanche Noyes triumphed in the otherwise all-male Bendix Race, the first time the coveted trophy had been captured by a woman.

On May 21, 1937, Amelia Earhart and her copilot, Fred Noonan, took off from Oakland, heading for Miami where her around-the-world flight would officially begin June 1, 1937. Traversing the Caribbean, the South Atlantic, the African continent, the Middle East, the sub-continent, and on to Australia and New Guinea, the Electra had covered more than 22,000 miles by July 2, when Earhart and Noonan took off from Lae, New Guinea. Their next stop on this longest leg of the journey was Howland Island;

from there they would journey to Honolulu and, finally, home to Oakland.

In one of the century's great and poignant dramas, the Electra vanished over the Pacific on July 2, 1937, following a final feeble radio transmission near Howland Island. The mystery surrounding the disappearance of the world's most famous woman aviator grew, fueling 40 years of speculation ranging from espionage to sabotage, and providing grist for books, articles, films, and television documentaries. Despite continued probings of Amelia Earhart's disappearance, the puzzle of her last flight will almost certainly remain forever unsolved.

AE in the early 1930s made an indelible mark as a woman in aviation. That mark, and the gauntlet it represented, was aggressively picked up by Jacqueline Cochran. Already a successful beautician in 1932, catering to New York and Miami socialites, Jackie Cochran met Floyd B. Odlum, Wall Street lawyer and investment genius, who would become her mentor and husband (Odlum later controlled Consolidated Aircraft, San Diego).

Jackie Cochran learned to fly in 1932 at Roosevelt Field, Long Island, later polishing her skills at the Ryan Flying School at San Diego. She became a converted Californian. By 1934 Cochran competed, albeit unsuccessfully, in a London-to-Melbourne, Australia, race. Although she started the 1935 Bendix Race, she had aircraft problems and did not finish.

But Amelia Earhart's 1937 disappearance caused Jackie Cochran to don the mantle of the world's leading woman pilot. By 1937 she was breaking one speed record after another. In concert with Russian-born Alexander P. de Seversky, who had been attempting to sell the U.S. Army Air Corps his new P-35, Jackie flew its civilian counterpart, an AP-7, in the 1938 Los Angeles-Cleveland Bendix Race, the only woman in a field of 10. She won the race in the amazing time of 8 hours, 10 minutes, flying at an average speed of just under 250 miles per hour. To show it was no fluke, Cochran took off immediately from Cleveland to fly nonstop to New York and set a new women's west-east transcontinental record. In 1939 she set a

women's altitude mark, became the first woman to make a blind landing, and in that year and 1940 set ever-faster international speed records. But Jackie Cochran had only just begun.

Although the U.S. had not yet entered World War II, Jackie convinced General "Hap" Arnold that she could ferry to England a new Lockheed Hudson bomber as part of the U.S. Lend-Lease Act. In June 1941 Jackie Cochran became the first woman to pilot a military aircraft across the Atlantic. She recognized the need for ferry pilots and the role women aviators could fill in what was certain to be a massive war effort. Since the U.S. was not yet at war, General Arnold proposed that Cochran recruit a small detachment of American women to serve Britain's Air Transport Auxiliary. With an elite group of 40 pilots Jackie Cochran led a contingent of American women aiding the Allied cause.

While Cochran was in England, another U.S. female flying detachment, the Women's Auxiliary Ferry Squadron (WAFS), had been organized as an element of the Army Air Force Air Transport Command. Although conflict between Jackie Cochran and Nancy Love, originator of the WAFS, was inevitable, it was ultimately solved. In 1943 the WAFS and Jackie Cochran's Women's Flying Training Detachment were merged into one organization known as the Women Airforce Service Pilots (WASP). Jackie Cochran was named Director of Women Pilots. By war's end WASPs had delivered 12,650 planes of 77 different types, including flying half the U.S. ferrying of high-speed pursuit planes. Women pilots under Cochran's direction flew 60 million miles.

Even while maintaining a successful cosmetics business and her marriage to Floyd Odlum, Jackie Cochran continued her record-breaking aviation assault following the war. She became the first woman ever to fly a jet aircraft, Northrop's T-38 Talon. In the 1950s and 1960s women's world aviation speed and distance records became a "battle of the Jackies." California's Jackie Cochran would set a record only to have it broken by France's Jacqueline Auriol, then later bettered by the American

Jackie. It was an intense, but overtly friendly competition between the tough, aggressive, outspoken American and the soft-spoken, charming, but dedicated Frenchwoman.

Although not officially classified as women aviators, California's "Rosie the Riveters," immortalized in a famed Norman Rockwell *Saturday Evening Post* cover, contributed perhaps as much to America's feminist movement as any other single group. In the Second World War 19 million American women joined the labor force. Breaking every known barrier, the Rosie force was comprised of whites, blacks, Latinas, singles, marrieds, and divorcées. According to an extensive 1983 study by Sherna Gluck at Cal State Long Beach, the Rosies "sowed the seeds for the women's movement 20 years later." As a result of her study, Ms. Gluck says, "I think there was a very personal effect in the home that translated to the next generation, perhaps not even consciously. I suspect it was the daughters of many of these women (of WW II) who became active in the women's movement of the '60s." Gluck points out that not nearly as many women entering the labor force during WW II were content to return home as many have been led to believe. From a peak of 19.4 million during the war, 16.6 million women were *still* in the U.S. labor force in 1947. Included in Gluck's study were women who spent 20 or more years, many until retirement, at Southern California's North American, Douglas, Lockheed, and Northrop plants. Because Los Angeles was the nation's WW II aircraft manufacturing center, 42 percent of all U.S. women aircraft workers were employed there. During the height of wartime employment one of every ten Los Angeles women worked in the aircraft industry. Many of WW II's Rosies earned starting salaries of 60 to 68 cents an hour; some worked up to $1.05 an hour by war's end.

Although she probably didn't think about it at the time, Rosie the Riveter in the 1940s opened entirely new vistas for women of the '60s, '70s, and '80s.

One California woman aviator—a WW II WAFS veteran—pioneered in helicopter advances and flight instruction. Lauretta Foy, a Warner Brothers dancer in the 1930s, received her pilot's license in 1940. Following WW II service Foy became a test pilot and flight instructor for North American Aviation. In 1961 she took her first helicopter ride; it generated an entirely new facet for her flying career. Foy became the world's 47th woman helicopter pilot, joined Hughes Helicopters to instruct police helicopter pilots from the U.S. and 21 foreign countries, and later became a pilot and heliport expert for Bell Helicopter. Foy today continues as an active aviation consultant.

A bright new star in California's galaxy of women aviators is Brooke Knapp. She earned her wings only five years before setting an around-the-world record of 50 hours, 32 minutes in February 1983 in her Learjet 35, appropriately named *The American Dream.* Knapp and her *American Dream* were thwarted in November 1983 when she attempted an under-60-hours pole-to-pole circumnavigation of the world. She was grounded in Recife, Brazil, by landing gear problems. In the spirit of her California aviation sisterhood, however, Knapp vows to continue her assault on long-distance flight records.

## HOLLYWOOD: A LIFELONG ROMANCE WITH AVIATION

Zoom. Spin. Climb. Pursue. Strafe. Dive. Even crash. The excitement of airplanes and aviation, of sleek, beautiful aircraft, of dashing pilots and the sweethearts awaiting their return to earth.

It was a natural "affair," the dramatic depiction of aerial action captured by the only medium capable of portraying the three-dimensional movement that is aviation's hallmark. It was a love affair between two fledgling industries, aviation and the movies, that began soon after the Wrights' first powered flight.

In 1909 at a small field outside Rome, Wilbur Wright demonstrated the brothers' amazing flying machine for King Victor Emmanuel III. On one flight Wilbur took along a Universal News cameraman, to record for the first time in history aerial maneuvers on film. The Wright flights in 1909 at Fort Myer, Virginia, and in

France and Italy were recorded on newsreel film. It marked the beginning of the link that today is evoked by special effects visualizing future air and space travel. The pioneering *2001: A Space Odyssey*, the blockbusting *Star Wars* series, and other science-fiction thrillers made possible by the combination of computers and modern film technology are modern exemplars of a heritage of nearly 80 years of filmed aviation features and dramas.

Southern California in the early 1900s was the site of not only aviation's roots but of the "Hollywood legend" as well. Movie moguls, notably Cecil B. De Mille, had enough surplus drive and determination to directly affect aviation and motion pictures. Even while laying groundwork for what was to become one of Hollywood's most powerful movie kingdoms, De Mille took time to personally plead the case for support of his Mercury Aviation efforts to the Los Angeles Chamber of Commerce.

In nearly 80 years of parallel growth of the aviation and motion-picture industries, hundreds of Hollywood stars and lesser lights were active flying avocationists. Intrigued by the romance and challenge of flight, they learned to fly, restored antique airplanes, and fought for their country in the aerial battles.

At Culver City Airport's flying school (run by Bob and Margaret Blair) such movie notables as Clark Gable, Jimmy Stewart, Ruth Chatterton, and Henry Fonda took their first flying lessons. Movie cowboy "Hoot" Gibson remodeled his own plane and flew in the 1927 Dole Race. Two men destined to enhance Hollywood's romance with flying, director William Wellman and writer John Monk Saunders, were members of the famed World War I Lafayette Escadrille. Jimmy Stewart, hero of many aviation films, was a World War II USAAF pilot and is now a retired Major General. Bob Cummings was a World War II flight instructor. Cliff Robertson and the late Steve McQueen restored, owned, and flew antique sport airplanes. George Kennedy, originator of the tough "Joe Patroni" airline mechanic from the *Airport* film series, is an active pilot, as was the timeless Wallace Beery, star of many flying films. In the 1935 classic,

*West Point of the Air*, Beery plays an Army flyer who brings up his son, Robert Young, in the best between-wars spit-and-polish tradition. Another "silver-screen idol," Wayne Morris, was a World War II U.S. Navy fighter pilot. George Peppard, anti-hero ace of *The Blue Max*, is an active pilot.

Despite this real-life flying fascination of Hollywood personalities, aviation truly blossomed in the "reel-life" dramas that emanated from the world's film capital. In their outstanding narration of Hollywood's love affair with aviation, *Stunt Flying in the Movies*, authors Jim and Maxine Greenwood characterized the magic that flying has brought to films:

*Be it good or evil, the airplane is, in Hollywood, a device imposing its own imperatives upon characters and story. Put an airplane on the silver screen and it dominates the scene. The movie easily becomes 'an airplane story,' the symbol of defiance, destruction or disaster. In the minds of viewers, at least, it is almost as if the flying machine itself had turned into a wild animal or an active volcano.*

Hollywood recaptured, recreated, and documented aviation milestones. The 1946 film, *Gallant Journey*, starring Glenn Ford, was a biography of California aviation pioneer John J. Montgomery. Jimmy Stewart's portrayal of Lindbergh in *The Spirit of St. Louis* forever enhanced that milestone event. The made-for-television movie, *Red Flag: The Ultimate Game*, revealed the previously mysterious role of USAF's Nellis AFB Aggressor squadrons, in which Air Force pilots assume the mantle of enemy pilots flying Soviet-marked airplanes in real-life air combat situations.

Although one of the first feature-length flying films, *The Great Air Robbery*, produced by Universal in 1919, was actually a story of U.S. Air Mail service hijackings set in the future (1930), it was the flying feats of World War I that established the first "era" of Hollywood airplane pictures. In the 1920s and 1930s, Hollywood, in effect, reprised "The War to End All Wars." The two best-known, and pacesetting, films of this era were *Wings*, winner of the first-ever Oscar in

1927 for best picture, and *Hell's Angels*. Directed by World War I pilot William Wellman, "Wings" was the first "big budget" aviation picture (estimated to cost $2 million) in film history. The movie starred Charles "Buddy" Rogers, Richard Arlen, and the "It" girl, Clara Bow. A bit player in *Wings* was a gangly young man destined to go on to greater things, Gary Cooper. Interestingly, even famed Hollywood columnist Hedda Hopper appeared in the film. Written by Wellman's compatriot from the Lafayette Escadrille, John Monk Saunders, *Wings* had an infusion of realism never before captured on the silver screen. Reminiscing in later years about the making of *Wings*, Buddy Rogers recalled that many of his flight sequences in World War I Spads were actually piloted by a young Army Air Corps lieutenant who squeezed into the cockpit with Rogers to do the actual flying. That lieutenant was Hoyt S. Vandenberg, later to become USAF chief of staff. Another of the approximately 300 pilots used in the film was "Hap" Arnold. Hard on the heels of the silent *Wings* was Howard Hughes' talkie, *Hell's Angels*.

The third famous World War I film was Howard Hawks' *The Dawn Patrol* first released in 1930, for which writer Saunders won an Academy Award. The original version starred Richard Barthelmess and Douglas Fairbanks, Jr. Using many of the original 1930 flight scenes, *Dawn Patrol* was remade in 1938, starring Errol Flynn, David Niven, and Donald Crisp.

Aerial dogfights and the mystique of daring World War I pilots continued in films such as *The Legion of the Condemned*, the first film in which Gary Cooper starred; *The Woman I Love*, in which Paul Muni played a World War I ace; and even carried into the mid-1960s with the release of *The Blue Max*, an anti-war film depicting war's impersonal brutality and the ambition of a WW I fighter pilot (George Peppard) to win the coveted German medal, the "Blue Max." As authors Greenwood noted about the film: "The flying scenes . . . were among the most spectacular ever created for an aviation-oriented motion picture."

In the years between the two world wars came an era of romantic dramas depicting aviation's evolution, particularly in the peacetime air services. *Men With Wings*, released by Paramount in 1938, traced the then 30-plus-year history of aviation from the Wrights to the development of multi-engine bombers of the mid-1930s. It starred Ray Milland, Fred MacMurray, Andy Devine, and Kitty Kelly. Jimmy Cagney and Pat O'Brien starred in two classics depicting aviation in the 1930s, *Devil Dogs of the Air* and *Ceiling Zero*. In 1938 the MGM release, *Test Pilot*, became not only a classic aviation film featuring Clark Gable, Spencer Tracy, and Myrna Loy but also "starred" an airplane that would become a major force in World War II, the B-17 Flying Fortress. Gable starred with the venerable Wallace Beery in another MGM epic of those between-war years, *Helldivers*.

With war in Europe a certainty and ample evidence that the U.S. would become involved, Hollywood flying films shifted to another era lasting through the Second World War, Korea, and even Vietnam. The 1939-1945 world conflict, like the 1914-1918 war before it, was a catalyst for a veritable "market basket" of flying films.

In 1941 Paramount's *I Wanted Wings*, starring Ray Milland, William Holden, Brian Donlevy, Wayne Morris, and the subtle beauty of Veronica Lake, was a major factor in recruiting flying cadets for America's military forces. Many films were produced with the enthusiastic cooperation of the War Department and individual services. *Air Force, Wing and a Prayer* (shot in 1944 during the shakedown cruise of the Navy carrier, USS *Yorktown*,) and *God is My Co-pilot*, the autobiography of Robert L. Scott, who originally gained fame as one of General Claire Chennault's "Flying Tigers" in China, were each supported by service locations and equipment.

Hal Roach Studios became known as "Fort Roach"; the facilities were used to produce motion pictures for the war effort. One serviceman assigned to "Fort Roach" was a young lieutenant named Ronald W. Reagan. The future U.S. president and his first lady appeared together in only one film during their individual

Hollywood careers, the 1957 flight film, *Hellcats of the Navy*.

Just as in the years following World War I, the late '40s and '50s saw a rash of films whose story lines were WW II aviation. *Men of the Fighting Lady, Command Decision,* and *Twelve O'Clock High* are notable examples. John Wayne, America's ultimate movie cowboy hero, portrayed a fearless flyer in a number of films, including *The Flying Tigers, Flying Leathernecks, Island in the Sky, The High and the Mighty,* and even the jet-age *Jet Pilot* in 1957. *Jet Pilot* was a Howard Hughes production that featured, as Jim and Maxine Greenwood wrote, " . . . some truly breathtaking air-to-air photography." The Greenwoods noted: "However, the spectacular footage of F-86s, T-33s . . . and even the Bell X-1 could not rescue the picture from an implausible plot and some of the silliest dialogue ever put on a sound track. The film was withdrawn from distribution shortly after its release and 'remained in the can' until after Hughes' death. *Jet Pilot's* first major public appearance didn't come until 1981, when it was shown on NBC TV."

The jet age and the Korean conflict spawned such aviation epics as *Breaking the Sound Barrier* and *The Bridges at Toko-Ri*.

In films such as *It's a Mad, Mad, Mad World, The Great Waldo Pepper, Around the World in 80 Days, Tarnished Angels,* and a film starring America's current male heartthrob, Tom Selleck, *High Road to China,* Hollywood recalled the nostalgic barnstorming and "devil-may-care" pilots of the 1920s and 1930s. These films represented another era and contributed to a renaissance of aviation's so-called golden age.

With the *Airport* series of films in the 1970s Hollywood practically made a career of aviation disaster movies. Because of massive challenges depicted in these films—midair collisions, ditchings at sea, and midair transfers of emergency pilots to bring crippled aircraft and their crews to safety—the *Airport* series enabled the movies to continue the long-standing tradition of portraying true heroes who saved passengers and planes and drew audience adulation and applause. However, like many other modern-day Hollywood epics, *Airport*

became the victim of a hilarious spoof: *Airplane*. The film satirizes almost every in-flight emergency and disaster ever attempted in the movies. And the "stars" fared no better.

California's aviation history is replete with pioneers who achieved mightily. Fortunately, California's aviation *motion picture* history is also replete with people who have documented that progress on the only medium that captures the inherent excitement of aviation in nearly eight decades of movies that graphically trace aviation's heritage.

## BY ANY OTHER NAME, THEY'RE STILL BUFFS

For some it's pure nostalgia. For others it's the discovery of the adventure of flight. For a select few it's an extension into today's modern world of the sometimes-forgotten entrepreneurial spirit that buoyed California aviation in the early days. No matter the motivation, the romance of flight compels aviation's "buffs."

Mix a soupçon of nostalgia with a large dose of adventure and a pinch of practicality: the result is a potion that feeds a hearty aviation appetite. Not all aviation today is comprised of giant corporations, computers, teams of design engineers, and the trappings of big business. For many Californian senior citizens and youngsters alike—working to create or restore airplanes is a labor of love. For many it is a lifetime of dedication.

Perhaps the top "buff" of them all, at least the individual who may hold the longevity record, is Stan Soderberg, "Mother Hen" to the Hughes Spruce Goose. Soderberg points out: "I'm the only one who was with it prior to the flight and who is still with it." The "it", of course, is the giant H-4 Flying Boat now on permanent public display in Long Beach. Soderberg has lived with the Spruce Goose for more than 37 years. Since 1946 he has been its rigger, janitor, painter, custodian, carpenter, consultant, grease monkey, engineer, crew chief, and baby sitter. Soderberg began with Hughes Aircraft that year as a $1.19-per-hour maintenance man who kept up military transports, polished the Lockheed Model 14 Howard Hughes used to set a 1938 around-the-world record, and was ultimately assigned to construction and maintenance of the H-4. He was a member of the original team and a confidant of Howard Hughes during visits to the construction hangar in the early morning hours. Soderberg later patroled Long Beach Harbor by boat to check for flotsam in advance of initial taxi runs and the Hercules' only flight, after which Soderberg joined the 300-worker H-4 maintenance and modification crew, each sworn to secrecy. When Hughes' Flying Boat interest waned in 1962, the crew was reduced to 50 workers. Following Hughes' death in 1976, negotiations began with the intent of cutting up and disposing of the plane. Soderberg retired from Hughes; he couldn't be part of its destruction. His retirement, however, was brief. The Aero Club of Southern California, under the leadership of Nissen Davis, moved quickly to save the Spruce Goose. The airplane was donated to the Club, then loaned permanently to Wrather Corporation for its permanent display. Soderberg was called out of retirement to supervise the Flying Boat's temporary move, restoration, and final trip to its spot of honor alongside the *Queen Mary*. Because there was some damage during the move, Soderberg recalled old skills and performed fabric and dope repair on the H-4's vertical stabilizer and a control surface. It was a surface he had first covered in 1946.

Soderberg now works for Wrather; his "baby" is still the Spruce Goose. But for the first time in 37 years his overseeing chores are "in the spotlight." It's a sharp contrast to the secrecy and mystique of the Hughes era. Nonetheless, the saga and intrigue of the Goose continues, abetted by Soderberg. If they have parts problems for the airplane, Soderberg says: "I can even get replacement parts because we were originally going to build three airplanes and I know where there are parts to the other two still in storage in a warehouse in Carson."

Military aviation has always provided a catalyst for aviation progress. As a result, many buffs are caught up in the nostalgia of military aircraft, from World War I to the jet age. Disdaining restoration of antique propeller

aircraft, Bruce Goessling, with his wife, Linda, has found a full-time vocation in the rehabilitation of military jets for flight use. In their Chino shop the Goesslings and eight mechanics work on such varied jets as a Lockheed T-33, a Douglas A-4 Skyhawk, a North American F-86 Sabrejet, and even a British Hawker Hunter.

For Goessling, however, his company, Unlimited Aircraft Limited (UAL), has become a business venture serving other aviation buffs. The top performance aircraft being restored by Goessling is a Northrop T-38 Talon for Chuck Thornton, a Los Angeles investment executive and pilot, who intends to use the two-place Mach 1.3 jet for business travel as well as for lease to companies looking for a high-performance flight-test aircraft.

UAL is also working on other high-performance jet aircraft for one of California's top aviation buffs, Dave Tallichet, owner of Specialty Restaurant Corp. Tallichet owns perhaps more vintage aircraft, scattered in locations around the state and nation, than anyone outside established aviation/aerospace museums. A WW II B-17 pilot with the 8th Air Force in Europe, Tallichet not only owns the Hawker Hunter, but also has a T-33, F-86, two De Havilland Vampire jets, three SAAB Lansens, and a fleet of other aircraft that, if assembled in one place, would rival some military squadrons. Other military jet owners are Gary Levitz (Levitz Furniture), with an F-86 and T-33, and Richard Bach (author of *Jonathan Livingston Seagull*), who owns a T-33.

For a dedicated collection of stalwarts at Van Nuys and Mojave airports, all of whom are aviation buffs, Lockheed's T-33 provides the base for an entrepreneural venture recalling California's aviation small-business halcyon days of the '20s and '30s. Forming a corporation headed by Russ O'Quinn, engineer and test pilot, and comprising a cadre of Kelly Johnson's top management from Lockheed's Skunk Works, including test pilot Tony Levier who test flew the first T-33, they are remanufacturing T-33s. The new airplane is the Skyfox military tactical trainer intended for use by a number of nations.

O'Quinn piloted the new Skyfox, re-engined with two Garrett turbofan engines and a new nose and tail built on the original T-33 airframe, into the sky at Mojave Airport for its first flight in August 1983. The high-performance jet is intended for remanufacturing by nations with aircraft production capability. O'Quinn calls the Skyfox "a hot airplane that will meet the needs of many countries around the world for the next 10 to 20 years."

At the opposite end of the performance scale Ernie Hawk heads a team of "hangar-retired guys from Lockheed, McDonnell Douglas, Northrop, and North American . . . who were bored stiff and relished the idea of building a new airplane by hand from scratch." Hawk has spent 10 years and nearly $3 million designing and constructing his "Flying Truck." The GAF (for General Aviation Freight) Hawk 125 is a short-haul, air-cargo, single-engine turboprop airplane that its designers and builders believe will meet the needs of air freight operators who have been trying to reduce the major cost differential between air and truck freight.

The Hawk 125 is being built and flight tested at Yucca Valley Airport under the direction of a WW II pilot who flew F6F Hellcats from Navy carriers. The entrepreneurial Hawk proudly notes that he has not used anybody's money but his own. He is "convinced this airplane is going to be a winner." The dedicated group of aircraft company retirees has had a wide variety of experiences in their 10-year saga. One of Hawk's original compatriots, Larry Stewart, described the time they were trying to create smoke in a wind tunnel to test a model of the Flying Truck. "We rigged up a gadget with 20 cigars. It didn't work. The cigars were sucked into the wind machine. That was the day Ernie and me got the nickname 'the Wrong brothers.'"

Gas turbine engines, including turboprops utilizing the latest technology propellers, are the epitome of modern aviation. But Art Fritzen, a technician and craftsman with unique skills, eschews the jet age. Fritzen's skills, recalling another era, may be unique. California Fritzen Propeller Company, a one-man Los Angeles shop, turns out wooden propellers for aircraft long since out of production. Plying his trade for more than 60 years, Fritzen first rebuilt a propeller for his Jenny in 1923. In the ensuing years Fritzen handcrafted propellers for Amelia Earhart and Fred Noonan, for Nieuports, Gypsy Moths, for the recreated Wright Flyer that flew at Kitty Hawk for the 75th anniversary of powered flight, and a B-25 for the Hollywood film *20 Seconds Over Tokyo*. In 1983, still proud of his ability to work wonders with wood, Fritzen produced a number of eight-bladed wind machines for the movie business.

Dotted across the state at airports, restoration shops, and antique airplane collections are small pockets of individuals whose interest is aviation nostalgia, but with actual flight as the objective. One group, headquartered in Paradise, California, calls itself "The Birds of Paradise." A chapter of the international Experimental Aircraft Association, the Birds work on home-built replicas of famous aircraft. Many are former Southern California aviation workers, now retired, who are recreating Piper Cubs, P-51s, and Pitts Specials. But they are also building the new, radical Vari-eze as well as some ultralights. One member is building an amphibious Osprey so he can fly to lakes across the West. In addition to keeping planes at Paradise Airport, some club members build and maintain aircraft at Chico Airport.

One "Bird of Paradise" is a truly dedicated senior citizen. Arthur York, 80 years old, is constructing his own home-built helicopter, using his skills as a former Lockheed and shipyard welder. With only helicopter manuals and a basic kit, York's helicopter resembles the early tubing-and-bailing-wire creations of helicopter pioneer Igor Sikorsky.

For many Californians aviation nostalgia becomes reality only if they are able to take aloft their antique aircraft to engage in aerial dogfighting or barnstorming. At John Wayne Airport in Orange County and Chino Airport in Riverside County, Bob Olson's Sunshine Aviation caters to aviators who want the thrill of going up in an open-cockpit craft to perform loops and rolls. In many cases, Olson's customers are not even pilots. They simply want to recapture the thrills experienced by the Curtisses, Martins, Doolittles, and others who earned their wings with an airstream in their face, their leather helmet and goggles firmly affixed and a white scarf trailing behind. For their first-hand open-cockpit experience, Olson provides the weekend warriors with Stearman biplanes, top speed about 90 mph. The Stearman with its fabric-covered wings and open cockpit provides a heady return to aviation's Golden Age.

In Madera, the heartland of California's San Joaquin Valley, military aircraft nostalgia was at its height in 1983. The 12th annual Gathering of Warbirds, sponsored by the Air Force Association, included a fly-in of operational P-51 Mustangs, P-47 Thunderbolts, B-26 bombers, PBY-5A Catalinas, Ryan trainers, Navy Bearcats, and even a German Messerschmitt Me 108. For a few glorious days at Madera Airport the pages of aviation history were turned back to World War II.

*Above: Called by the* Los Angeles Examiner *in 1949 "the area's outstanding flying instructor of the 1920s," Burdett Fuller (shown here about 1927) included among his hundreds of students Bobbie Trout, Jack Frye, Paul Richter, and Jake Moxness. Courtesy, Nixon Galloway*

*Above left: Burdett Air Lines and School of Aviation at 94th and Western Avenue in Los Angeles opened in 1922 and was sold by Burdett Fuller to Jack Frye and his colleagues in 1927 and 1928. Courtesy, Nixon Galloway*

*Left: Union Air Terminal (present Glendale-Burbank-Pasadena Airport) is pictured here in the late 1920s, when Boeing Air Transport ran it. Courtesy Gordon S. Williams.*

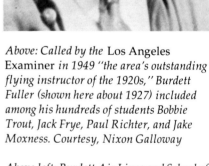

*Above: Partly because of his outstanding management of the 1928 National Air Races hosted at Mines Field, Cliff Henderson was named the first Los Angeles Director of Airports, with a salary of $400 per month. Courtesy, Smithsonian Institution*

*Above left: To enable LAX to serve the 40 million annual passengers anticipated by 1990, a $700 million modernization project began in 1981. The program, completed in 1984, included double decking the airport roadway and adding such new buildings as the 963,000-square-foot International Terminal. This view from the west shows construction in November 1982. Courtesy, Los Angeles Department of Airports*

*Above: Los Angeles' Mines Field (today's LAX) began operations in 1928, but was not officially dedicated until June 1930, when this picture was made. The original hangar still stands on the field's south perimeter, Imperial Boulevard. Courtesy SPNBPC/ LAPL*

*Right: During the past 25 years two Airport Department general managers have shaped Los Angeles' municipal airport development and operation: Francis T. Fox (left), from 1958 until 1968, and Clifton A. Moore (right). Fox supervised the massive building program that brought LAX to world-class status in the 1960s. Under Moore's guidance the department has navigated the rapids of noise, pollution, and expansion with good success. Courtesy, Los Angeles Department of Airports*

*Right: Electrical installer Olive E. Bacon works on an instrument panel wiring harness for a Lockheed Hudson bomber, one of 3,000 that would be turned out at the Burbank plant for Britain's Royal Air Force by May 1943. Courtesy, CALAC*

*Opposite, top left: The most famous working woman pilot in Hollywood annals was Florence Lowe "Pancho" Barnes, granddaughter of pioneer balloonist Thaddeus S.C. Lowe. Socialite, actress, stuntwoman, animal trainer, script girl, and immensely skilled pilot, Barnes set several important records in her legendary career. Courtesy, SPNBPC/LAPL*

*Opposite, top right: Jackie Cochran, shown here around 1934, learned to fly in 1932 at Long Island's Roosevelt Field. She polished her skills at the Ryan Flying School at San Diego and became a converted Californian. By 1964 Cochran held 85 world flying records—more than any pilot in the world at that time. Courtesy, Burbank-Glendale-Pasadena Airport*

*Repeating a drama staged all around America in 1927, Charles A. Lindbergh flew the* Spirit of St. Louis *to Sacramento in September, where local pilots escorted the once Lone Eagle to his touchdown. Courtesy, California State Library Collection, Sacramento History Center*

*Development of a municipal airport for Oakland began in 1927 on a site (shown here near the end of the decade) selected by the Army for its first transpacific flight. On June 28, 1927, an Army Fokker monoplane with a crew of three took off from Oakland, reaching Hawaii the next day. Courtesy, Smithsonian Institution*

*Amelia Earhart and Paul Mantz, two of the era's finest aviators, are shown beneath the wing of the record-setting Vega during a visit to Lockheed's plant in August 1935. Courtesy, CALAC*

*Twenty-three-year-old Californian Bobbi Trout (left) and 17-year-old New Yorker Elinor Smith set an in-flight endurance record. After taking off from Metropolitan (now Van Nuys) Airport on November 27, 1929, the pair stayed aloft 42 hours and were the first women to refuel an aircraft in flight. Courtesy, SPNBPC/LAPL*

# CHAPTER NINE

# EPILOGUE

Powered flight is little more than 80 years old. In that miniscule span of world history man has gone from the sands of Kitty Hawk to the dust of the moon. In the 12 seconds consumed as the Wright Flyer traversed 120 *feet*, the space shuttle *Challenger* covered 56 *miles*.

In the face of the naysayers in history who said "It can't be done," California's aviation pioneers literally belied that notion. They forged a path, a solid highway, leading to man's future in the atmosphere and in outer space. In only 80 years they carefully set in place building blocks for a road leading even farther than the eye can see. These pioneers were seers, able to perceive that powered flight provided a vehicle pointed directly into the future.

What would these giants of the Golden Age of Aviation think if they were suddenly plunked down into the world of the 1980s, in a world of supersonic flight, travel in one day to almost anywhere in the world, into an age of instantaneous communications? Because they were visionaries, few would be surprised.

Igor Sikorsky, father of the modern helicopter, would certainly not be awed by today's achievements. In 1930 he was asked to look ahead 50 years (to 1980). Sikorsky was particularly prescient about air transport:

*Travel will be comfortable and passengers will feel as if the craft were entirely motionless. In the heated and nicely arranged interior the rooms of the ship will be kept at a constant atmospheric pressure of say, two-thirds that on ground level. There will be no air pockets and no motion of any sort will be felt except for a slight vibration given by extremely powerful*

*motors, or rather turbines.*

That projection of jet travel was made nearly 10 years before the first-ever jet flight and more than 20 years before commercial jet travel.

In 1982 Sir Frank Whittle, credited (along with Hans von Ohain of Germany) with the invention of the modern jet engine, looked back on more than 50 years since he first dreamed of gas turbine-powered aircraft. Sir Frank mused: "Everyone thought I was a crazy optimist. As it turned out, I was actually a crazy pessimist." Assessing the future, Sir Frank said, "There's still plenty of room for development."

## TECHNOLOGY: THE WAVE OF THE FUTURE

The contrast is vivid between aeroplanes flown in 1910 at Dominguez Hills and the civil transports, military fighters and bombers, and space shuttles that have evolved over three-quarters of a century. Nonetheless, some of aviation's earliest achievements are finding their way into aircraft designs for the future. California's Rutan brothers, Burt and Dick, were among the first to demonstrate the aerodynamic advantages of the canard (the forward airfoil) to flying characteristics of modern aircraft. Jack Northrop first demonstrated in 1929 the advantages of his clean flying wing. Aircraft studies for the future by NASA and airframe manufacturers such as Boeing, McDonnell Douglas, and Lockheed include giant air ships based on what has become known as the "span loading" principle. In the late 1970s the NASA director said, "We have, in effect, rediscovered the flying wing."

New materials from which airplanes can be built are high on the future's priority list. Composite materials, largely graphite, are being used in today's commercial and military aircraft. These materials, derived from graphite epoxy similiar to that used in sporting equipment, offer not only lighter weight but also increased strength in many cases. Some observers see an all-composite aircraft in the future.

Military and civil aircraft cockpits are transitioning from mechanical dials and meters to the "all-glass" front office with digital readouts and television-type screens providing all basic flight information. Modern mini-computers enable flight crews to enter flight information, including weather and navigation, before takeoff. A computer then plans the most accurate and efficient route.

Investigations are underway to utilize solar power for flight propulsion. California's Paul MacCready designed and achieved success with the Solar Challenger, a lightweight aircraft that made aviation history by flying across the English Channel fueled only by sunlight. Lockheed Missiles and Space Company is studying a solar-powered high-altitude platform that could loiter for months at altitudes of 60,000-80,000 feet to provide weather and intelligence surveillance.

Aviation advances have not been limited to large civil transports and military aircraft. More than 3,000 Californians are taking to the skies in what are called "ultralights." Powered by engines of about the same size as those in a snowmobile, the tiny aircraft, made of aluminum tubing, steel cable, and Dacron fabric, weigh little more than their pilots.

## MILITARY AVIATION: ANOTHER GROWTH CYCLE

Altered world political conditions and a changed federal administration combined in the early 1980s to emphasize defense programs into the next century. With five top defense contractors' major operations in California, the state has realized the benefits of this restored interest in defense development. Rockwell is prime

contractor for the USAF B-1B bomber; Northrop is prime contractor on the futuristic Stealth bomber provides guidance systems for the MX missile; McDonnell Douglas produces KC-10 tankers and the projected USAF C-17 transport; Rockwell and Lockheed are major contractors on the NASA space shuttle program; Hughes Aircraft is the nation's leader in space technology and electronics; Hughes Helicopters is providing the U.S. Army's next-generation attack helicopter. A host of subcontractors form a second tier of the defense business in California.

## SPACE SHUTTLE: A BUSINESS VENTURE

NASA's space shuttle has become a logical extension of private sector use of aviation as a cargo/passenger-carrying transport system. The only difference between the space shuttle and giant passenger and cargo-carrying transports produced by California manufacturers is that this airframe, designed by Rockwell in Los Angeles and built at the company's Palmdale facilities, is carrying its payload into space.

From the first space shuttle flight in April 1981, the program has demonstrated its capabilities to transport payloads—a crew, commercial payloads for America and its allies, and ultimately passengers. Brigadier General James Abramson, NASA's deputy director in charge of the space shuttle, said in 1983: "It is the means to make America a space-faring nation."

A logical extension of aviation's leadership in passenger and freight transportation, the shuttle represents California's next giant step in aerospace progress.

## AVIATION/AEROSPACE: AMERICA'S EXPORT LEADER

From the years immediately prior to World War II, American aviation development, production, and operational achievements have set a standard against which the rest of the world is measured. As a result, the aerospace industry is the number one U.S. exporter of products to other nations of the world, accounting for 7.4 percent of the total of U.S. exports. With

$7 billion in U.S. aircraft exports in 1982, aviation was responsible for nearly 45,000 production jobs in the United States.

Because of the staggering cost of development and production of major aircraft programs and a shrinking world made possible by the jet transport itself, more aviation programs are taking on an international hue. The leading international challenger to traditional U.S. leadership of large civil transports, Airbus Industrie, boasts that one-third of its current A300 and A310 Airbus is made in America. In fact, according to Alan S. Boyd, chairman and president of Airbus Industrie of North America, "There's more American content than French content, and also more American content than British or German (in the Airbus)." Boyd says, "Every time we sell an airplane, anywhere in the world, we sell American labor." One of Boyd's projections for the future of international civil transport business is: "Perhaps one day we will read about an Airbus/Boeing/Douglas con-sortium, should I include Lockheed? to build a twin-aisle space shuttle."

There is no doubt about future civil world transport business. The world's airlines will need 6,700 new aircraft in the years between now and the turn of the next century. That calls for an investment of about $300 billion. According to James E. Worsham, president of McDonnell Douglas Aircraft, there will be twice the number of commercial aircraft in the year 2000 as those flying today. He sees many more international "gateways," cities with major airports providing international service. By the turn of the next century, Worsham envisions operational service of supersonic transports, including a supersonic executive jet. In the year 2000 Worsham projects individual airplane utilization of up to 3,000 hours per year; an increasing number of twin- and three-engine transports that will be considerably more cost effective than today's four-engine airplanes; a continued use of the propeller-type airplane, but with what are called "propfans" (multiple bladed propeller-like devices driven by highly efficient gas turbines); and super-quiet, fuel-efficient power plants propelling transports

carrying from 100 to 600 passengers.

The greatest challenge facing the aviation industry is greater productivity. With airplane *performance* pushed to its highest level short of supersonic flight, aircraft manufacturers are concentrating their efforts on increasing operating efficiencies of the total aircraft system. Fuel-efficient engines, airplanes designed to carry larger payloads more efficiently, electronic systems to make flight safer and more reliable, and production, manufacturing, and materials advances to lower relative cost per pound of aircraft delivered are principal targets of these manufacturers. The next target is the cost of labor inherent in not only the manufacture of aircraft but operations of passenger and freight-carrying airlines as well. Industry leaders and observers alike agree that increased productivity, and the resultant high-quality, high-value product or service at a relatively lower price, is the *only* way in which American aviation will remain internationally competitive.

## CALIFORNIA WINGS: THE PAST A PROLOGUE FOR THE FUTURE

California's aviation heritage has paralleled world progress in the air. Through man's evolution in flight, aviation achievements made in the Golden State have led the way. The gargantuan strides made by California aviation developments were accomplished by giants who were born here or adopted California as their headquarters. Over the years of the 20th century, they demonstrated the philosophy expressed by Joseph Conrad in 1902: "The mind of man is capable of anything, because everything is in it, all the past as well as all the future." Anne Morrow Lindbergh, writer, aviation pioneer, and wife of America's best-known aviator, writing in 1940, might well have been speaking of California aviation approaching the end of the 20th century when she said: "The wave of the future is coming and there is no fighting it."

*Above and top: Riding high on the crest of the aviation interest that swept the nation after Lindbergh's 1927 transatlantic flight, two California projects enjoyed enormous success. The 1928 National Air Races, hosted by Los Angeles, earned nationwide headlines, and Howard Hughes' $4 million 1930 epic film,* Hell's Angels, *grossed $7 million. Courtesy, NASM and Larry Edmunds Bookstore*

*Above: A superb example of cooperation among the men and women for whom vintage airplanes and the romance of aviation are never obsolete is WAE's 1926 Douglas M-2 mailplane, which was reconstructed during 1973-1977 and then flown to the National Air and Space Museum. Here, with Don Lykins in the cockpit,* Old Red *makes an early test flight over Long Beach after its resurrection. Courtesy, MD*

*Right: Photographed high above Edwards AFB in October 1967, North American's X-15 rocket-powered research plane generated an enormous body of data relating to aerodynamics and structural techniques for hypersonic flight. Courtesy, EAFBHO*

*Below: Resplendent in house colors, the demonstration McDonnell Douglas DC-10 Series 10 gleams in this early afternoon photograph taken above Santa Catalina Island's Avalon Bay in 1971. Courtesy, MD*

*Bottom: The final variant of the Lockheed Constellation was the Model 1649A Starliner, which first flew on October 11, 1956, and is shown on a blustery day at Burbank. Only 43 were built (for TWA, Air France, and Lufthansa). Courtesy, CALAC*

*Opposite: In a fine example of Boeing's justly admired predelivery photographs, one of AirCal's 15 Boeing 737s dazzles the eye in its 1968-vintage livery. Courtesy, the Boeing Company*

*Below: In 1980, prior to acquisition by Republic, the Hughes Airwest fleet included 41 Douglas DC-9s painted in a memorable scheme. Hughes planes were popularly called the "Flying Bananas." Courtesy, Clinton Groves, ATP Incorporated*

*Above: During a 1982 visit to Beale AFB with Clarence "Kelly" Johnson, Lockheed's chief photographer Robert C. Ferguson made this fine informal portrait of the great designer. Courtesy, CALAC*

*Top: Photographed at Beale AFB in 1982, Lockheed's Mach 3 SR-71 Blackbird, the world's fastest airplane since its debut in December 1964, is powered by twin 32,500-pound-thrust P&W J58 turbojets with afterburners that operate continuously during flight. Courtesy, CALAC*

# PART FOUR: PARTNERS IN INDUSTRY

*In this circa 1912 view of the Glenn L. Martin factory on South Los Angeles Street, engineers and craftsmen work on a seaplane. At right is a completed float showing the step design which allowed the plane to break free of the water during takeoff. Courtesy, MD*

California's aviation industry first rose on wings, usually of fabric, but 50 years later was soaring mostly on fins, occasionally of exotic metals. The wings had been on manned aircraft. The fins were on unmanned satellites and missiles; the industry had become more aerospace than aviation. Moreover, most of its very largest companies had become that way by concentrating less on things that flew and more on their electronic innards. The advent of the aerospace age worked a far more profound change on the aviation industry than had the arrival of jet engines in the piston era.

To be sure, there still were wings and human beings on the space shuttles of the 1970s and 1980s, and conventional aircraft manufacture in California set records. In 1984, for example, the Long Beach plants of McDonnell Douglas won a $3.3-billion order from a single U.S. carrier for 100 new-design airliners, representing the largest single order in history to that time. Deliveries were to start in 1985 and continue through 1991.

Meanwhile, Rockwell International commenced work in the early '80s at its Palmdale plants on B-1 bombers, with deliveries scheduled into the '90s—when Northrop was to start rolling out the so-called Stealth bombers.

Basically, however, since the *Sputnik* turning point of 1957, the aerospace aspects gradually overtook the parent aviation industry. Despite its name, Hughes Aircraft, for instance, had not built an airplane since the '40s—yet by 1984 had become California's leading manufacturing employer. And such other firms as Lockheed and Litton, traditionally associated with aviation, were building ships as well.

Aerospace's growing dominance over aviation was shown clearly by a 1983 study by the Aerospace Industries Association, a national trade group. Industry sales that year, including aircraft manufacture, totaled nearly $75 billion. Sales of more than $82 billion were forecast for 1984.

Sales of space hardware in 1983 gained 30.5 percent over those for the previous year—but the sales increase for civilian aircraft was only 2.3 percent.

Government defense spending played a major role in the shifting emphasis within California's skies-oriented industry. Noting that the state received 22 percent (or $26.3 billion) of all U.S. military spending in 1982 (though not solely for aerospace/aviation), Sacramento estimated that state companies would be getting 30 percent by 1986. It reported that one of every three manufacturing jobs in California already was aerospace-connected, with half of those workers employed on military projects.

Aerospace corporations in four California counties—Los Angeles, Orange, San Diego, and Santa Clara—were receiving more than 65 cents of every federal defense dollar reaching California in 1983.

In the '80s the majority of companies in the state's aviation industry were dealing in systems, components, and support, such as some of the firms profiled in the ensuing pages. Cammacorp, for one, thrived by converting engines to add life to the classic DC-8 into the 21st century. Aviall, for another, handled aviation services, gas-turbine engines, and parts worldwide. Other firms were active in both aviation and aerospace. Parker Hannifin and

Western Gear made their respective components and systems for aircraft, satellites, and missiles. California Avi-Tron, whose 10 founders made airplanes with wooden spars in the '30s, grew to hundreds of experts who helped put *Surveyor* on the moon.

Even more than the manufacturing and support facets of the California aviation industry, its essence in the public mind has doubtless been its services: the carriers. Turbulence afflicted them, especially in the early '80s.

The pattern of the carriers' steady growth since the '30s was disrupted in 1978, paradoxically as a result of deregulation. Taking advantage of it, more than a dozen airlines sprang up in California. Few lasted. The commuter airlines were hardest hit; of nine in the nation that had filed for bankruptcy by 1984, six were California carriers. Even long-established, long-haul carriers ailed, and one of them, Continental, ceased to be California-based, having been acquired by a smaller, Texas airline.

Cost-cutting and improved efficiencies, however, went far toward rescuing the major carriers. Pan American, ingrained in California history through its fabled China Clippers, was a leader in achieving them, and also supplied a dramatic pivot of recovery. In 1982 its chairman pledged to turn back his salary (then $350,000 yearly) if the airline did not turn a profit in 1983.

He didn't have to.

Aerospace Industries Association predicted its members would lay out $5.8 billion nationally in 1984 for capital improvements. With California expected to account for the major portion of that, the state estimated that during the five-year period to end in 1986, more than 700,000 new jobs would be created.

The climate for such growth nurtured both hard-headed fiscal figuring and a resurgence of confidence. Pan Am's acquisition of National Airlines in 1980 exemplified the former; McDonnell Douglas' purchase of Hughes Helicopters in 1984, the latter. In the closing decades of the 20th century, California's aviation industry appeared to be nearing once again the glory days of peacetime manufacturing when the state Chamber of Commerce could trumpet in 1936: "California Aircraft Plants Make Three-Fifths of All the Country's Planes."

Another example of the industry's seeming to come full circle was bound to delight those traditionalists who felt more at home in white scarves and open cockpits than with ultra-jet aircraft and aerospace's electronic wizardry. That was the disclosure in 1984 that both Lockheed and McDonnell Douglas were intensifying efforts to make aircraft propulsion more fuel efficient in the 1990s. They were studying—propeller-driven planes.

# CALIFORNIA CHAMBER OF COMMERCE

The California Chamber of Commerce's powerful boost to the state's fledgling aviation industry began with the printed word.

As early as September 1924 its *California Journal of Development,* with statewide circulation from its San Francisco headquarters, was promoting air shows, air mail, and "flying fields for commercial planes and the machines for aerial tourists." The magazine showcased such aviation advances as a 1925 carrier flying three "cabin planes," each roomy enough for four passengers, between Los Angeles and San Diego. It lauded the Checker Cab Company's plan to operate nine planes, every one adorned with the taxi firm's distinctive markings, from San Francisco to Los Angeles "at 100 miles per hour."

The *Journal* featured an enthusiastic aviation article by Herbert Hoover, then Secretary of Commerce. His son, the late Herbert Hoover, Jr., became a distinguished member of the Chamber's board in the '50s and '60s. Other 1926 stories profiled such organizations as Western Air Express, the Douglas Company, and Ryan Airlines. The recurring theme was "What Can the Business Men of California Do to Assist in the Development of Aviation?"

Meanwhile, the Chamber formed an Aeronautical Committee comprised of business executives and restless World War I flyers, which convened the first statewide conference on commercial aviation in May 1926 in Los Angeles. It emphasized the need for airports throughout the state.

The conference became an annual event, with the *Journal* chronicling the expanding agendas: "Industry Adopts the Airplane," "Financing Aeronautical Enterprises," and "Problems of Aviation Insurance."

In 1930 the Chamber spurred the state legislature into forming its own Aviation Committee, to make uniform a welter of laws regulating both commercial and private aviation in California. The remainder of the decade saw the *Journal* faithfully reflecting the growing sophistication of the industry with articles on airfield proliferation, flying schools, meteorology, airliner interior design, and marketing.

Retitled *California, the Magazine of the Pacific,* it devoted most of its 1940s coverage to World War II production and postwar planning—for vast international airports capable of handling jumbo jets, as well as "Airports for Recreation" and a "Downtown Heliport for Los Angeles." The '50s and '60s brought forth articles on additional topics like subsidies, trade routes, air freight, and charters.

*Starting in 1926, the California Chamber of Commerce's magazine devoted an entire issue to aviation each year.*

On May 24, 1963, the Chamber's board of directors prophetically resolved to obtain a federal Space Recovery Center in California. In the early '70s the Chamber sponsored and financed a Space Shuttle Task Force, the efforts of which helped North American Rockwell of El Segundo secure the prime contract to build the shuttles. In addition, the work of the task force influenced the decision to designate Edwards and Vandenberg Air Force bases as shuttle operation sites. The project promised over 70,000 jobs in California.

The Chamber and its magazine (renamed *Pacific Business* by 1970) entered the '80s with great momentum to further California's key role in the national space program, while proudly maintaining the standards of the earlier aviation era when the *Journal,* in 1936, was able to proclaim: "Flight Builders: California Aircraft Plants Make Three-Fifths of All the Country's Planes."

# ROCKWELL INTERNATIONAL CORPORATION

J.L. Atwood (left), chief executive of Rockwell's predecessor, North American Aviation, although retired, continues to serve as an advisor. Robert Anderson (right) is chairman and chief executive officer of Rockwell International Corporation.

Rockwell International Corporation traces its days as a major California aerospace company back almost five decades, when North American Aviation, a predecessor company, built a new plant adjacent to the Los Angeles International Airport.

Since the plant—one of the first in the nation designed to mass-produce airplanes—opened in 1935, the company has built more military airplanes than any other in the world and has produced most of the nation's manned spacecraft as well as the rocket engines that carried them into space.

Just as California has grown and become more diverse, so has Rockwell International. The merger in 1967 of North American Aviation

and Pittsburgh-based Rockwell Standard Corporation has resulted in an $8-billion, multi-industry organization that applies advanced technology to a wide range of products in aerospace, electronics, automotive, and general industries.

Rockwell's aerospace activities continue to be centered in California. With approximately 45,000 employees, the firm is one of the state's largest employers.

The company is building the B-1B strategic bomber for the U.S. Air Force, the Space Shuttle orbiters and their rocket engines for the National Aeronautics and Space Administration, and major elements of the Peacekeeper intercontinental ballistic missile.

The first production B-1B, which will replace the aging B-52 as the manned bomber of the nation's defensive force, is scheduled for rollout in the fall of 1984 at Rockwell's Palmdale facility. The Air Force has said it will order 100 of the sleek new bombers.

The B-1B continues the heritage of such famous Air Force aircraft as the P-51 and B-25 of World War II; the F-86 Sabre Jet, which mastered the Russian-built MiG in Korea; the F-100, the first fighter to fly super-

Rockwell International's heritage of excellence in aviation, electronics, space, and rocketry.

sonic in level flight; and the X-15 rocket research aircraft that first took man to the fringes of space.

Delivery of the fourth Space Shuttle orbiter is scheduled to occur in 1984. The fleet of manned spacecraft is the key element of the nation's space transportation system, which is demonstrating that space can provide practical benefits for everyone on earth.

Earlier, a Rockwell-built Apollo spacecraft carried the first American astronauts to the moon, and its engines were in all three stages of the Saturn launch vehicles.

The company's Rocketdyne division is developing the fourth stage for the Peacekeeper, continuing rocket engine production which began with Redstone and Explorer I, two of America's first space projects.

Originally a spinoff from its aircraft business, Rockwell's Defense Electronics Operation (DEO) is one of the largest in the United States. Headquartered in Anaheim, California, the organization built the guidance and control system for all three generations of the Minuteman intercontinental ballistic missile and is now providing similar systems for Peacekeeper. DEO is the principal supplier of inertial navigation systems for the Navy's attack submarines.

A revolutionary new navigation satellite is being produced in Seal Beach that will enable users anywhere on or above the earth to determine their exact location and speed. Called the Navstar Global Positioning System, the program involves the production of 28 satellites.

The California aerospace industry has clearly demonstrated it has the capability to accept and solve any technical challenge. Rockwell International, as a part of this industrial stronghold, will continue to accept the challenge of making the impossible into the possible.

# AVIALL

Andrew G. Galef, chairman, was among the private investors who reacquired Aviall's key California component in 1979.

Frank D. Hintze, Aviall's vice-chairman in the 1980s, was founder and chief executive officer of Burbank's Aviation Power Supply.

Aviall, as its name implies, is an all-in-one aviation services firm: a major worldwide supplier in the 1980s of gas turbine engine support for aircraft and industrial applications, aircraft parts distribution, and general aviation aircraft and terminal services. Approximately two-thirds of its business involves general aviation, with the remainder in the airline and industrial gas turbine markets.

Aviall's earliest corporate component dates back to 1932 at Love Field, Dallas, where aviation pioneer Edwin F. "Doc" Booth formed a company to provide aircraft maintenance and engine overhaul services. Aviall's largest plants and heaviest employment are still in the Dallas area, and it has substantial West Coast operations based in Burbank, California, which were established in 1952 as Aviation Power Supply, Inc. (APS).

APS—contributing to California's wings for more than 30 years—was founded by Frank D. Hintze and Elmer M. Hanson, industry leaders dedicated to serving the needs of corporate, commercial, and private aircraft in all phases of engine overhaul, parts distribution, and sales. Its success made it a significant international factor in the aviation industry, repairing, maintaining, and overhauling gas turbine engines for

customers around the globe.

APS was acquired by the Ogden Corporation in 1969, but Frank D. Hintze, APS' founder and longtime chief executive officer, and a group of private investors led by Californian Andrew G. Galef bought it back in December 1979.

Things moved quickly after that. Within two years APS acquired Cooper Airmotive, the Texas firm that ultimately succeeded the original Texas-based companies, and APS and Cooper were combined in December 1981 into a single new organization called Aviall.

Aviall's growth has continued with its acquisition in 1983 of Bradair, Inc., originally of Houston, a distributor of mechanical and hydraulic parts and supplies for widely used commercial aircraft. Bradair is now based in Dallas.

A dramatic index to Aviall's

expansion in California: In 1952 APS' monthly sales were less than $50,000; by 1984 Aviall's original Burbank operations were contributing more than $3 million a month to the company's annual combined sales of some $300 million.

As another measure, there were fewer than 20 California employees when APS was founded in 1952. At the start of 1984 Aviall employed more than 400 in its 176,000-square-foot-Burbank plant, and more than 1,700 people were employed in the Dallas area and elsewhere throughout the United States and overseas. There were also California sales offices in Sacramento, San Diego, San Leandro, and Van Nuys (as well as engine specialists at the Palmdale and Edwards Air Force bases).

The total corporation has more than 40 distribution division sales offices on five continents, nearly 1.5 million square feet of plant space in the United States, some 300 direct and indirect service centers serving customers around the globe, and six regional turbine shops covering the general aviation community across the United States.

Aviall—having marked its 50th anniversary in 1982—has a proud history of continuing growth in the West Coast's aviation community. Its second half-century promises even greater contributions to California's and the world's wings!

The West Coast headquarters of Aviall is located in Burbank.

# CAMMACORP

The versatile DC-8, first commercial jetliner to surpass the speed of sound, faced legislative extinction. Although none had been built since 1972, more than 200 still were in service a decade later. They were targets, however, of increasingly stringent anti-noise regulations, and seemed doomed to premature retirement.

General Electric and SNECMA in France, through a joint venture, had developed a new power plant that could be the DC-8's salvation. The high-bypass-ratio CFM-56 engine not only was 25 percent more fuel efficient but also reduced noise to levels below those required for a new-generation aircraft. In 1976 GE was asking around the industry for airlines interested in preserving the DC-8 by re-engining.

Two men came forward. One was Jackson R. McGowen, a veteran engineer who had retired in 1973 as president of the Douglas Aircraft Company. He perceived that, with re-engining, many years of life remained for the DC-8 Series 70 and pronounced them "the only 200-plus passenger aircraft available through the 1980s that can be economically utilized over both medium- and long-range routes."

The other founder was Leroy Cooper, a Navy pilot in World War II and then a Lockheed executive and engine specialist. Together they envisioned "a unique arrangement in aviation" which they likened to an architectural firm that raises money for a building, has it built, and then leases and manages it. "It had not been done before," they recalled years later. "It took something new."

McGowen and Cooper, with an associate, incorporated the privately held CAMMACORP on February 3, 1977, and, with a secretary, moved into small offices above a bank on Sepulveda Boulevard in Los Angeles. Their new firm assumed a prime contractor and program management

*The first production pylon and CFM-56 engine pod is readied for installation in 1981. The engine, an example of international cooperation arranged in El Segundo, is produced at two locations in Ohio—and three in France.*

role using the McDonnell Douglas Corporation and CMF International (a joint company of GE and SNECMA, a French enterprise) in re-engining DC-8s with the new CFM-56 plant.

Also involved during the conversion process was the replacement of air conditioning and auxiliary power systems. In sum, CAMMACORP enabled DC-8 operators to solve what McGowen diagnosed as "the dilemma of meeting the requirement for fuel-efficient, quiet aircraft while maintaining control over the mounting investment required." Success was demonstrable. Operators' return on investment began to run 50 to 80 percent higher, due to the minimal capital outlay enabled by CAMMACORP's unique role.

The first roll-out of a re-engined and converted DC-8-71 occurred on August 15, 1981. By early 1983 CAMMACORP had contracted for more than 98 conversions for U.S. and

*Re-engined DC-8s may also have their interiors converted for corporate executives or heads of state. Versatility extends to 200-plus seating arrangements for carriers, or a cargo configuration, or a combination.*

foreign operators. Individuals among them included the Sultan of Oman and the President of Gabon.

CAMMACORP itself was expanding. Its staff, which had grown tenfold by 1983, moved to the recently completed LAX Business Center in El Segundo. There, as McGowen has put it, "Our work will continue the versatile DC-8's reputation as a practical, dependable jetliner throughout the 1980s and 1990s and into the 21st century."

*Founders Jackson R. McGowen (right) and Leroy Cooper, president and executive vice-president, respectively, congratulate each other at the roll-out of their firm's first conversion in Tulsa, Oklahoma, in August 1981.*

# AIRPORT PARK HOTEL

*The Airport Park Hotel, on the grounds of the Hollywood Park Thoroughbred Racetrack, is flanked by the Forum at left. Hotel vans provide regular service to the Los Angeles International Airport, only eight minutes away.*

*Guests can enjoy a respite from travel—or business meetings inside—at the pool. The ocean is nearby and such attractions as Marineland and Marina del Rey (and not forgetting Disneyland) are easily accessible.*

Airports are the crossroads of the modern world and, like the crossroads inns of yore, their contemporary hotels are far more than lodging places. They play an integral part in the movement of mankind—and its commerce. At the Los Angeles International Airport, with its 100,000 travelers daily, the Airport Park Hotel is literally outstanding. It rears 10 stories from the grounds of the Hollywood Park Thoroughbred Racetrack in Inglewood and is immediately adjacent to the sports and entertainment arena aptly called the "fabulous" Forum.

Acreage for the hotel was made available by the track and, in the since-passed era when carriers were complementing their airborne services with accommodations below, Pacific Southwest Airlines was the management when Airport Park opened its doors on July 31, 1973. "But airlines aren't hoteliers," an executive of the 1980s noted, and both ownership and management of the hotel eventually passed to International Innkeepers, Inc.

An international flavor came with that, ranging from the red, Spanish-mission-type tiles in the lobby to the guests. The hotel is favored by pilots of foreign airlines, as well as sports figures from the racetrack and Forum, who often overlap at the hotel. An example was the 1979 reception for Muhammad Ali, receiving an award from Anheuser-Busch. The firm honored the champ by parading six giant Clydesdale beer-wagon horses for him on the portico—to the delight of all.

Entertainers playing the Forum may be circus stars or world-renowned rock groups. The latter often take entire floors, and provide their own security. Nonetheless, the hotel was once besieged by 600 eager fans. They were held at bay.

The management clubs of the Northrop and Rockwell International corporations meet at the hotel monthly. So do municipal, school, and military associations, and service clubs. A California governor brought his entourage. Corporate executives and businessmen perhaps predominate among guests. They observe the growing practice of flying out again—without having to brave the metropolis itself. If they wish otherwise, however, they find that the Airport Park, by its location, provides the easiest access to Los Angeles freeways of all the LAX hotels.

The Airport Park offers 350 rooms and executive suites. Its 11 meeting and banquet areas can accommodate groups from 10 to 1,000 persons (and up to 800 diners in the Hall of Champions). The hotel is affiliated with the Best Western reservations systems. Its shops, salons, and boutiques tastefully augment its restaurants, lounges, and amenities of pool and spa.

Spouses of persons engaged in business meetings at the hotel are not ignored. Airport Park supplements its regular van service to LAX with trips to the nearby and fashionable Fox Hills shopping mall. And, for all guests, there are trips to the Fitness Center at a neighboring hospital so that a cutting edge for business sessions can be maintained.

# LOCKHEED-CALIFORNIA COMPANY

Within a decade of the Wrights' epochal flight, two other brothers growing up as sky-struck teenagers on a ranch in California had designed and built their own aircraft. Launched from a garage on San Francisco's waterfront, the three-seater Model G seaplane first flew on June 15, 1913. Allan Loughead, at the controls, was 26. Malcolm Loughead was 24.

Profits earned by taking up visitors for rides in the Model G at the 1915 Pan-Pacific Exposition allowed the brothers to establish the Loughead Aircraft Company at Santa Barbara in 1916. With contracts for Navy seaplanes, the company blossomed to 85 workers. But the World War I armistice ended military production and war surplus aircraft eliminated the civil market, so the firm closed its doors in 1921.

Allan Loughead reentered the aircraft industry in 1926. His new Hollywood-based venture was called the Lockheed Aircraft Company to reflect proper pronunciation of the name. Its first product was a winner—the historic Vega monoplane.

Flown by such legends as Amelia Earhart, Charles Lindbergh, and Wiley Post, the Vega became so popular that in 1928 the company moved to larger production facilities in Burbank, where the headquarters remains.

With production of the Vega (and ensuing models such as the Sirius and Orion) booming, Lockheed entered the 1930s as a subsidiary of the Depression-doomed Detroit Aircraft Corporation. Its failure in 1931 also brought down Lockheed, but only for a matter of months. On June 6, 1932, a small group of investors led by Robert E. Gross, having bought the subsidiary's assets for $40,000, reincorporated it as the Lockheed Aircraft Corporation.

A key move for the new corporation was the immediate development

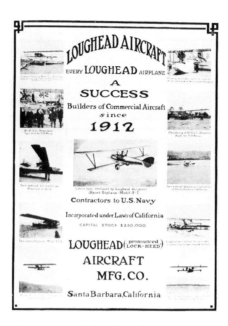

*When its sports biplane (center) didn't take up postwar production slack, the original company folded, to be reborn in the late '20s with the highly successful Vega.*

of the Model 10 Electra—the country's first all-metal airliner. Lockheed built more than 500 aircraft in this family during the '30s and military derivatives like the Hudson, Ventura, and Harpoon bombers were prominent among the more than 19,000 planes it produced for World War II service. Wartime products also included the famed P-38 Lightning

and the first P-80 Shooting Stars that ushered in the Jet Age.

Postwar civilian production was dominated by the celebrated Constellations and later, in the 1970s, by the equally renowned L-1011 TriStars, which were not phased out until 1983.

Meanwhile, in 1952, Lockheed designated its Burbank operations as its California Division, the first of many to be created as the corporation diversified. In 1977 the Lockheed Aircraft Corporation dropped its middle name to better reflect its overall aerospace involvement.

During the '60s, '70s, and '80s, military production at the Burbank-based Lockheed-California Company included U-2 and SR-71 reconnaissance aircraft, the P-3 Orion, and the S-3 Viking maritime patrol craft.

More than 17,000 persons worked for Lockheed-California at Burbank and three other Southern California locations in 1984. Still headquartered in Burbank, the corporation's worldwide operations employ more than 75,000.

*Some of the 50-man factory force making wooden fuselages at Lockheed's original Burbank location. A completed aircraft is in center background.*

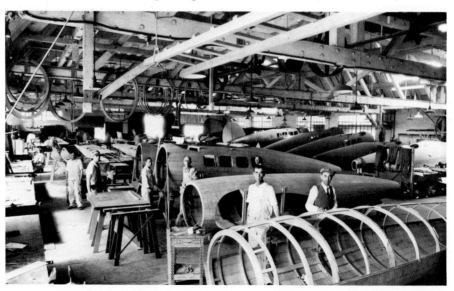

# WESTERN GEAR CORPORATION

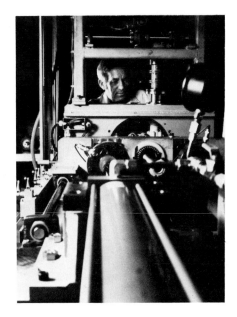

*Sophisticated actuation equipment is made by Western Gear for Boeing's 707s through 767s, McDonnell Douglas' DC-10, Lockheed's L-1011, and DeHavilland's DASH-7.*

Western Gear Corporation manufactures a wide range of aerospace products including primary and secondary flight actuators, airframe and engine-mounted accessory gear drives, helicopter personnel hoisting systems, helicopter transmissions, on-board cargo handling systems, advanced weapons delivery systems, aircraft structural assemblies, and

refrigerators and ovens for in-flight food service.

Western Gear won its first aviation laurels in 1933, when it supplied the flight-control systems for Boeing's famed P-26 fighter. A decade later it was supplying multiple systems for Boeing's even more famous B-17 bombers.

Military production was handled at the company's Vernon plant, closed after the war when aviation and aerospace work was moved to its Lynwood complex. Production there included gearboxes for the counter-rotating propellers on the Northrop Flying Wing and supercharger prototypes for the Lockheed Constellation.

Western Gear helped foster the fledgling helicopter industry with special transmissions for Hiller, Kaman, and Hughes. It provided an immense boost to airlifter capabilities, making cargo winches for the C-130, C-141, and C-5A Galaxy.

In the Jet Age, Western Gear products flew on the first Boeing 707s and aboard all successive generations;

*With Western Gear's flight-control system, Boeing's P-26 fighter of 1933 could streak at 234 miles per hour.*

plus Convair's 880 and 990s; Lockheed's Electras and L-1011s; McDonnell Douglas' DC-8 and DC-10s; Airbus Industries' A-300 and A-310s; DeHavilland's DASH-7s; Lear Fan jets; and, indeed, virtually every commercial and military aircraft in the Free World.

Military work in the mid-1980s included systems for F-14s, F-18s, F-20s, A-6s, and the experimental X-29. Western Gear is the prime contractor for bomb-release assemblies enabling supersonic aircraft to drop their "stores" at speed, without having to slow in order to let them escape the jet's airstream.

The missile age found the company at work on the Minuteman, Titan, and Harpoon. (In the mid-1980s the associated Western Gear Machinery Company was producing components for the MX missile.)

Originally founded in San Francisco in 1907 as the Pacific Gear and Tool Works, Western Gear adopted its present name in 1954. In 1980 it ranked 128th among California's top 500 companies in terms of revenue ($270.3 million). The Bucyrus-Erie Company of South Milwaukee, now part of Becor Western Inc., acquired it on September 30, 1981, for $183 million. Retaining its name, Western Gear contributes substantially to Becor Western's programs for aerospace and industrial products.

In 1983 Western Gear numbered some 2,600 employees. With its subsidiaries, it has eight manufacturing plants, three of them abroad.

Its historic continuing association with Boeing is only one reason Western Gear will remain in the forefront for the rest of the 20th century. As John T. Edelman, president and chief executive officer of Western Gear, has pointed out, new-generation aircraft such as the 757-767 series "are expected to set industry standards through the year 2000."

# HUGHES AIRCRAFT COMPANY

The year was 1932. Howard Hughes, a pilot and aviation enthusiast, assembled about a dozen engineers and technicians in a hangar at Grand Central Terminal in Glendale. His objective was the design and construction of innovative, experimental aircraft. The small group called itself the Hughes Aircraft Division of the Hughes Tool Company, an oil-drilling equipment firm owned by Hughes.

The group was the forerunner of today's vast Hughes Aircraft Company, a world leader in electronics and its associated fields.

While at Glendale Hughes and his team built a unique aircraft, the H-1 *Racer*—and began a pioneering, inventive tradition that has marked Hughes' operations to the present day.

The *Racer* incorporated more

design "firsts"—among them a power-driven retractable undercarriage and flush rivets—than any aircraft up to that time. With Hughes at its controls, the *Racer* also established numerous world records. The *Racer* is now on display at the Smithsonian Institution in Washington, D.C., where a plaque notes that it was a milestone on the road to development of many famed aircraft of World War II.

A noted successor to the *Racer* was the legendary H-4 flying boat, also known as the *Spruce Goose*, built of birch wood, and still the largest plane ever to fly. Designed to carry 750 fully equipped combat soldiers, the flying boat has a wingspan of 319.92 feet—longer than a football field. It is on public display at Long Beach.

In 1953 Hughes Aircraft Company began operations under its own name. At the same time the Howard Hughes Medical Institute, a not-for-profit medical research organization conceived many years earlier by Howard Hughes, was created and

given all the stock of the newly formed Hughes Aircraft Company. The institute remains the sole owner of Hughes Aircraft Company.

Hughes Aircraft Company has no legal, financial, or other connection with Hughes Helicopters, Inc., the Summa Corporation, or the Hughes Corporation. The only commonality shared by these organizations is that each stemmed from a single origin, the Hughes Tool Company.

During the 1940s electronic equipment produced by Hughes gradually eclipsed the firm's role in the design and manufacture of aircraft. The result is that, despite its name, Hughes Aircraft Company is no longer involved in making aircraft.

Expanding into the field of electronics instead, Hughes has since become engaged in about 1,500 projects involving 12,000 separate products—each of them in the electronics and related fields.

In the process Hughes has consistently developed its reputation as a leader and innovator in a complex

*Hughes Aircraft Company headquarters and labs in Culver City, California, as they looked in 1954. At right center is the 9,000-foot runway, believed to be the longest privately owned landing strip in the world.*

*Two of the many Space Age projects conceived at Hughes Aircraft are the HS 376 (left), a communications satellite capable of being launched from a Space Shuttle, and a prototype of SYNCOM.*

*Late in 1982 the company moved into new headquarters at 200 North Sepulveda Boulevard (tower in foreground), El Segundo.*

and sophisticated industry.

In 1950 the company, a pioneer in aviation communications, built America's first air-to-air guided missile, the Falcon. Three years later Hughes built the world's first operational laser. Hughes built SYNCOM, the world's first synchronous-orbit communications satellite, in 1963. The firm built Early Bird, the world's first commercial communications satellite, in 1965.

The following year the Hughes-built series of Surveyor spacecraft made soft landings on the moon, paving the way for the manned landings to come.

In 1971 two U.S. Navy aviators in an F-14 Tomcat became the first military crew to attack multiple targets simultaneously with multiple

missiles from a single fighter aircraft—by using Hughes-built Phoenix missiles and the Hughes-built AWG-9 weapons control system.

Hughes made unprecedented advances in radar in 1977. With JTDS, the Joint Tactical Information Distribution System, the firm provided U.S. surface and airborne units with secure, jam-resistant, high-capacity, radar-based communications. In another new radar system, Hughes has enabled U.S. units to pinpoint the location of enemy artillery in seconds.

Hughes designed and built the pioneer Venus mission spacecraft that, in 1978, probed the Venusian atmosphere, about 26 million miles from earth.

History was made in 1982, when two Hughes-built communications spacecraft became the first to be launched from an orbiting vehicle, the Space Shuttle, rather than by

rocket from the ground—at a savings of millions of dollars.

Howard Hughes died on April 5, 1976. Lawrence A. (Pat) Hyland, an early expert in electronics who had joined the company in 1954 as vice-president and general manager, became president and later chairman of the board. On Hyland's retirement in 1978, Dr. Allen E. Puckett was named chairman and chief executive officer.

From building the H-1 *Racer* in the Glendale hangar to working in electronics before the word was widely known, being "first" has repeatedly characterized Hughes Aircraft Company.

Company officials are confident that this hallmark of innovation will continue to be associated with Hughes as it moves toward the 21st century.

171

# PARKER HANNIFIN CORPORATION

Charles A. Lindbergh had a problem. His *Spirit of St. Louis* suffered from persistent fuel system leaks that surely would preclude the transatlantic flight he planned. Lindy sought help, and a fellow midwesterner—Arthur L. Parker of Cleveland—came to his aid. Parker invented a series of leak-proof fuel fittings. They worked perfectly, and Lindbergh flew into history in May 1927.

That was Parker Hannifin's first, but by no means last, famous link with aviation. The association has continued into the Space Age, with the company now providing key components for the Space Shuttle, as well as fluid system components on virtually every aircraft manufactured in the Free World.

*Arthur Parker's growing involvement in aviation led him in 1935 to add wings as one of the firm's symbols.*

The launching pad for what has long been known as "the fluid power company," the only worldwide, full-line supplier of fluid systems and components, was the small Parker Appliance Company which Arthur Parker had founded in Cleveland in 1924. It grew with aviation and the technology related to it until the firm became large enough to incorporate on December 30, 1938.

During World War II Parker employed 5,000 people in the greater Cleveland area, engaged exclusively in making tube fittings and fuel valves for military aircraft. The end of that war was in many ways a mixed blessing, however. Parker's single customer, the United States government, wasn't buying anything, and the company's employment dropped overnight to 300. But Arthur Parker's widow, Helen Parker, remained resolute. She resisted liquidation. New management was recruited, and research into new-product development began. The firm continued to expand, acquiring the Hannifin Manufacturing Company by merger in 1957 and adopting the name Parker Hannifin Corporation.

The concern's dedication to aviation deepened in June 1959, when it established the Parker Aircraft Company in Inglewood, California, within earshot of Los Angeles International Airport. Within 10 years, however, far more space was needed to fulfill the swelling demand for Parker's aerospace products and services, and in 1971 it moved south to Irvine, in Orange County.

Meanwhile, another company that was to vault Parker Hannifin even higher into the realm of aviation technology was also thriving. That was Bertea Corporation, specialists in hydraulic flight-control technology and computerized system design techniques. Founded in 1939, Bertea Corporation had moved to Irvine in 1964 from its original facility in Pasadena, California.

*Arthur Parker, founder of the Parker Appliance Company (forerunner of the Parker Hannifin Corporation), expanded the firm from pneumatics into fluid power.*

*The company's first facility, in Cleveland, Ohio, in the 1920s, generated worldwide operations during the next half-century.*

Bertea was a natural complement to Parker Hannifin, which acquired 96.6 percent of its stock in June 1978, and formally brought it into the corporate fold that December. In the mid-1980s the founders of both companies were still represented on the Parker Hannifin board by their sons: Patrick S. Parker as chairman and chief executive officer, and Richard Bertea as a director and senior vice-president.

Because Parker Hannifin Corporation, overall, represented such a broad spectrum of fluid power undertakings in the early '80s, the Parker Bertea Aerospace Group was formed. This sector became the leading edge for the firm's fluid systems technology. By 1983 Parker fluid systems and components were in use on every major military and commercial aircraft.

Parker is also recognized as a world leader in designing and supplying valves and nozzles for fuel systems, from storage tanks to the heart of jet engines to hydraulic components that actuate landing gear, doors, and flaps; primary flight-control systems for commercial airliners, helicopters, and military aircraft; as well as components for ground support and sophisticated controls for aircraft environmental systems.

For general aviation, Parker supplies wheels, brakes, and pneumatic systems. The company's aircraft refueling technology is also being used in marine systems, for ship-to-ship refueling, and in revolutionary hydrofoil craft, which use Parker parts in both their control and jet engine systems.

Parker's business mix during 1983 was roughly two-thirds production

*Typical aircraft hydraulic components produced by Bertea Products (later Bertea Corporation) in the late 1940s and early 1950s.*

of original equipment and one-third maintenance, repair, and overhaul. Aerospace Group operations that year accounted for 22 percent of the parent corporation's sales.

Staff growth has necessarily kept pace. In 1983 it totaled approximately 3,000 employees at Parker Bertea's headquarters complex in Irvine, and about 1,200 elsewhere.

Long-deserved recognition has grown as well. "Cycle the Parker valve," said astronaut Harrison Schmidt from the moon, on December 11, 1972. As he guided *Apollo 17*'s lunar excursion module down to the surface with the circuits open to worldwide radio, a valve the company had made was put to the test.

Like the fitting that Arthur Parker had made for Lindbergh a generation before, it performed flawlessly. Thus, Parker Hannifin has the distinction of having the first radio and television commercial produced on and transmitted from another planet. Indeed, Patrick Parker once exclaimed, "We've been on nearly everything that flies . . . and we can't wait for tomorrow."

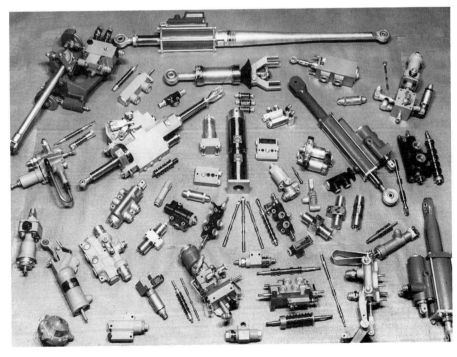

# AVIONICS SYSTEMS, INC.

In 1960, having completed their respective tours of duty in the U.S. Navy, Clifford W. Archer and Patrick W. Bell met each other for the first time inside Oakland Airport's spacious Hangar 8, which then housed an avionics enterprise named Bayaire. Bell, well versed in naval supply and procurement, had joined the small firm two years earlier as its purchasing agent. Archer was just joining the company as a radar specialist.

On returning to civilian life, Archer had maintained his close ties to flying, becoming certificated by the Federal Aviation Administration for airline transports, commercial rotary-wing flight, and commercial gliding. Already steeped in the growing field of avionics, he was destined to serve as director of the Aircraft Electronics Association, of which Bell was also a member.

Their key roles in the early '60s, however, were played in Hangar 8. Bell became manager of purchasing and distribution for the company. Archer became service manager in 1962—and president the next year.

The ensuing decade was uncertain for Avionics Systems' predecessor company. Supplying a few airframe manufacturers concentrated on the West Coast, it faced the same headwinds that were buffeting the entire aircraft industry in the 1960s. Deep cuts in the national defense budget were slowing prime contractors almost to a stall. The small firm in Hangar 8, so dependent on them, was greatly affected.

Archer and Bell felt that by diversifying the organization's services and broadening its geographical scope, it could escape its overdepen-

*Joseph "Red" Barrows (right), holding Air Transport license 255, owned Pacific Coast Air Service and flew commercially until his retirement in 1962. Co-pilot Harry Blunt (left) still lived in Spokane, Washington, at the age of 94 in 1983.*

dence on supplying military avionics to only a few western manufacturers. Accordingly, in what soon proved to be a successful move, the two men formed Avionics Systems, Inc., in 1973—and bought out Bayaire.

Archer was president of their new venture, and Bell the vice-president. There were only 12 other employees.

Diversification began almost at once. Avionics Systems established two subsidiaries: XL Avionics and Tower Avionics. A third, TASA, was to follow in 1982. All remained headquartered in Hangar 8, now merely on the periphery of the airfield which had itself grown into the sprawling Oakland International Airport.

Avionics Systems, the parent concern, dealt primarily with the procurement, assembly, and modification of avionics products; it did not manufacture them.

The subsidiary XL dealt with the sales, especially overseas, of aircraft components and systems to airlines, the government, and the business-jet "aftermarket" worldwide. Spare parts comprised a large part of its business. XL also provided "turnkey" maintenance facilities worldwide to aircraft operators, both governmental and commercial.

*Avionics' historical photo collection, a veritable "who's who" of early aviators, includes this shot beside a Comet-engined Waco at Oakland Airport in 1928 of (left to right) Joseph "Red" Barrows, Milo Campbell, and Willie Willingham.*

*Clifford W. Archer, founder and president, in the cockpit of Avionics' corporate jet, personally visits key customers around the world.*

Tower handled domestic sales and services in several major fields: design and installation standards in medium and heavy jet transports; complete aircraft instrument calibration, repair, and overhaul in Hangar 8 laboratories; complete avionics calibration, repair, and overhaul; accessory repair and overhaul; and airframe and turbine-engine

repair and overhaul.

TASA devoted itself, amid the rising popularity of executive jets, to the buying and reselling of previously owned corporate jets and rotary-wing aircraft.

Entering the 1980s, two of the subsidiaries alone—XL and Tower—had grown to more than 60 employees, and annual sales exceeded $20 million. In 1983 about 20 percent of them were to the U.S. civilian market. Overseas sales, to governments and businesses, were 70 to 80 percent military.

By 1984 Avionics and its three subsidiaries together had more than 100 employees, and overall sales were growing by more than 30 percent annually. Besides those in Hangar 8, complete service facilities had been established in Buenos Aires, Argentina, in support of several ongoing South American contracts. Fully staffed offices were also maintained in Washington, D.C., Amsterdam,

Bogota, and Singapore.

The enlarged geographical scope that Archer and Bell envisioned in 1973 had come to pass. The pattern continued; Archer thinks little of making a personal trip to Ankara, for example, in pursuit of the kinds of avionics business "that the really big companies just can't get around to."

Avionics Systems' relatively modest size enables it to tailor its collective services to clients' particular needs. "The huge aerospace corporations simply don't have time to fill them," the president feels. "We do."

Avionics' accomplishments have ranked, nevertheless, with those of the giants. It is particularly proud, for example, of its pioneering the avionics for the Piper Aerostar, in conjunction with the late Ted Smith. The company also has an acute sense of aviation history—and of responsibility to the overall business community. Archer serves on the California Advisory Board on Economic Development, and is a member of the National Aviation Club, Washington, D.C.; and Bell is a member of the Oakland Aviation Council and the Oakland Airport Aviation Business Association.

The sense of history is reflected by Avionics' collection of photographs of early airplanes, air meets, racers, experimental planes, and derring-do pilots. One of the nation's leading assemblages, it is on permanent display in Hangar 8.

In sum, Avionics Systems in the mid-'80s was soaring ever higher in its endeavors, although, according to Archer, "We are not into spacecraft—yet." He predicted corporate growth to 300 employees by 1990, however, to conduct additional services and operations.

*Patrick W. Bell, vice-president and co-founder, was instrumental in the diversification of the company and the extension of its geographical scope.*

# CALIFORNIA AVI-TRON CORPORATION

From repairing the spars and canvas of wooden, fabric-covered airplanes in the 1930s to fashioning the major tubular structure for the *Surveyor* which still reposes on the moon in the 1980s—that has been the partial history of the California Avi-Tron Corporation. Moreover, in 1984, the company neared its half-century mark with ever-greater versatility. The Inglewood firm was making components for both the B-1 Bombers and the Space Shuttles. Continued growth through the remainder of the 20th century was assured.

The saga began in 1938 when 10 men, calling themselves the California Flyers and operating a flying school near Mines Field, the predecessor of Los Angeles International Airport, formed a venture to manufacture monoplanes and biplanes as well. They pooled their money to acquire and equip a building for that purpose at 9020 Aviation

Boulevard. That structure remains corporate headquarters.

As World War II approached, the 10 California pilots and the small factory force they had assembled began to look into the possibilities of producing sheet-metal subassemblies for prime contractors making what would be America's air armada after the attack on Pearl Harbor.

"We began to teach our people how to rivet," one old-timer recalled, "and we expanded our building."

A major order arrived early in 1942 from the Boeing Company to make ailerons for its B-17s. More contracts flowed in. The California Flyers incorporated as the California Avi-Tron Corporation to handle them.

During World War II Avi-Tron supplied all major companies, a practice that has continued to date. Along the way it earned the government's MIL-Q-9858A military rating for specifications, a standing coveted by many but possessed by few. An example of performance that won that rating is the firm's ability to produce regularly machine-welded as-

semblies, ranging from 1/2 inch to 30 inches in size, with tolerances of plus/minus .001 inch; all heli-arc welding is of radiographic quality.

The list of corporations now relying on Avi-Tron for components reads like a "who's who" of the aerospace industry: Garrett Turbine Engine, Pratt & Whitney, Avco Lycoming, Bendix, Boeing, Ford Aerospace, Hughes Aircraft, General Dynamics, McDonnell Douglas, Northrop, Rockwell International, Bell Helicopter, Honeywell, and the U.S. Army and Air Force.

Such top-market acceptance also recognized Avi-Tron's dedication to what it styled as its "single-source responsibility." That stemmed from its having built its own tooling, to support its own in-house forming, cutting, and machining, with all welding and riveting, assembly, and painting done under its own roof. Further, few shops have had as much experience

---

*Nose cone containers for Polaris missiles leave the Avi-Tron plant in the '60s for Lockheed's facility in Sunnyvale.*

*A partial array of precision sheet-metal components and assemblies Avi-Tron was making in the early 1980s for aerospace and the military.*

with titanium, Inconel, Waspaloy, Hastelloy, and other exotic metals. Avi-Tron stood almost alone in 1983, for example, in its industry successes with felt-metal welding.

Avi-Tron has combined various operations to produce small aluminum ducts of complex shape which require bending, welding, machining, and drop-hammer forming; or hydraulic reservoirs representing machining, welding, and dip brazing, a total assembly process not offered by most companies in the field.

Still another unusual, tailored service from Avi-Tron has been its Value Engineering program, whereby its own engineering staff will analyze clients' drawings, a procedure that often results in savings of time, cost, and weight.

By the mid-1980s Avi-Tron had become the sole supplier of electronic data link pods for the F-4, F-15, F-16, F-18, A-7, B-52, and F-111 military aircraft. It also was the sole supplier to the industry of Helicopter IR sup-

pressor cowlings—components of aluminum and stainless steel that provided a good example of the company's ability to bring out complicated assemblies requiring both welding and riveting.

During its first half-century, Avi-Tron garnered industry accolades for its pioneering. In the 1960s, for example, it developed the engine nacelles and cowlings for the T-39, which later became the celebrated North American/Rockwell Sabreliner executive airliner. The concern also perfected certain components for the original B-1s in the early '70s. Its versatility has ranged from installations in Air Force One to sound-attenuation programs to suppress jet engine noise.

The company thrived. In the late '60s monthly billings had approximated $50,000 for custom work. By 1983 those sales had grown to $7 million annually. Projected sales for 1984 were estimated at $12 million, mostly in the United States but some in Canada. Much of that growth came during the guidance of

Jack E. Randall, who assumed the presidency of Avi-Tron in 1983.

Contributing were extraordinarily skilled, longtime specialists. Avi-Tron had some 125 employees in 1983; several were veterans of the days of making canvas-covered biplanes. Indeed, in the early '80s, tool and die makers had averaged 15 years with the company. "Turnover in that critical department is almost nonexistent," observed Ray W. Schneider, chief engineer.

Today Avi-Tron's mix is custom manufactured, to all aspects of customers' specifications, of components for missiles, the military, and commercial aerospace, the latter including airliners, helicopters, and general aviation. The company provides assemblies for electronics, but not electronics per se—although Avi-Tron is keeping all its options open to at least 2000 A.D.

*Five decades earlier, this plant space was devoted to the repair of fabric-covered airplanes. Here a worker puts finishing touches on an electronic data link pod, of which Avi-Tron is the sole supplier.*

*Jack E. Randall, president.*

# PAN AMERICAN WORLD AIRWAYS

On November 22, 1935, eight years after Pan American Airways began flying between Florida and Cuba, founder Juan Terry Trippe stood a continent's breadth away, watching another historical takeoff. He saw the fabled China Clipper churn the waters of San Francisco Bay and soar over the Golden Gate Bridge on its maiden flight to the Philippines. It marked the most dramatic of Pan Am's early links to California.

It was not the first one. A subsidiary, Aerovias Centrales, S.A., had begun service between Los Angeles and Mexico City the year before.

The limelight, however, was held by San Francisco, birthplace of trans-pacific air service and destined to become Pan Am's major West Coast gateway. The 1935 mail flights were followed within months by passenger service to Manila and, in 1937, to Hong Kong.

The Pacific operations, involving distances as great as the Clippers' popularity, enabled Pan Am to pass the 400-million-passenger-mile mark overall in July 1938. Routes were extended steadily, reaching Noumea and New Zealand in 1940.

World War II interrupted the growth. Pan Am became, worldwide, the largest air transport contractor to the U.S. military—a role it was to resume in lesser degree for the ensuing Korean and Vietnamese conflicts. But on November 16, 1945, the airline returned commercially to Pacific skies, with major expansions during the Jet Age.

By 1977 Pan Am had won 26.3 percent of the entire Far East market and 29.1 percent of the Oceania market.

During the decades, the firm experienced few changes in its hierarchy. Founder Trippe, at the helm for 37 years, yielded the presidency—but remained as chairman and chief executive officer—in July

*The first China Clipper, shown clearing the Golden Gate Bridge, carried mail to Manila on its maiden flight. Passenger service began on October 21, 1936.*

*Transpacific service after World War II resumed in 1945. By 1949 routes featured such luxurious pre-jet liners as the Stratocruiser "Clipper America" shown here, speeding over Alcatraz.*

1964 to Harold E. Gray, a Pan Am veteran, who also had been first officer on that historic transpacific passenger flight in 1936. Gray eventually became chairman and chief executive officer, serving until May 1970, when he was succeeded by Najeeb E. Halaby, who served until March 1972.

Leadership then fell to William T. Seawell, a former Air Force general and commandant of the Air Force Academy, who served as chairman and chief executive officer until his retirement in August 1981. He would shepherd an epochal development for Pan Am.

That was the firm's $436.8-million acquisition of National Airlines of Miami. Founded in 1934 as an intra-Florida carrier, National had developed a country-wide network—its flights reached San Francisco and Los Angeles in June 1961—and had become an international airline after being awarded routes to Europe in 1970. Its foreign flights complemented those of Pan Am, which itself had no domestic routes. A merger seemed ideal. After 16 months of negotiations, it was federally approved. The "new" Pan Am took off officially at 5 p.m. on January 7, 1980, when it became owner of 100 percent of National's stock.

In 1979 several divisions of Pan Am were consolidated into Pan Am World Services, Inc., operating in 17 foreign countries and at 18 U.S. locations. A California facility is at the Navy's China Lake Weapons Center.

C. Edward Acker, former chief of two other major airlines and a financial and marketing expert, joined the firm in September 1981, succeeding Seawell as chairman and chief executive officer. In 10 months he also became president, the first to hold the three top titles simultaneously since Halaby in 1971.

Acker did not stint California. His attentions to the Pacific division increased its operating revenue to more than $770 million in 1982, second only to Pan Am's Atlantic division among all international activities. San Francisco remained the hub; in June 1982 more than 2,200 employees (out of 29,000 for the global carrier overall) were handling 190 arrivals and departures weekly. The previous year those operations had aggregated 1.3 million passengers and more than 81,000 tons of mail and cargo.

As 1985 approached, the firm was paring its costs and employees and was phasing out its scheduled, all-cargo jet flights and was disposing of its DC-10 fleet in an aircraft swap with American Airlines, continuing an efficiency pattern which had returned the company to operating profitability two years before. Inter-Continental Hotels, formed as a subsidiary in 1946, already had been divested—but not before Pan Am's benevolent ownership of the Mark Hopkins in San Francisco during its hostelry era had further endeared it to the city.

For the remainder of the 20th century, other close and traditional ties between Pan Am and California were to be perpetuated, including purchases from the Lockheed-California Company in Burbank, designation of California banks as transfer and registrar co-agents, and selection of prominent Californians to serve on the global carrier's board of directors and International Advisory Board.

*Juan T. Trippe (right), not yet 30 years old, hired Charles A. Lindbergh in 1929 to help survey the Pacific routes Pan Am was to fly six years later.*

# BIBLIOGRAPHY

Allen, Oliver E. *The Airline Builders.* Alexandria, VA: Time-Life Books, 1981.

Anderson, Fred. *Northrop: An Aernautical History.* Los Angeles: Northrop Corporation, 1976.

Austin, Edward T. *Rohr: The Story of a Corporation.* Chula Vista, CA: Rohr Corporation, 1969.

Ball, John, Jr. *Edwards: Flight Test Center of the USAF.* New York: Duell, Sloan and Pierce, 1962.

Barlett, Donald L., and James B. Steele. *Empire: The Life, Legend, and Madness of Howard Hughes.* New York: W.W. Norton Company, 1979.

Barton, Charles. *Howard Hughes and His Flying Boat.* Fallbrook, CA: Aero Publishers, 1982.

Bean, Walton. *California: An Interpretive History.* 2nd Ed. New York: McGraw-Hill, 1973.

Bender, Marylin, and Selig Altschul. *The Chosen Instrument: Pan Am, Juan Trippe, The Rise and Fall of an American Entrepreneur.* New York: Simon and Schuster, 1982.

Biederman, Paul. *The U.S. Airline Industry: End of an Era.* New York: Praeger Publishers, 1982.

Briddon, A.E., and E.A. Champie. *Historical Fact Book, A Chronology, 1926-1963.* Washington, D.C.: Federal Aviation Administration, 1966.

Bright, Charles D. *The Jet Makers: The Aerospace Industry from 1945 to 1972.* Lawrence, KS: The Regents Press of Kansas, 1978.

Brooks, Peter Wright. *The Modern Airliner: Its Origins and Development.* London: Putnam, 1961.

California Institute of Technology. *The Guggenheim Aeronautical Laboratory at the California Institute of Technology: The First 25 Years.* Pasadena, CA: CIT, 1954.

———. *75: An Informal History of the California Institute of Technology.* Pasadena: CIT, 1966.

Cameron, Frank. *Hungry Tiger: The Story of the Flying Tiger Line.* New York: McGraw-Hill, 1964.

Carron, Andrew S. *Transition to a Free Market: Deregulation of the Air Cargo Industry.* Washington, D.C.: The Brookings Institution, 1981.

Casey, Louis S. *Curtiss: The Hammondsport Era 1907-1915.* New York: Crown, 1981.

Cassagneres, Ev. *The Spirit of Ryan.* Blue Ridge Summit, PA: TAB Books, Inc., 1982.

Caves, Richard E. *Air Transport and Its Regulators.* Cambridge, MA: Harvard University Press, 1962.

Chant, Christopher. *Aviation: An Illusrated History.* London: Orbis Publishing Limited, 1978.

Cherington, Paul W. *Airline Price Policy: A Study of Domestic Airline Passenger Fares.* Cambridge: Harvard University Press, 1958.

Christy, Joe. *American Air Power: The First 75 Years.* Blue Ridge Summit, PA: Tab Books, Inc., 1982.

Cleveland, Reginald M. *America FledgesWings: The History of The Daniel Guggenheim Fund for the Promotion of Aeronautics.* New York: Pitman Publishing Corp., 1942.

Combs, Harry, with Martin Caidin. *Kill Devil Hill: Discovering the Secret of the Wright Brothers.* Boston: Houghton Mifflin Company, 1979.

Convair Aerospace Division of General Dynamics. *Fiftieth Anniversary.* St. Louis: General Dynamics Corporation, 1973.

Corn, Joseph J. *The Winged Gospel: America's Romance with Aviation, 1900-1950.* New York: Oxford University Press, 1983.

Crouch, Tom D. *A Dream of Wings: Americans and the Airplane 1875-1905.* New York: W.W. Norton & Company, 1981.

———, ed. *Charles A. Lindbergh: An American Life.* Washington, D.C.: NASM, The Smithsonian Institution, 1977.

Cunningham, William Glenn. *The Aircraft Industry: A Study in Industrial Location.* Los Angeles: Lorrin L. Morrison, 1951.

Daley, Robert. *An American Saga: Juan Trippe and His Pan Am Empire.* New York: Random House, 1980.

*Dateline Lockheed.* Burbank: Lockheed Corporate Communications, 1982.

Davies, R.E.G. *Airlines of the United States since 1914.* London: Putnam & Company, 1972.

———. *A History of the World's Airlines.* 2nd Ed. London: Oxford University Press, 1967.

Douglas, George W., and James C. Miller III. *Economic Regulation of Domestic Air Transportation: Theory & Policy.* Washington, D.C.: The Brookings Institution, 1974.

Dwiggins, Don. *Flying the Frontiers of Space.* New York: Dodd, Mead & Co., 1982.

Eads, George C. *The Local Service Airline Experiment.* Washington, D.C.: The Brookings Institution, 1972.

Elliott, Arlene. "The Rise of Aeronautics in California,1849-1940." *Southern California Quarterly,* Volume 52, pp. 1-32, March 1970.

Fleet, Dorothy. *Our Flight to Destiny.* New York: Vantage Press, 1964. Rev. ed.

"Aviation: Past, Present, and Future" (50th Anniversary Issue) *Flying Magazine,* September 1977, Volume 101, Number 3. New York: Ziff-Davis Publishing Company.

Flynn, William. *Men, Money and Mud, the Story of San Francisco International Airport.* San Francisco: Mercury Press, 1954.

Foxworth, Thomas G., ed. *The Historical Aviation Album, Volume XVI.* Temple City, CA.: Historical Aviation Album (produced by Paul R. Matt), 1980.

Francillon, Rene J. *Lockheed Aircraft Since 1913.* London: Putnam and Company, 1982.

Freudenthal, Elsbeth E. *The Aviation Business from Kitty Hawk to Wall Street.* New York: McGraw-Hill, 1940.

Friedman, Paul D. "Birth of an Airport." *Journal of American Aviation Historical Society.* 1978

———. "Fear of Flying: The Development of Los Angeles Airport and the Rise of Public Protest Over Jet Aircraft Noise." Unpublished Master's Thesis, University of California at Santa Barbara, 1978.

Gablehouse, Charles. *Helicopters and Autogiros.* New York: J.B. Lippincott Company, 1969.

Garrison, Omar. *Howard Hughes in Las Vegas.* New York: Lyle Stuart, Inc., 1970.

Gibbs-Smith, Charles H. *The Invention of The Aeroplane (1799-1909).* New York: Taplinger, 1965.

Gilbert, James. *The Great Planes.* New York: Grosset and Dunlap, 1970.

Gill, F.W. and G.L. Bates. *Airline Competition.* Cambridge: Harvard University Press, 1949.

Gleason, Spencer. *Moffett Field: From Lighter-than-Air to Faster-than-Sound.* San Jose: Globe Printing, 1958.

Goldberg, Alfred, ed. *A History of the United States Air Force 1907-1957.* Princeton: D. Van Nostrand Company, 1957.

Gray, George W. *Frontiers of Flight: The Story of NACA Research.* New York: Knopf, 1948.

Gray, Jeanne. "Naval Aviation Hall of

Honor: Glenn L. Martin." *Naval Aviation News*, October 1982.

Greenwood, Jim and Maxine. *Stunt Flying in the Movies*. Blue Ridge Summit, PA: TAB Books, Inc., 1982.

Gurney, Gene. *A Chronology of World Aviation*. New York: Franklin Watts, 1965.

Hall, R. Cargill. "Theodore Von Karman, 1881-1963." *Aerospace Historian*, Vol. 28, No. 4, December 1981, pp. 253-258.

Hallion, Richard P. *Designers and Test Pilots*. Alexandria: Time-Life Books, 1983.

_____ . *Legacy of Flight: The Guggenheim Contribution to American Aviation*. Seattle: University of Washington Press, 1977.

_____ . *Test Pilots: The Frontiers of Flight*. Garden City: Doubleday & Company, 1981.

_____ . *On the Frontier: Flight Research at Dryden: 1946-1981*. Washington, D.C.: National Aeronautics & Space Administration, 1984.

Hanle, Paul A. *Bringing Aerodynamics to America*. Cambridge: The MIT Press, 1982.

Hatch, Alden. *Glenn Curtiss: Pioneer of Naval Aviation*. New York: Julian Messner, 1942.

Hatfield, David D., ed. *Aeroplane Scrapbook No. 2, 1911-1939*. Inglewood: Northrop Institute of Technology, 1971.

_____ . *Howard Hughes' H-4 "Hercules."* Los Angeles: Historical Airplanes, 1972.

_____ . ed. *Los Angeles Aeronautics 1920-1929*. Inglewood, CA: Northrop University Press, 1973.

_____ . ed. *Dominguez Air Meet*. Inglewood, CA: Northrop University Press, 1976.

Heiman, Grover. *Jet Pioneers*. New York: Van Rees Press, 1963.

Heinemann, Edward H., and Rosario Rausa. *Ed Heinemann: Combat Aircraft Designer*. Annapolis: Naval Institute Press, 1980.

Hereford, Jack and Peggy. *The Flying Years: A History of America's Pioneer Airline*. Los Angeles: Western Air Lines, Inc., 1946.

Hopkins, George E. *Flying the Line: The First Half Century of the Air Line Pilots Association*. Washington, D.C.: Airline Pilots Association, 1982.

Ingells, Douglas J. *The L-1011 TriStar and the Lockheed Story*. Fallbrook, CA: Aero Publishers, 1973.

_____ . *The Plane that Changed the World*. Fallbrook, CA: Aero Publishers, 1966.

_____ . *The McDonnell Douglas Story*. Fallbrook: Aero Publishers, Inc., 1979.

Jablonski, Edward. *America in the Air War*. Alexandria: Time-Life Books, 1982.

Jackson, Donald Dale. *Flying the Mail*. Alexandria: Time-Life Books, 1982.

Jackson, Ronald W. *China Clipper*. New York: Everest House, 1980.

Johnson, Kenneth M. *Aerial California: An Account of Early Flight in Northern and Southern California, 1849 to WW I*. Los Angeles: Dawson's Book Shop, 1961.

Johnston, Moira. *The Last Nine Minutes: The Story of Flight 981*. New York: William Morrow, 1976.

Jordan, William A. *Airline Regulation in America: Effects and Imperfections*. Baltimore: The Johns Hopkins Press, 1970.

Josephy, Alvin M., Jr., ed. *The American Heritage History of Flight*. New York: American Heritage Publishing Company, 1962.

Kane, Robert, and Allan Vose. *Air Transportation*. Eighth ed. Dubuque: Kendall/Hunt, 1982.

Keats, John. *Howard Hughes*. New York: Random House, 1966.

Kelly, Fred C. *The Wright Brothers*. New York: Bantam Books, 1983.

Knowlton, Hugh. *Air Transportation in the United States: Its Growth as a Business*. Chicago: The University of Chicago Press, 1941.

Komons, Nick A. *Bonfires to Beacons: Federal Civil Aviation Policy under the Air Commerce Act 1926-1938*. Washington, D.C.: U.S. Department of Transportation, 1978.

Kucera, Randolph P. *The Aerospace Industry and the Military: Structural and Political Relationships*. Beverly Hills: Sage Publications, 1974.

LaMond, Annette M. "An Evaluation of Intrastate Airline Regulation in California." *Bell Journal of Economics* 7 (Autumn 1976): pp. 641-657.

Lewis, W. David, and Wesley Phillips Newton. *Delta: The History of an Airline*. Athens, Ga: The University of Georgia Press, 1979.

"Seventy-five Years of Flight." *Life Magazine*. November 1978, Volume 1, Number 2. Chicago: Time, Inc., 1978.

*Lockheed Horizons Magazine*. Burbank: Lockheed Corporation, 1983.

Loening, Grover. *Takeoff into Greatness: How American Aviation Grew So Big So Fast*. New York: G.P. Putnam's Sons, 1969.

Lougheed, Victor. *Vehicles of the Air: A Popular Exposition of Modern Aeronautics with Working Drawings*. Chicago: The Reilly & Britton Company, 1910. Second edition.

Lowenfeld, Andreas F. *Aviation Law: Cases and Materials*. New York: Matthew Bender, 1981. 2nd edition.

Mandell, Robert W. *Financing the Capital Requirements of the U.S. Airline Industry in the 1980s*. Lexington, MA: Lexington Books, 1979.

Martin, Paul K., ed. *The Airline Handbook*. 7th and 8th eds. Cranston, RI: Aerotravel Research, 1982 and 1983.

Mason, Herbert Molloy, Jr. *The United States Air Force: A Turbulent History, 1907-1975*. New York: Mason/Charter, 1976.

Maynard, Crosby, ed. *Flight Plan for Tomorrow: The Douglas Story, A Condensed History*. Santa Monica, CA: Douglas Aircraft Company, 1966. 2nd ed.

Messimer, Dwight R. *No Margin for Error: The U.S. Navy's Transpacific Flight of 1925*. Annapolis, MD: Naval Institute Press, 1981.

Meyer, John R., and Clinton V. Oster, eds. *Airline Deregulation: The Early Experience*. Boston: Auburn House, 1981.

Millar, Richard W. Various interviews, 1979-1983.

Miller, Jay. *The X-Planes: X-1 to X-29*. Marine on St. Croix, MN: Specialty Press, 1983.

Miller, Jeffrey R. *The Airline Deregulation Handbook*. Wheaton, IL: Merton House Publishing Company, 1981

Miller, Ronald, and David Sawyer. *The Technical Development of Modern Aviation*. London: Routledge and Kegan Paul, 1968.

Millikan, Clark B. "Advanced Education and Academic Research in Aeronautics." *Journal of The Royal Aeronautical Society*, Vol. 61, No. 564, December 1957, pp. 793-810.

_____ . "Theodore Von Karman—His American Period." *Journal of The Royal Aeronautical Society*, Vol. 67, No. 634, October 1963.

Moolman, Valerie. *The Road to Kitty Hawk*. Alexandria: Time-Life Books, 1980.

_____ . *Women Aloft*. Alexandria:

Time-Life Books, 1980.

Moore, Clifton A. "Report of the General Manager." Los Angeles Department of Airports *50th Anniversary Magazine.* 1978.

———. Interview at Los Angeles, December 1983.

Morris, Lloyd, and Kendall Smith. *Ceiling Unlimited: The Story of American Aviation from Kitty Hawk to Supersonics.* New York: The Macmillan Company, 1959.

Munson, Kenneth. *Airliners between the Wars 1919-1939.* New York: The Macmillan Company, 1972.

———. *Airliners since 1946.* New York: The Macmillan Company, 1972.

Murray, Russ. *J.H. Kindelberger.* Los Angeles: North American Rockwell Management Association of Southern California, 1972.

———. *Lee Atwood . . . Dean of Aerospace.* Los Angeles: Rockwell International Corporation, 1980.

National Academy of Engineering. *State of the Nation's Air Transportation System: Summary Proceeding of a Symposium, 3-4 June 1976.*

Nava, Julian, and Bob Barger. *California: Five Centuries of Cultural Contrast.* Encino, CA: Glencoe Press, 1976.

*Naval Aviation News.* "Pioneers Set Out to Show Navy 'Flying Machines' Can Go to Sea." January 1961.

Nevin, David. *Architects of Air Power.* Alexandria: Time-Life Books, 1981.

Newhouse, John. *The Sporty Game.* New York: Alfred A. Knopf, 1982.

Northrop, John K. Various interviews, 1979-1980.

O'Neil, Paul. *Barnstormers and Speed Kings.* Alexandria: Time-Life Books, 1981.

Oakes, Claudia M. "U.S. Women in Aviation: the 1930s." *Air and Space.* Winter 1980.

Odekirk, Glenn E. *Spruce Goose.* Glendale, CA: Aviation Book Company, 1983.

Palmer, Henry R., Jr. *This Was Air Travel.* New York: Bonanza Books, 1962.

———. *The Seaplanes.* Fallbrook, CA: Aero Publishers, Inc., 1980.

Prendergast, Curtis. *The First Aviators.* Alexandria: Time-Life Books, 1981.

Rae, John B. *Climb to Greatness: The American Aircraft Industry, 1920-1960.* Cambridge: MIT Press, 1968.

Raymond, Arthur E. *"Who? Me?" [An] Autobiography of Arthur E. Raymond.* Los Angeles, CA: privately printed,

1974.

Reinhold, Ruth M. *Sky Pioneering: Arizona in Aviation History.* Tucson: The University of Arizona Press, 1982.

Rochester, Stuart I. *Takeoff at Mid-Century: Federal Civil Aviation Policy in the Eisenhower Years 1953-1967.* Washington, D.C.: U.S. Department of Transportation, 1976.

Roseberry, C.R. *Glenn Curtiss: Pioneer of Flight.* Garden City: Doubleday & Company, 1972.

Schoneberger, William A., et al. *Seven Decades of Progress: A Heritage of Aircraft Turbine Technology.* Fallbrook: Aero Publishers, 1979.

Seidenbaum, Art. *Los Angeles 200: a Bicentennial Celebration.* New York: Harry N. Abrams, Inc., 1980.

Serling, Robert J. *Loud and Clear: The Full Answer to Aviation's Vital Question: Are the Jets Really Safe?* Garden City: Doubleday, 1969.

———. *Maverick: The Story of Robert Six and Continental Airlines.* New York: Doubleday & Company, 1974.

———. *The Only Way to Fly: The Story of Western Airlines, America's Senior Air Carrier.* New York: Doubleday, 1976.

———. *The Jet Age.* Alexandria, VA: Time-Life Books, 1982.

———. *Howard Hughes' Airline: An Informal History of TWA.* New York: St. Martin's/Marek, 1983.

Sherrod, Robert. *History of Marine Corps Aviation in WW II.* Washington, D.C.: Combat Forces Press, 1952.

Simonson, G.R. *The History of the American Aircraft Industry.* Cambridge, MA: MIT Press, 1968.

Smith, Elinor. *Aviatrix.* New York: Harcourt Brace Jovanovich, 1981.

Smith, Henry Ladd. *Airways: The History of Commercial Aviation in the United States.* New York: Alfred A. Knopf, 1942.

Smith, Richard A. "How A Great Corporation Got Out of Control: The Story of General Dynamics Part I." *Fortune.* (January 1962).

Smith, Richard K. "Aerospace Profile: a Douglas Decision." *Aerospace Historian.* (Autumn 1968).

Smith, Vi. *From Jennies to Jets: The Aviation History of Orange County.* Fullerton, CA: Sultana Press, 1974.

Solberg, Carl E. *Conquest of the Skies: A History of Commercial Aviation in America.* Boston: Little, Brown, 1979.

Stadlman, Anthony. Interview, 1982.

Stanley, Max. Various Interviews, Los Angeles, 1981-1983.

Still, Henry. *To Ride the Wind: A Biography of Glenn L. Martin.* New York: Julian Messner, Inc., 1964.

Sudsbury, Elretta. *Jackrabbits to Jets: The History of North Island, San Diego, California.* San Diego: Neyenesch Printers, Inc., 1967.

Sunderman, James F., ed. *Early Air Pioneers 1862-1935.* New York: Franklin Watts, 1961.

Taylor, Frank J. *High Horizons: Daredevil Flying Postmen to Magic Carpet—The United Airlines Story.* Rev. ed. New York: McGraw-Hill, 1958.

Thruelson, Richard. *Transocean.* New York: Henry Holt, 1952.

Tomlinson, Captain D.W. "Tommy." TWA interview, 1983.

Trans World Airlines Flight Operations Department. *Legacy of Leadership: A Pictorial History of Trans World Airlines.* Marceline: Walsworth, 1971.

Tryckare, Tre. *The Lore of Flight.* Alexandria: Time-Life Books, 1970.

Turnbull, Archibald D., and Clifford L. Lord. *History of U.S. Naval Aviation.* New Haven: Yale University Press, 1949.

United States Civil Aeronautics Board. *Air Carrier Traffic Statistics.* Washington, D.C.: CAB, 1980.

———. *Airport Activity Statistics.* Washington, D.C.: CAB and Department of Transportation, Federal Aviation Administration, 1979.

Van Vleet, Clarke, and Armstrong, Wm. J. *United States Naval Aviation 1910 to 1980.* Washington, D.C.: U.S. Government Printing Office, 1980.

Vivian, Robert E. *The U.S.C. Engineering Story.* Los Angeles: University of Southern California Press, 1975.

Von Kármán, Theodore, with Lee Edson. *The Wind and Beyond: Theodore Von Karman, Pioneer in Aviation and Pathfinder in Space.* Boston: Little, Brown and Company, 1967.

Vorderman, D.M. *The Great Air Races.* Garden City: Doubleday & Company, 1969.

Wagner, William, with Lee Dye. *Ryan the Aviator: Being the Adventures and Ventures of Pioneer Airman and Businessman Claude T. Ryan.* New York: McGraw-Hill, 1971.

———. *Reuben Fleet and the Story of Consolidated Aircraft.* Fallbrook, CA: Aero Publishers, Inc., 1976.

Whittle, Sir Frank. Interview. London: 1982.

Wigton, Don. *From Jenny to Jet.* New

# INDEX

York: Bonanza Books, 1963.

Wiley, Frank W. *Montana and the Sky.* Helena, MT: Montana Aeronautics Commission, 1966.

Wilson, John R.M. *Turbulence Aloft: The Civil Aeronautics Authority Amid Wars and Rumors of Wars 1938-1955.* Washington, D.C.: U.S. Department of Transportation, 1979.

Wolko, Howard S. *In The Cause of Flight: Technologies of Aeronautics and Astronautics.* Washington, D.C.: Smithsonian Institution Press, 1981.

Wooldridge, E.T. *Winged Wonders: The Story of the Flying Wings.* Washington, D.C.: Smithsonian Institution Press, 1983.

Woolley, James G. and Earl W. Hill. *Airplane Transportation.* Hollywood, California: Hartwell Publishing Company, 1929.

Young, Warren R. *The Helicopters.* Alexandria: Time-Life Books, 1982.

*Italic* page numbers indicate illustrations.

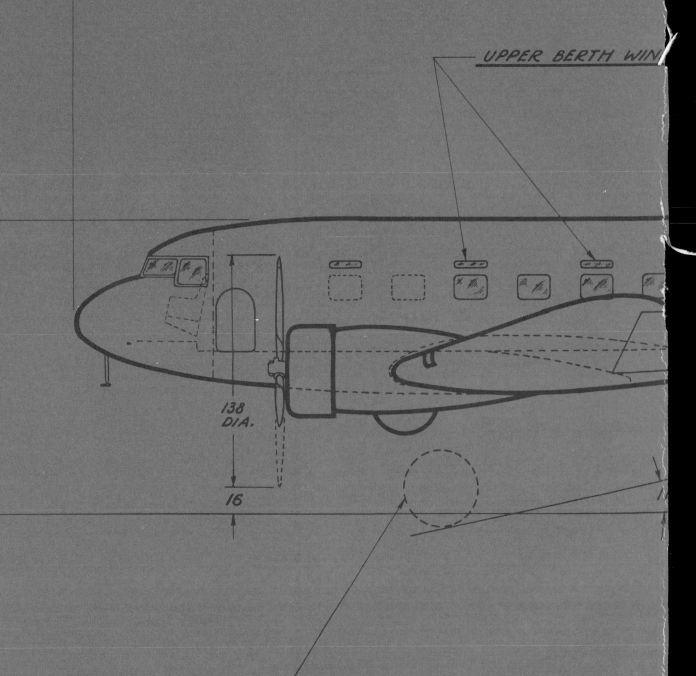

64'-5½"

UPPER BERTH WIN

179½

138
DIA.

16

17.00:16 TIRE (GOODRICH) OR
20:10 GOODYEAR AIRWHEEL